Border
Rhetorics

Border
Rhetorics

Citizenship and Identity on the US-Mexico Frontier

EDITED BY
D. ROBERT DECHAINE

THE UNIVERSITY OF ALABAMA PRESS
Tuscaloosa

821736247

Typeface: Bembo and Ryo

∞

The paper on which this book is printed meets the minimum requirements of American National Standard for Information Sciences—Permanence of Paper for Printed Library Materials, ANSI Z39.48-1984.

Library of Congress Cataloging-in-Publication Data

   Border rhetorics : citizenship and identity on the US-Mexico frontier / edited by D. Robert DeChaine.
      p. cm. — (Rhetoric, culture, and social critique)
   Includes bibliographical references and index.
   ISBN 978-0-8173-5716-0 (alk. paper) — ISBN 978-0-8173-8605-4 (ebook)
 1. Mexican-American Border Region—Emigration and immigration—Political aspects. 2. Mexican-American Border Region—Emigration and immigration—Social aspects. 3. Citizenship—Political aspects—United States. 4. Rhetoric—Political aspects—United States. 5. Illegal aliens—United States. 6. Border security—United States. I. DeChaine, D. Robert (Daniel Robert), 1961–
 JV6477.B67 2012
   304.80972′1—dc23

                                                                    2012005534

Cover photograph: "Barbed Wires" © Diego Vito Cervo | Dreamstime.com
Cover design: Gary Gore

Contents

Acknowledgments

The conceptualization and contents of *Border Rhetorics* emerged over a number of years and across diverse discursive contexts. I owe a great many debts of gratitude for its existence, several of which deserve special acknowledgment. The intellectual impetus for the volume owes heavily to the scholarship of Kent Ono and John Sloop, whose co-authored book, *Shifting Borders: Rhetoric, Immigration, and California's Proposition 187,* established a pathbreaking agenda for the critical study of immigration discourse in the United States. An exemplar of engaged communication scholarship, Ono and Sloop's work has decisively influenced the designs of the project as well as my own understanding and thinking about border matters. Another primary source of inspiration for the volume has been its contributors. The pioneering analyses undertaken by the authors have both individually and collectively informed its direction at all stages of its development. I am thankful to have had such a stellar group of scholars rally around the project, and their work continues to inspire me as they break new ground in communication studies. The Western States Communication Association (WSCA) 2009 preconference, "Border Rhetorics: Mapping American Citizenship, Cultural Space, and Identity," served as a productive forum for the development of a number of the volume's guiding questions and themes. I also wish to acknowledge my students at California State University Los Angeles, both undergraduate and graduate, who provided an important milieu for developing and testing ideas during the book's formative stages. Their spirited dialog and tough questions have influenced it—and me—in more ways than they could know.

Several particular individuals provided helpful commentary and criticism at various stages of the book's development. At a 2009 WSCA panel on border politics, Karma Chávez supplied valuable feedback on an early iteration of arguments I advance in the volume's introductory chapter. Dan Brouwer offered incisive commentary at an early point in the volume's development that helped me to clarify and rethink a number of its conceptual and structural aspects. Both directly and indirectly, John Lucaites has provided me with an invaluable editorial education, and his insights regarding the rhetorical crafting of civic culture animate the volume's central thesis. Last, but certainly not least, Mike Willard, my colleague in the department of Liberal Studies, has been a stalwart supporter, a generous interlocutor, a deft critic, and a provoking agent throughout the project's evolution. To each of these fine folks, I offer my sincere gratitude.

Along with the individuals named above, a number of others share credit for this volume as a result of their assistance, wise counsel, encouragement, and friendship. These include Bryant Alexander, Kevin Baaske, Lena Chao, Steve Classen, Dionne Espinoza, Diana Fisher, Jenny Faust, Julia Johnson, Michelle Ladd, Alejandra Marchevsky, Ulises Moreno, David Olsen, Kent Ono, Scott Rodriguez, Ranu Samantrai, Patrick Sharp, and Victor Viesca. I offer heartfelt thanks to Dan Waterman at The University of Alabama Press for his unwavering belief in the project, to Lady Smith and Joanna Jacobs for their expert editorial assistance, and to the crack production staff and the anonymous reviewers at UA Press for their many improvements in the volume's quality. I also wish to acknowledge the American Communities Program at California State University Los Angeles and its director, Maria Karafilis, for awarding me a fellowship that funded a portion of the research, writing, and editing of the volume.

This book is for Cindy, my best friend, my patient guide, and my most brilliant teacher.

Border
Rhetorics

Introduction

For Rhetorical Border Studies

D. Robert DeChaine

The figure of the border animates the language of social relations in the United States today. Symbolic and material, affective and performative, the border is an omnipresent force in our everyday lives, materializing and shifting across registers of geography, history, politics, economics, citizenship, identity, and culture. Variously invoked as a geographical term for delineating territories, a political expression of national sovereignty, a juridical marker of citizenship status, and an ideological trope for defining terms of inclusion and exclusion, the border circulates as a robust spatial metaphor in the public vernacular. And crucially, as *Border Rhetorics* aims to demonstrate, the border functions as a powerful site of rhetorical invention.

Gaining force from a history of shifting meanings over the last century, the border's discursive reach extends from local discussions on immigration reform to congressional debates over national security, from courtrooms to classrooms, and from presidential town hall meetings to boisterous street protests. Individuals, groups, and governments call upon symbolism of the border in order to mobilize communal allegiances, negotiate boundaries of civic identity, construct unities and divisions, and, often enough, craft understandings of "us" and "them." Border symbolism is used to draw lines, mark off boundaries, and effect different kinds of crossings. Perhaps ironically, it also underwrites appeals to "a world without borders" and various claims to deterritorialized spaces and places. Given both its ubiquity and its polyvalence as a signifier, it is indeed difficult to imagine a world without borders, or at least a world without border symbolism.

Across all of its invocations, a border operates as a bounding, ordering apparatus, whose primary function is to designate, produce, and regulate the space of difference (DeChaine, "Bordering the Civic Imaginary" 44). While symbolic ascriptions of borders can provide people with a sense of safety, identity, belonging, and home, they also "constitute institutions that enable legitimation, signification and domination through which control can be exercised" (Newman 148). Regardless of their form or function, borders are thus always invested in power. Moreover, it is important to remember that since borders are human symbolic constructs, the power that they hold, or wield, does not issue from borders per se, but rather from specific persons who call upon the figure of the border in specific ways in order to do specific things.[1] In short, border symbolism constitutes a powerful form of social sense-making—a public *doxa,* or structure of belief, that informs cultural values, shapes public attitudes, and prescribes individual and collective actions.

Civic Identity and Bordering Practices

In the context of the US nation–state, borders and border symbolism are formative in shaping public understandings of citizenship and identity. The production of civic identity reflects intense struggles over the cultural politics of recognition, struggles that often involve fraught negotiations of race, ethnicity, class, gender, and sexuality. Such struggles and negotiations bear profoundly on ways that people view each other and are viewed by others as members of, or outsiders to, the national community (Kymlicka and Norman; Rosaldo, "Cultural Citizenship"; Taylor). Borders and their zones of contact serve as spaces of identity and empowerment for those who willfully or forcibly inhabit them (Anzaldúa). At the same time, inhabitants of borderlands are regularly cast as aliens and transgressors, a subjugated status that invariably exacts legal and moral penalties (Henderson). Moreover, public understandings of "the American people" reflect often-heated debates regarding who is and is not a legitimate American subject, debates that rhetorically stack the deck against the racialized, alienized migrant (Cisneros, "Contaminated Communities"; DeChaine, "Bordering the Civic Imaginary"; Flores, "Constructing Rhetorical Borders"; Ono and Sloop). National identity, a subject now thoroughly contextualized by the "immigration problem," commonly turns on the question of citizenship, a status premised on a juridical conception of the natural or natural*ized* US citizen-subject. Rarely are values of respect, belonging, and tolerance for difference included in the definition of national identity (Alejandra Castañeda; Parekh).

The doxastic, world-making function of the border signals its preeminence as a rhetorical mode of enactment. That is to say, borders are produced, defined, managed, contested, and altered through human symbolic practices. In their pathbreaking study of the media's role in the passage of California's Proposition 187 in the 1990s, Kent Ono and John Sloop argue that rhetorical appeals to the nation and its borders such as those surrounding Proposition 187 have the power not only to influence people's perceptions of immigrants and immigration but, more importantly, to shape the very meanings of "nation" and "border." As Ono and Sloop explain, "such rhetoric *shifts* borders, changing what they mean publicly, influencing public policy, altering the ways borders affect people, and circumscribing political responses to such legislation. . . . Rhetoric shapes understandings of how the border functions; taken further, because of its increasingly powerful role, rhetoric at times even determines where, and what, the border is" (5).

Such a view of the rhetoricity of borders and of their power in public discourse marks an important shift in focus: from borders to *bordering*. While it is of course accurate to say that borders affect people in real ways, the majority of extant scholarship on the subject assumes the existence of borders as static entities, as given objects to be examined for their effects on individuals and populations. Rarely acknowledged in such scholarship is the fact that whatever else they may be, borders are products of human symbolic action, created by human agents through particular and often complex rhetorical practices.

Following Ono and Sloop's lead, what is needed—what this volume presses for—is a move beyond a traditional view of borders as given, pre-symbolic entities to their recognition as dynamic rhetorical *enactments*. The analytical turn from borders to bordering is crucial because, we contend, it is through examining how borders are symbolically enacted that the shifting meanings of "citizen" and "alien," "American" and "outsider," and "us" and "them" may be held to the light of critical reflection.

This volume aims to uncover the fundamental role of rhetorical bordering in defining the boundaries of civic identity in the United States. From a diversity of perspectives, the chapters that comprise *Border Rhetorics* explore the interrelationship between rhetorical enactments of citizenship and identity, particularly as they concentrate on and around the US-Mexico border, with emphasis on how such enactments give shape to democratic life in contemporary US society. Outside of this volume, in their discussion of the construction of a vernacular US Chicano/a nationalism in the book *Politics, Communication, and Culture,* Lisa A. Flores and Marouf A. Hasian Jr. together argue that nationhood is at its heart a rhetorical achievement, explaining that "Nations and 'peoples' are brought into being through the acceptance or rejection of invitations to believe in particular symbolic creations" (190). In their function as invitations to belief, border rhetorics, we argue, figure instrumentally as shapers of US national culture. There is at present a paucity of scholarship that explicitly examines the rhetoricity of borders and bordering practices. This volume seeks to redress this situation, and to advance an agenda for critical studies of border rhetorics as an important and heretofore neglected field of communication studies.

The Bordering of Border Studies

Although attention by scholars to the rhetorical practices of bordering has been scant, interest in the social significance of borders is far from novel within the academy. Indeed there is at present a proliferation of "border studies" research and scholarship spanning humanistic and social scientific modes of inquiry. A principal source of border scholarship began to emerge within the field of geography as early as the 1950s. Although its theoretical purview has broadened over time, a traditional geographical perspective has regarded borders as fixed and stable entities delineating territories, national identities, and social-state relations (Newman 146). Along with geography, anthropology has figured prominently in the development of border studies since the 1970s. Scholars who engage "the anthropology of borders" have examined how borders influence cultural processes, reflect communal values and traditions, and bear upon "issues of nationalism, political economy, class, migration and the political disintegration of nations and states" (Wilson and Donnan 4). Several other disciplines have also advanced conceptions of borders and studied their social effects, including political science, sociology, and economics. Common among all of these, argues geographer David Newman, is the assertion that "borders determine the nature of group (in some cases defined territorially) belonging, affiliation and membership, and the way in which the processes of inclusion and exclusion are institutionalized" (147).

The advent of postmodernity, and in particular its role in ushering the "spatial turn" in social theory, has had a significant impact on the conceptualization of borders across a number of disciplines (DeChaine, "Imagined Immunities" 264–69). By and large, prior to the 1970s scholars considered space, territory, and borders to be given, static entities. Beginning in the 1970s, postmodern theorists began to vigorously critique the traditional spatial logic, prompting a refiguration of the study of space to include a focus on its character as socially produced and practiced (Lefebvre; Massey; Soja). In the decades since postmodernism's entree, the theoretical emphasis on the social character of space has been influential in forging two significant areas of border research. The first gives attention to the construction of border identities and the experiences of bordered subjects. This area of research views the border and its spatialized "borderlands" as a dynamic site of hegemonic struggle over terms and conditions for the formation of national and ethnic identities (see Anzaldúa; Fox; Rosaldo, *Culture and Truth;* Saldívar; Vila). A second, often overlapping emphasis draws upon multidisciplinary engagements with discourses of globalization and transnational culture, focusing attention on the social-spatial politics of movement, mobility, migration, and displacement (see Appadurai; Bhabha; García Canclini; Grewal). Together, these two areas of ongoing research in border studies have influenced contemporary understandings of the place and power of borders in people's everyday lives. Both, in short, have contributed to a recognition that "the geography of the world is not a product of nature but a product of histories of struggle between competing authorities over the power to organize, occupy, and administer space" (Ó Tuathail 1).

As is the case with every field of inquiry, the field of border studies evinces particular disciplinary histories, epistemological assumptions, areas of focus, and methods of investigation that define its present form. As such, it operates as a discursive formation, producing particular knowledge and "regimes of truth" (Foucault, *Power/Knowledge* 134) that prescribe what borders are, how they operate, and the appropriate way(s) to study them. That is to say, the discursive formation of border studies effectively defines and delimits what border studies can be. To be sure, the aforementioned disciplinary perspectives and theoretical moves have broadened the study of borders beyond traditional static conceptualizations and opened up important areas for analysis. Be that as it may, a significant blind spot exists in the current articulation of the field—namely, a lack of attention to the consummately rhetorical function of borders. While several disciplines such as anthropology, sociology, and literary studies have included the symbolic study of borders within their purview, very few attend with specificity to the rhetorical processes and practices of bordering, and fewer still bring a critical perspective to bear in their scholarship.

As the contributors to this volume make clear, an inattention to border rhetorics impoverishes our understanding of the conceptual, historical, legal, performative, and mediated processes of civic identity-making. A rhetorical border studies offers scholars, critics, and activists useful strategies for investigating the array of linguistic, visual, and aural resources through which understandings of citizenship, national identity, belonging, and otherness are publicly negotiated. It provides a means of investigating how institutional, majoritarian, and vernacular discourses shape and are shaped by border(ing) rhetorics, and how, in turn, border(ed) conditions and spaces spur resistive politics and unique forms of social critique. A rhetorical approach to concepts, for example, sheds light on ways in which bordering produces public knowledge and "truth" about people, places, social statuses, and communal allegiances. Focusing on the sense-making function of rhetoric, it reveals how discourses of racism, nativism, sexism, and homophobia fund terminologies of otherness that cast border-crossing subjects as abject, unassimilable outsiders to the US national body. A rhetorical approach to history helps to illuminate how bordering practices have shaped and continue to shape social collectivities, and how they function as modalities of social action. Such an approach entails careful analysis of how historical modes of bordering influence current practices and how, in turn, contemporary bordering practices re-present border histories. A rhetorical approach to law affords critics an understanding of the symbolic power of legal discourses in shaping social attitudes about citizenship status and the role of the state in the maintenance of "true American" values. Infusing rhetorical studies with the rich field of performance studies enables modes of investigation that illuminate the performative power of borders, how the affect of borders is infused in both individual and collective memory, and ways that border performativity is infused in the practices of everyday life. Finally, a rhetorical approach to media offers a variety of methods for examining how mediated representations of borders both direct and reflect ideological positions and institutional forms of power.

In short, a neglect of the rhetorical dimensions of borders elides important questions about how people use borders to reinforce values, inculcate beliefs, mobilize attitudes, and provoke action. Furthermore, all too rarely do the disciplines that currently engage in border studies engage each other in their analyses,[2] thereby limiting the ability of each to inform, enrich, and learn from the others. To wit, the current state of border studies underscores the need for critical interdisciplinary investigations of rhetorical bordering practices. It is here that the multiperspectival field of communication studies offers a rich contribution to—and thus a rebordering of—existing scholarship.

Citizenship and Identity on the US–Mexico Frontier

The frontier separating Mexico and the United States is an exemplary site for examining both the localized and the diffused politics of bordering. A mostly rugged terrain extending approximately 1,954 miles from the California Baja through Texas and to Tamaulipas, the US-Mexico border is at once the world's most heavily traveled land crossing (Andreas, *Border Games* 141) and one of the most well-known, serving as "the model of border studies and borderlands genre throughout the world" (Alvarez 451). Numerous cities both large and small flank it on both sides, marking it as not only a physical geographical boundary but a space of cultural contact and exchange. It is also one of the world's most heavily fortified border zones, guarded and policed by reinforced steel fences, video cameras, remote sensing equipment, militarized border checkpoints, aerial surveillance, governmental personnel, and civilian border patrol groups. Beyond its significance as a site of localized activity, the US-Mexico border's influence extends outward, pulsing through the US national imagination. The circulation of mediated images, popular narratives, and official knowledge about what kind of place the border is, what kind of people inhabit and cross it, and the kinds of events that transpire there gives form to a constellation of normative and often prescriptive ideas about where America ends and something "other" begins. In this sense, as Guillermo Gómez-Peña poignantly notes, "The US-Mexico border is wider than ever" in terms of its ideological reach (200).

Prevalent attitudes about the US-Mexico border, border inhabitants, and border crossers have taken shape within a particular conjuncture of predominantly US state-centered political, economic, and social-cultural discourses, policies, and practices. The articulation of the political-economic conjuncture is in fact quite recent,[3] and chiefly tracks the US government's increasing desire since the early twentieth century to control the flow of transborder labor (Nevins 43–44). Over the past two decades, regulation of the US-Mexico border has been profoundly influenced by the intersecting movements of economic globalization, neoliberalist philosophy, and governmental policy that attempt to mitigate the flow of transborder capital and trade. In particular, the North American Free Trade Agreement (NAFTA) established between Canada, Mexico, and the United States in 1994 has been at the center of US border policy and practice. Ostensibly an agreement aimed at promoting the free flow of goods and decreasing migration across borders, NAFTA's liberalization of labor, environmental, and trade regulations has in fact led to a relaxation of worker safety standards and protections; spurred the rapid growth of low-wage factories (*maquiladoras*) in border zones; exacerbated environmental degradation, human health issues, and crime; and contributed to a depressed Mexican labor market that has increased the rate of migration to the United States (Romero 42–44). The ongoing disjunction between the US government–led effort to create an integrated transborder market and the lack of a concomitant integration of transborder labor has had serious implications for people living on and around the border as well as for the national economies that are affected by the neoliberal rhetoric of "free trade." As Toby Miller aptly emphasizes in his chapter in this volume, we surely ignore the political economy of border rhetorics at our collective peril.

Whereas the historical conjuncture of political and economic discourses, policies, and practices that circulate on and around the US-Mexico border is relatively recent, the social and cultural history that shapes contemporary border rhetorics in the United States is extensive, reaching back to the founding of the nation. Anti-immigrant sentiment, rooted in nativism and materialized in processes of racialization, has long influenced US public attitudes toward migrants and other border crossing subjects (Feagin; Reimers). Along with its racist and nativist underpinnings, the alienization of border(ed) subjects is also predicated on a state-directed discourse of migrant illegality, a mode of subjectivity that constructs the "illegal alien" as one who is by nature out of place, a problem, and a threat to the national body (Chávez, "Border (In)Securities"; Cisneros, this volume; Flores, "Constructing Rhetorical Borders"; Inda, *Targeting Immigrants;* Nevins; Ngai). Ramped up post-9/11 and fueled by the proclaimed Global War on Terror, alienization surfaces most prominently in the rhetoric of "national security" that dominates contemporary US immigration discourse. In effect, the bordering practices of alienization collude in the production of an eth-nonationalist form of civic identity—a way of seeing, experiencing, and distinguishing between the true American and the illegal Outsider that is "made real" through the authority and control of the US state (Andreas, *Border Games;* Pickering). Put another way, borders and border subjectivities are constitutive, state-choreographed performances (Wonders 66). Gesturing to the power of the US government to normalize discursive categories and conceptions of American civic identity, Joseph Nevins argues, "the power of state discourse vis-à-vis the national citizenry illustrates the ability of the state to construct not only political-juridical categories, but also ways of seeing. . . . By subjecting people to the law, the state produces subjects and identities, which become 'discursive facts' that inform how people interact and perceive one another" (150).

The articulation of political, economic, and social-cultural discourses operating on and around the US-Mexico border bears profoundly on popular understandings and experiences of citizenship and identity in the United States today. Public attitudes regarding migrants, border inhabitants, and other border-crossing subjects are conditioned by prevalent narratives and imagery that depict the US-Mexico border as a badlands that is out of control—an unruly space in dire need of containment from the ravages of criminals, illegal aliens, terrorists, and other undesirable threats to the national body (Nevins; Néstor P. Rodriguez). Such narratives and imagery provide symbolic grist for normalizing a view of boundary-making as a necessary and natural function of the state (Demo, "Sovereignty Discourse"). Once inscribed, normative constructions of "proper" border relations reinforce normative prescriptions of the US citizen-subject, a condition that can spur anxiety, unrest, and violence. As Ronald Greene notes, "The modern legacy of citizenship locates the citizen within the political space of the nation-state whereas the circulation of immigrants constantly transgresses these borders. In so doing, immigrants are often vulnerable to intense anxieties about how their arrival disrupts the national imaginary" (165). In their role as shapers of public knowledge about the propriety of people, places, and social statuses, border rhetorics function as an index for gauging social meanings of the true American citizen and the terms and conditions of membership in the national political community.

A critical engagement with the rhetorical practices of civic identity-making on and around the US-Mexico frontier reveals its place and power in the US national imagination. In the face of numerous historical and current appropriations of "true American"—a hegemonic strategy all too regularly employed to malign, alienize, and dehumanize human beings—a rhetorical border studies offers the potential for a counterhegemonic intervention. It seeks to demystify, denaturalize, and thus refigure the trope of citizenship as an object of critique, underscoring its vital role in the crafting of national identity.

Overview of the Volume

In the thematic sections and chapters that comprise *Border Rhetorics,* the contributors explore a variety of issues, texts, contexts, and acts to illuminate how the figure of the border both animates and limits human social life. The chapters are organized around five thematic perspectives for engaging border rhetorics. The first section, "Conceptual Orientations," includes three chapters that together propose a set of starting points, openings, and strategies for interrogating the rhetoricity of borders and the impact of bordering practices on civic life. In the first chapter, entitled "Borders That Travel: Matters of the Figural Border," Kent A. Ono sets out to chart the pervasiveness of what he terms "the figural border," which he describes as a deeply consequential counterpart to the literal borders that predominate the majority of discussions about border matters. For Ono, borders are inherently social constructions whose meanings are defined and shifted through discourse and discursive practices. These practices, he argues, include various disciplining mechanisms and modes of regulation and control of migrant individuals and communities. As discursive productions, borders travel beyond their literal locations, mapping onto the bodies and identities of subjects. Thus, insists Ono, tracking the figural movement of the border across people, places, and practices is crucial to understanding its social and politi-

cal power. In her chapter "Bordering as Social Practice: Intersectional Identifications and Coalitional Possibilities," Julia R. Johnson announces her
aim to explore "the processes of constructing borders, the differences that
are fundamental to bordering practices, and the construction of border(ed)
bodies as perverse and beyond normalized citizenship." Orienting her discussion to the many "inters" that inform processes of individual and collective identification in, on, between, and across borders, Johnson endorses
intersectionality as a critical-theoretical perspective. She argues that an intersectional perspective enables a richly contextual interrogation of social
practices of domination and oppression. In turn, it holds potential strategic value for migrants and other bordered subjects, encouraging movements
across identificatory lines to challenge forms of oppression and create new
subjectivities and coalitional formations. In the section's final chapter, entitled "Border Interventions: The Need to Shift from a Rhetoric of Security to a Rhetoric of Militarization," Karma R. Chávez argues that the current emphasis on "national security" in public and scholarly discourse serves
to obfuscate symbolic and material violences committed against migrants
and bordered others in the name of state and conservative appeals to safety,
privacy, and the Global War on Terror. By way of an analysis of the US governmental publication *Secure Border Initiative Monthly*, Chávez exhorts rhetorical scholars to work actively to reframe discussions about US national
values and interests in ways that call attention to the violence of border
militarization and that challenge the current discursive regime.

The volume's second section, "Historical Consequences," includes two
case studies that consider historical border rhetorics and their contemporary
relevance. In "A Dispensational Rhetoric in 'The Mexican Question in the
Southwest,'" Michelle A. Holling traces present US national anxieties concerning what Samuel Huntington has termed "the Hispanic challenge"
through the antecedent "Mexican problem" that took shape during the
1920s and 1930s. Engaging the 1939 political work "The Mexican Question
in the Southwest" by Emma Tenayuca and Homer Brooks, Holling identifies the deployment of a "dispensational rhetoric," which she describes as
a rhetorical process "to rectify the position of an oppressed national group
through 'rearticulation'" of political, economic, and cultural relationships.
In the section's second chapter, entitled "Mobilizing for National Inclusion:
The Discursivity of Whiteness among Texas Mexicans' Arguments for Desegregation," Lisa A. Flores and Mary Ann Villarreal focus on responses by
Mexican community members in Corpus Christi, Texas, in the late 1940s
to legal efforts to segregate students of "Mexican extraction." Flores and
Villarreal argue that a careful examination of Texas Mexicans' public dis-

course reveals a complex negotiation of whiteness and citizenship that mobilized community members and mounted a strategic challenge to prevalent racial and class attitudes regarding Mexicans' "fitness for citizenship."

The two chapters that comprise the third section, "Legal Acts," consider the political and legal as well as social implications of border rhetorics for public perceptions of migrants, immigration policy, national security, and non/governmental relations. In the first chapter of the section, "The Attempted Legitimation of the Vigilante Civil Border Patrols, the Militarization of the Mexican-US Border, and the Law of Unintended Consequences," Marouf Hasian Jr. and George F. McHendry Jr. examine efforts by border patrol groups, particularly the Minuteman Project (MMP), between 2002 and 2007 to gain legal legitimacy. Their efforts, Hasian and McHendry argue, drew upon longstanding metanarratives of US American exceptionalism[4] in the crafting of a "state of exception" (Agamben) as a discursive response to the perceived immigration problem in the United States. Offered as an instructive example of the law of unintended consequences, Hasian and McHendry conclude that the MMP's efforts to establish itself as a solution to governmental failures to control immigration contributed to both the rapid surge and the subsequent dissolution of MMP's public ethos. In the section's final chapter, entitled "Shot in the Back: Articulating the Ideologies of the Minutemen through a Political Trial," Zach Justus offers an appraisal of public responses by members of the Minuteman Civil Defense Corps (MCDC) to the trial and conviction of Texas Border Patrol agents Ignacio Ramos and Alonso Compean, accused of violating procedural guidelines and shooting an alleged drug trafficker on the Texas-Mexico border. Employing articulation theory to analyze particular positionalities and modes of redress expressed by MCDC online forum participants, Justus demonstrates how the MCDC's rhetorical "'battle' over the border spilled onto the bodies and stories of salient parties" in its attempt to (re)articulate nongovernmental politics in the public sphere.

In the fourth section of the volume, "Performative Affects," contributors draw upon a variety of theoretical frameworks and modes of writing to explore ways in which subjectivity is negotiated in and through bordering practices. In the first chapter, "Looking 'Illegal': Affect, Rhetoric, and Performativity in Arizona's Senate Bill 1070," Josue David Cisneros critiques the discourses implicated in the passage in 2010 of Arizona Senate Bill 1070, titled the "Support Our Law Enforcement and Safe Neighborhoods Act." Identifying "a moment of articulation in an affective economy about citizenship, the border, and Latina/o immigrants," Cisneros argues that the Arizona legislation enacts a rhetorical ascription of specifically

Mexican-Latina/o immigrant bodies as dangerous and threatening to US national culture and, further, construes migrant illegality as a performative affect of the Latina/o subject rather than a product of juridical state discourse. Moreover, Cisneros contends, in its entangling of conceptions of border enforcement and civic engagement, Senate Bill 1070 effectively recasts citizenship as a national value structure entirely congruent with current practices of border vigilantism. In her chapter entitled "Love, Loss, and Immigration: Performative Reverberations between a Great-Grandmother and Great-Granddaughter," Bernadette Marie Calafell attends to the affective, embodied character of personal narrative in her encounters with her maternal great-grandmother, Teresa Carbajal Benavides. In her desire "to flesh out the story of a woman whom I knew, but never *really* knew," Calafell uses strategies of performative writing and poetry to stage a dialogic negotiation of the deeply felt, always-conflicted boundaries of identity, family, citizenship, memory, self, other, and home. In the section's final chapter, "Borders without Bodies: Affect, Proximity, and Utopian Imaginaries through 'Lines in the Sand,'" co-authors Dustin Bradley Goltz and Kimberlee Pérez are likewise interested in teasing out the affect and fraughtness of border-(ing) encounters. Assessing the effects of whiteness and anti-migrant sentiment in establishing social-cultural boundaries between self/other and us/them, Goltz and Pérez turn inward to consider "how border rhetorics produce non-immigrant and white signifying bodies through reflecting on how border rhetorics produce *bodies,* namely ours." In recounting their individual and collaborative experiences developing and performing "Lines in the Sand: Fear, Loss, and Whiteness in Contemporary US Representation of Mexican Immigration," the authors engage in a reflexive form of social critique, simultaneously identifying and working to overcome their own positions of privilege and complicity in discourses of domination.

The chapters in the final section, "Media Circuits," examine border rhetorics as they are produced, circulated, represented, and contested in media culture. In their chapter entitled "Transborder Politics: The Embodied Call of Conscience in *Traffic,*" Brian L. Ott and Diane M. Keeling analyze the political, cultural, corporeal, and ethical dimensions of Steven Soderbergh's 2001 feature film, *Traffic,* assessing its significance as a mediated border rhetoric. Ostensibly a film about the destructive world of drug trafficking on the US-Mexico border, the authors discover within it an array of complex border(ing) negotiations. Ott and Keeling argue that through its framing techniques and the moral positioning(s) of its main characters, an embodied "rhetoric of conscience" emerges in *Traffic*—an ethical perspective that, although deeply conflicted, "generally fosters and promotes a transborder politics rooted in the protection and nurturing of children." In the section's second chapter, "Decriminalizing Illegal Immigration: Immigrants' Rights through the Documentary Lens," Anne Teresa Demo engages the emergent genre of immigrant rights documentaries to explore how filmic representations of migrants resonate with and/or challenge prevalent political attitudes toward immigration. Demo surveys nineteen documentary films produced between 2001 and 2010, identifying among them a set of visual and narrative strategies that, she argues, function as rhetorical resources for critiquing dominant immigration policies and practices. Demo concludes that despite their relatively marginal status and visibility in mainstream media culture, immigrant rights documentaries may provide a viable textual alternative for future immigration rights advocacy efforts. The section concludes with a bookending chapter by Toby Miller entitled "The Ragpicker-Citizen." In it, Miller offers an orientation to the study of mediated border rhetorics in which political economy figures centrally. Examining ways in which neoliberalism, global capitalism, and the culture industries have contributed to an abject underclass on the US-Mexico border epitomized by the *maquiladora* worker and the ragpicker, Miller assesses the impact of market-driven consumer electronics, and specifically its by-product, e-waste, on the environment; labor practices; human health; and conceptions of citizenship. At the same time, Miller's analysis issues a caution against modes of investigation that neglect material conditions of human life, privilege text over context, and engage in abstract theorization at the expense of those whose lives are (often profoundly) impacted by bordering practices.

The volume's chapters are followed by an afterword by John Louis Lucaites, in which he argues for the heuristic value of "the optic" as a means of rendering visible the numerous borders and boundaries "that constitute our civic life and that might otherwise remain invisible or go unnoticed, treated as altogether natural, ordinary, and apolitical." In placing emphasis on the ways in which borders enact ways of seeing and not seeing individuals as citizens, Lucaites underscores the performative character of civic identity and, more broadly, the attendant tensions of identity-making on, around, and beyond the US-Mexico frontier. Given the diversity of theoretical, methodological, and epistemological perspectives that inform *Border Rhetorics,* common among all of the contributors' engagements is our decisive turn from borders to bordering—a reorientation in analysis from descriptive accounts of static forms to critical interrogations of dynamic, power-laden enactments. Underlying this shift is our collective conviction that whatever forms they assume, border rhetorics are crucial to the formation of civic culture. We regard rhetorical bordering as an agency of power, an arena of struggle, and a performative mode of contestation. In a word, each of us makes the case that as formative shapers of civic life, border rhetorics matter.

Border Rhetorics, Democracy, and the Civic Imaginary

The time has come to treat the rhetoricity of borders seriously. As I have argued here, symbolic ascriptions of the border function doxastically in public culture. They provide a community with a structure of belief and thus a framework for gauging the truth about the nature of people, places, and social statuses. As such, they bear directly on the quality and character of human social life. Moreover, the effects of rhetorical bordering are not "merely" symbolic; they have real consequences for those toward whom their influence is directed. To overlook the materiality of border rhetorics is to underplay the intimate link between human symbolicity, attitudes, and actions. Put quite simply, we cannot afford to ignore the place and power of border rhetorics in our lives.

Spurred by the cultural and political tensions marking our present moment, *Border Rhetorics* calls for an emergent, critical project of rhetorical border studies. Engaging the conceptual, historical, legal, performative, and mediated power of the border, the contributors underscore the intimate link between symbolic bordering practices and human social relations. Both individually and collectively, they reveal bordering to be a discursive and affective mode of civic identity enactment rife with tension, conflict, ambivalence, and social drama. Robert Asen has argued that citizenship enactment is "always conditioned by social status, relations of power, institutional factors, and material constraints" (204). Adopting a critical orientation toward bordering enables an examination of the contexts and specificities as well as the contradictions and paradoxes of civic identity enactment in a multipublic sphere. It encourages a scholarly perspective that questions prevalent understandings of borders, citizenship, identity, and the conditions of their articulation. Beyond its scholarly contribution, *Border Rhetorics* hopes to make a meaningful intervention in public discussions about immigration, public policy, social activism, and the place of the border in social life.

Ultimately, border rhetorics speak to both the quality of our conduct toward one another and our aspirations of the kinds of citizens we desire to become. As such, they figure instrumentally in the formation of the US civic imaginary. Donovan Conley and Greg Dickenson have contended that "the semiotics of democracy are articulated spatially and ingrained historically. . . . Social spaces, material conditions, and signifying practices make up the very texture of our political horizons" (2). As a project invested in the social-spatial character of human experience, a rhetorical border studies is especially alert to questions concerning the ideals and practices required for the maintenance of a vibrant, democratic, and socially just civic imaginary. As Karma Chávez rightly observes, "In addition to indicating to a population who it is, an imaginary also functions to identify to a population who it is not" ("Embodied Translation" 20). The formation and health of the civic imaginary depend on how we envision not only its contents but its boundaries. As I have proposed, and as the subsequent chapters attest, a rhetorical border studies is particularly adept at charting these formative constituents of public culture, both on the US-Mexico frontier and beyond.

Notes

1. Here and subsequently, I am mindful of scholars' varied conceptualizations and deployments of the terms "border," "boundary," and "frontier," which often reflect different etymologies, assumptions, emphases, and attitudes depending on who uses which term (Ono, this volume; also see Ceccarelli).

2. In the past few years, there have been encouraging signs from some border scholars of a movement away from disciplinary insularity toward a more interdisciplinary engagement with border issues. I draw from a number of these noteworthy scholars in this introduction.

3. This does not mean to deny the much longer history of political and economic factors and influences that predates and informs it. See Vélez-Ibáñez (20–87).

4. In this introduction and in several chapters, the terms "US America" and "US American" are deployed as a political rebuke to the terms "America" and "American." Such terms are often used unself-consciously and/or ethnocentrically in scholarly discourse and serve to generalize and homogenize an entire continent and its populations.

I
Conceptual Orientations

1

Borders That Travel

Matters of the Figural Border

Kent A. Ono

Unsurprisingly, national attention is once again focused on the US/Mexico border. Each time this happens (some might say, "Has this ever not happened?"), historically minded scholars remind us this is a recurring state of affairs. Not only is it the most crossed national border in the world,[1] but at the end of the Mexican-American War in 1848 and subsequently the Gadsden Purchase of 1853, Mexican nationals existed on both sides of the border.[2] To this day, citizenship along the border is a blurry matter.

If we stop to think about it, however, "border" is a hard word to define. Some see it primarily in terms of social regulation; hence the border is a "bounding, ordering" apparatus and construct (DeChaine, "Bordering the Civic Imaginary" 44). As Rob DeChaine writes, "a border exists as a given entity whose contours can be cleanly and clearly recognized, measured, and mapped" (44). For him, its "primary function is to designate, produce, and/or regulate the space of difference" (44).

Others remark on its physical materiality. As Shoshana Magnet has suggested, the US/Canada border is sometimes a strip of land, with actual areas that laborers have to maintain and protect from the seasonal elements—snow, rain, wind, and the like—constantly clearing a path in order to make the border visible ("Using Biometrics" 360, 365). So, especially when covered in blown and drifted snow, or when it is in water, where the border is, precisely, is often difficult to determine. So, for instance, at the US/Mexico border, geologists tell us the Rio Grande (like all rivers) changes course over time; with maturation, new rivulets appear, riverbeds erode, and overall the river becomes wider and possibly shallower. Eventually it may even disappear altogether.

The meaning of the border is unclear even at the linguistic level. People use other words to define the border, each of them metaphorical, and therefore figural, such as "strip," "edge," "limit," and "boundary." Each of these terms has a different emphasis: "strip" implying three-dimensionality, "edge" denoting a dividing line between realms or that which cuts, a "limit" signifying a point not to go beyond, and a "boundary" meaning an enclosure or the outer extremity of a container. Depending on who uses which term, one can impute to each one a general attitude toward and about the border, some more friendly to migration, others less so. For instance, Joseph Nevins demonstrates how different terms imply different political positions regarding the border when he describes "a *boundary* as a strict line of separation between two (at least theoretically) distinct territories, *a frontier* as a forward zone of contact with the uncontrolled or sparsely-settled, and a *border* as an area of interaction and gradual division between two separate political entities" (8; emphasis in original).

Depending on one's stance, a border may mean a boundary needing to be crossed, or alternatively it might mean a dividing line that, if crossed, becomes an act of moral, ethical, and political trespass.[3] Taking this logic further, John Sloop and I have suggested that what we say about the border shifts the border's meaning, changes how it functions, and determines both its relative porosity and impermeability.[4] Discourse makes phenomena meaningful, as Stuart Hall has so compellingly suggested.[5] In the case of the border, discourse is intrinsic to its meaning and the uses to which it is put. Furthermore, a definition of the border can convey more broadly attitudes and perceptions about social relations.

In this chapter, I concentrate on defining the border figurally. I do this in order to extend humanistic thinking about the border, addressing the contingency of social and public matters—contingency being a traditional province of rhetoric—and thereby encouraging questioning and introspection about a matter of fundamental significance to our collective futures. More specifically, I am interested in the border *not at the border* or, rather, the *border that travels.*

In his discussion of the ways the Southwestern United States is and is not exceptional with regard to neoliberal surveillance and control, Gilberto Rosas has suggested that processes that have historically been exceptional now are traveling to other locations in the United States. He writes, "The vast flows of largely Mexican immigrants across the United States perhaps cause the borderlands condition to likewise migrate, evidenced by two arrivals: the transnational immigrant social movement and the naturalization of anti-migrant paramilitary vigilantism on the national stage" (401). Central to the argument of this chapter is that discourse not only represents migration occurring at the border. Nor does it simply shuttle between material experiences and the epiphenomenal representation of that experience;[6] rather, discourse constitutes migration and border processes in such a way that not only do the border processes move, but *the US/Mexico border itself exists beyond the Southwest.*

Besides the intellectual argument for why we might theorize the border in this way, one practical reason is to help draw attention to border practices *across* the US nation-state and therefore to highlight and emphasize that borders are being established all over the place—not only in Arizona, but also now in Michigan and North Dakota, for instance.

Typically, in discussions of Latina/o and Mexicana/o migration to the United States, border simply refers to where one state ends and another begins. Those on the US side have rights as determined by US law. Those on the Mexican side have rights as assigned by Mexican law. Defining the border, determining where it is, and deciding who is properly on one side of it or the other is therefore consequential and determinative of where one nation-state begins and another ends. In this way borders are intimately interlinked with national rights. Complicated processes ranging from social policy, court hearings, surveillance, interrogation, transport, imprisonment, and medical inspections become part of border enforcement.

Furthermore, which side of the border one is on, and from which side one comes, is determinative of identity and whether or not one will be included or excluded from particular activities, or from society in general, as a result. If a border is, as DeChaine suggests in "Bordering the Civic Imaginary," a site of regulation, that site is also then affectively one of anxiety, anxiety for those fearful that regulation will be applied to them, as well as anxiety for those seeking greater and greater regulative control. Furthermore, a border functions as a mechanism for control, elimination, and/or ejection; its role as marker of space in certain respects is secondary to its role in determining who should be included and who should be excluded. Thus, what constitutes a border has to do with the practices that create the conditions for exclusion. Defining the border as both a site and product of anxiety, and a means by which exclusion is made possible, helps to understand the boundary not only in geographical terms but also in terms of both effect and affect: how borders affect lives, both materially and spiritually. Such a definition disarticulates the notion of the border from constraints of spatial and geographical location that sometimes serve to overdetermine it.

While discussion of the literal meaning of the border has been extensive, discussion of its figural counterpart has not. Borders go beyond borders, and so does their function. Paradoxically, once one has crossed the border, one is no longer at the border. The momentary crossing of the border is, thus, necessarily fleeting and objectively unisolatable, yet a discourse of "at the border" saturates media, policy, and quotidian discourse—a discourse ostensibly about a consequential but nevertheless theoretically imagined, fleeting moment.

What we might call "border effects" therefore transcend geographical space and physical sites. Fences, both literally "on the ground" and figuratively and conceptually "in words" and "on bodies," are used to restrict entry. Both literal and figural fences become reified through application and praxis. Borders migrate, and so do their effects. This chapter theorizes the figural dimension of borders, emphasizing their material effects beyond the immediate ones ordinarily discussed in scholarly, political, and news media contexts. While the focus of much research and public discourse is about the crossing of the border, this chapter argues that the effects of the border do not end when the border is crossed. In fact, it is at that point that they may begin.

If a border is something that separates one from another, we might do well to begin any exploration of the border by asking what effects that separation? What in fact constitutes the border between people? Whereas transnational capitalism may benefit from policies such as the North American Free Trade Agreement (NAFTA)—hence giving the appearance of borders having been eliminated or made invisible and as creating what Masao Miyoshi has called a "borderless world"—for those on the flip side of transnational capitalism's privileges and pleasures (predominantly the working-class transnational labor force) the world is far from borderless. Rather than experiencing the borderless world of cosmopolitan capitalism, workers face borders to inclusion, employment, housing, health, education, and welfare not because of a literal border but because there is a figural divide seemingly immanent between contiguous nations. As such, a border acts as a separator or divider of people with different social, economic, and political affiliations, as a signifier of inclusion and exclusion, and as a way of determining one's worthiness as a living being, what Foucault might call one's "biopower" (*Power/Knowledge*).

With regard to California's Proposition 187, which passed in 1994, anti-immigrant activists defined the border as in need of protection from lawbreakers, as a site of hard-won national division between the United States and Mexico, and as a mechanism one could use to say who should and who should not be a member of the nation-state. Advocates conceived of Mexicans as illegal and the undocumented as not American and therefore excludable (Robin Dale Jacobson). Proponents of Proposition 187 sought to discourage immigration by eliminating health, education, and welfare benefits, seeing those crossing the borders as invaders, soaking up resources, and, through population growth and political power, ultimately seeking "reconquista" (Robin Dale Jacobson 34).

Pro-immigrant discourse also defined the border as in need of protection from outsiders and as a site of national division between the United States and Mexico. The difference, however, was that in this discourse, once the border was crossed migrants became wards of the state who required health, education, and welfare benefits to ensure against the spread of disease, criminality, and moral corruption, and in order to ensure that successful productive labor would continue. In a sense, one could argue that those opposing Proposition 187 conceived of the literal border as more central to their definition of borders, whereas, those proposing Proposition 187 sought to enact more figural borders, since they saw the literal one as ineffective at repelling unwanted migrants.

One reason for making the argument that discourse shifts borders is to further illustrate the ways the border is socially constructed and to reflect on how this socially constructed border impacts human beings. The US/Mexico border is the effect and aftereffect of war, but it is also an outcome of policy, and of law, which means it is the product of discourse. For example, even after the court rejected implementation of Proposition 187, tragic stories of migrants afraid to purchase food at grocery stores and not going to, or taking sick children to, the hospital appeared. The meaning of the border became real or realized through the discourses that circulated, regardless of the proposition's legal standing. Discourse's power to produce realities, including laws and rules of enforcement, is tremendous, no less so in its ability to define the border and render realities material.

In this chapter, I want to reiterate that borders are discursively defined and constructed by ever-changing rhetorics. In addition, I also want to go one step beyond that argument to suggest not only that borders have to do with lines of demarcation separating nation-states, the real or imagined dividing lines between nations, but also that borders follow migrants. Surveillance, disciplining, and control of migrants take place within the nation-state, enforcing border effects.[7] As with the border, a new era of what Gilberto Rosas calls "policeability" is at hand beyond the border, in which illegal surveillance and control practices are justified because of the overall logic that undocumented migrants' lives and civil rights are simply not as important as the lives and rights of documented citizens. As Rosas writes:

> Policeability thus also captures the daily evaluations of the cumulative effects of numerous, historically configured, ideological processes that dehumanize a population to the point that state violence, merciless disposability, and other forms of population management appear appropriate or inevitable. . . . Popular ontological signifiers of race, such as the speaking of subordinated languages, hygienic practices, forms

of dress, as well as phenotype, render immigrants and sometimes those who resemble them subject to such official and extra-official scrutiny. Policeability thus captures the politically organized investment in fixing difference. It thus renders race in the borderlands an ideologically charged social and political relation instead of an attribute or simply "color." (405)

The border already exists, sometimes incipiently and sometimes manifestly, where migrants move and on all of our bodies. The border moves with migrants into those social spaces where they live: in the interior of the nation, their workplaces, and their homes.

One way to get at this notion of a figural border, which I suggest has no less meaningfulness than its literal counterpart, is to consider where the border is enforced. We know the border is enforced at a "literal border" and have some sense of how that works, with security checkpoints, fences, sometimes walls, and the like, but where else is it enforced?

Border Enforcement without Borders

Just because someone crosses the border does not mean that the Immigration and Naturalization Service (INS), Homeland Security, the FBI, and other enforcement and surveillance agencies are not very much continuing to patrol the border on the streets of Los Angeles, in the fields of the Imperial Valley, on the Onion Farms of New York, and in poultry plants throughout the US South and Midwest.[8]

We all know about Doctors without Borders, but now we have Minutemen without borders. Pictured with guns and waiting for undocumented migrants to cross, Minutemen are well known for patrolling the US/Mexico border, as scholarship has addressed (DeChaine, "Bordering the Civic Imaginary"; Holling, "Patrolling National Identity"), and the relevant chapters in this volume amply demonstrate, but Minutemen groups have also emerged throughout the United States, such as in Tennessee, home of the "Tennessee Minutemen Project." While INS raids have been widespread, the site of the raids has not been limited to the West or Southwest. For example, on August 26, 1999, news media reported that the INS led a raid at the Mall of America, not aimed at employers but at undocumented workers, part of the longstanding immigrant-busting processes and practices of the state.

Just as the destruction of the World Trade Center buildings on September 11, 2001, became the rationale for the US war against Iraq, with Iraqis having had no discernible connection to the attacks, so too did 9/11 serve as the rationale for widespread surveillance of the general population of US Americans, and, conspicuously, of all migrants, not to mention difference generally. In a sense, 9/11 emerged as the raison d'être for the massive fortification of the surveillance state. The goal of controlling terrorists comes to stand in for a larger and more extensive application of surveillance and control systems of migrants, to name one central focus of such scrutiny.

To take this argument further, the production of a supply to meet the economic demand for laborers, which has been fundamental to both US economic and immigration policy—indeed, they are inextricably intertwined—is more easily regulated as a result of post-9/11 discipline and control mechanisms. The surveillance and control systems help to ensure that large numbers of new laboring bodies come into the nation to do work ordinary citizens may not want or have the skill to do, and to help ensure that those bodies leave when the work is done or when they are no longer needed. As Hardt and Negri have suggested about contemporary processes of empire, the control of the flexibility of the labor supply comes to be a taken-for-granted logic of how things have to be today in order to meet the demands of transnational capitalism.[9] To create a system that efficiently processes the arrival and departure of day-wage laborers, seasonal workers, and trade and domestic workers who help out trend, bubble, or boom-and-bust economies and who do not appear to be citizens, establishing a large-scale system of surveillance and control under the heading of "National Security," works more effectively and more efficiently than taking the time to argue for even more inhuman neoliberal policies in chambers of Congress.

The Border beyond the Border

The movement of migrant workers to the midwest, east, and south United States is increasingly gaining interest. Some of this migration is considered a secondary migration from the more historically populous southwestern and western regions, as well as other initial migration points in and outside of the nation. It goes without saying that migrants have crossed national borders to get to those locations, as they would to any location in the United States. But, extending the logic of this chapter, their border struggles hardly end there.

Those living in cities, suburbs, and even rural areas have often reacted in a startled fashion, not unlike the way Californians have reacted for well over a century and a half, expressing concern about the influx of new migrants into what they previously understood either to be their place/space, a (at least relatively) racially and culturally homogenous space. A not unusual outcome of this reaction is the establishment of organizations to reduce migration to these locations. One example is the "Midwest Coalition to Reduce Immigration." Started in 1995, the organization is located in LaValle, Wisconsin, about halfway between Madison and Eau Claire, in relative terms not far from the US/Canada border. Despite the town's close proximity to Canada, however, based on the articles on the organization's website, its concern is not the lengthy US/Canadian border but the US/ Mexico one. LaValle is, as of 2008, 97.5 percent white and 2.1 percent Latino. It is, by car, approximately 2,114 miles away from Tijuana, Mexico. The organization says it is a non-profit "charitable" organization "dedicated to educating Americans regarding the long-term consequences of present immigration laws. The evidence is overwhelming that it is in the best interests of present and future Americans to reduce annual immigration from the present unprecedented level of 2 million immigrants (half of them illegal) a year to our historic average of 300,000 a year." Characterizing immigration as an "invasion," the organization expresses concern both for the Midwest and the nation. The website makes hyperbolic predictions about devastating effects of population growth, and uses typical rhetorical strategies such as characterizing migrants through water metaphors, figuring Mexican women as breeders, appealing to health and crime fears, and of course making economic appeals.

The influx of migrants is seen and discussed as an intrusion on the nation, albeit at sites far away from the actual US border. The border that is enforced in these locales is a palpable one that migrants bring with them into communities, like LaValle. Undocumented people living, breathing, and traveling within the United States are constantly reminded that they have crossed a border, even if that border is far away from where they are now. Furthermore, they are reminded of how they represent the border. As Lisa Flores suggests, Latina/o immigrants' "suspect bodies carry the border on them. These bodies, even when present at physical locations quite distant from the geopolitical border, are susceptible targets" ("Constructing Rhetorical Borders" 381).

Another example of the border beyond the border appears in Annabel Park and Eric Byler's *9500 Liberty,* a documentary about Prince William County, Virginia's local response to the Latino community. The film explores the emergence of the "immigration resolution," a precursor to Arizona's Senate Bill 1070, which requires police to use probable cause as a rationale for investigating people's immigration status. Aided by a blog site, titled *Black Velvet Bruce Li,* anti-Latino members of Prince William County demonized Latinos in the community and led a movement for the approval of the resolution. The film documents both the supporters of the resolution and the activism (first primarily Latino, then eventually not Latino) opposing the resolution. Far away from the border itself, the film documents anti-Latino community members' frustrations with the effect of the Latino presence in their community. This frustration centers around anxieties and fears about educational quality, increased crime, disorderliness, housing, culture, economics, health services, and language. Because of all of these factors, the film suggests that the local community opposing the Latino presence effectively lobbies the county government, at least initially.

What happens after the resolution's initial passage, however, appears in the film to be shocking and devastating. The Latino residents of Prince William County seemingly disappear, abandoning their jobs and homes, as well as grocery stores, the post office, and other civic establishments. Latino activists, for the most part, are no longer seen protesting in numbers against the legislation; instead, they have chosen to leave. Then, primarily white residents against the resolution realize the economically devastating impact the resolution has had on them and their community now that the Latino community has left. It becomes apparent to them that, by leaving, their fellow Latino residents have removed from Prince William County their economic support of the county. Thus, a largely white group of activist community members seeks to overturn the legislation and eventually are successful at doing so.

What is clear in the film is that, far away from the literal border, the local anti-Latino community seeks to raise and enforce a figural border by passing legislation legalizing greater surveillance of immigration status. The Latino community is effectively repelled, but to dramatic economic effect. The border erected by anti-Latino activists then is effective at regulating inclusion and effecting exclusion, but the argument of the film is that such exclusion is ultimately self-defeating and counterproductive.

The film helps us to reorient our understanding of "border matters" as occurring far from the literal border. Migrants feel the sting of prejudice, as well as ungenerous and unkind reactions to their language. Yet, they contribute economically and culturally to the community. In addition to both seasonal and nonseasonal heavy farm labor—labor in packing plants, railroads, and other industrial sites—migrants in such locations may establish Mexican restaurants, bakeries, grocery stores, and Spanish-language radio stations and newspapers, among other community services. Furthermore, local governments may be either resistant or slow to respond to the movement of increasing numbers of migrants to the area. Translators for 911 operators, police, education, and the like may be necessary. Bilingual instructors may be needed. It may take a number of years, but the community adaptation processes may include the establishment of policies about student attendance at public schools and services that address the needs of native Spanish-speaking community members.

Thus, as 9500 *Liberty* indicates, once migrants move to locations interior to the United States, borders may exist and then may be employed in a way to prevent further crossing, to inhibit access, and, perhaps, to render the crossing of the national inconsequential, all while the moving border transforms the economy, culture, community, and government of the places to which it travels.

Whereas immigration is often thought of, then, as a national issue or a state issue (e.g., for Texas, Arizona, New Mexico, and California), in fact one way border discourses come into play is through the regulation, disciplining, and control of migrants in their communities of residence. It is here that a secondary, alternative, or what I call figural border comes into play, one without the overt danger the national border poses, at least initially, but one that has the potential to be felt just as palpably over time.

Bodily Borders

As I have suggested, migrants carry borders with them. This means not only that the issues about the border continue long after the border crossing, but that the threat of deportation and of control and surveillance akin to that at the border continues, as well. Thus, in this final section, I discuss the body, specifically, in terms of the border and the way borders follow bodies and the way bodies come to function, figurally, as borders themselves.

Historically, the body has served as an apt metaphor for the nation.[10] The "national body" has symmetrical and asymmetrical dimensions to the body of its citizens. For instance, the body, itself, has a border—with skin and hair, contours, and, thus, a shape. Race, gender, and sexuality can be read onto bodies, as they can onto nations. A body, or a representation of a body, such as the Statue of Liberty, can symbolically stand in for the nation, as women and women's bodies can generally serve iconically as emblems of national identities, morals, convictions, and such abstract notions as purity. Nations are also asymmetrical. So, for instance, bodies travel—they migrate—whereas nations regulate bodily movement through migration policies. Furthermore, nations are imagined, in the way Benedict Anderson describes, and yet bodies have actual, perceivable materiality and can thus be seen and experienced directly.

But, there has also always been a degree of commensurability between the body and citizenship. Thus, in order for citizens to be separated from immigrant noncitizens, so too do citizen bodies have to be differentiated from immigrant noncitizen bodies. As Shoshana Magnet has suggested, researchers and entrepreneurs have been working to produce facial recognition technologies and other biometric technologies that can help isolate that dimension of the physical body that can lead to successful differentiation from other bodies, so that one can confirm the identity of the citizen and the noncitizen immigrant ("Bio-Benefits"). Such dividing practices have not only physical but psychological effects, as DeChaine suggests when he writes, "Defining clear and self-evident lines between American citizen and alien invader, as the [Minuteman Civil Defense Corps] does, reveals the ease with which psychic territories and their cultural investments map onto and reinforce physical territories and their geopolitical investments. More importantly, the us/them binary that such bordering practices work to cement into place all but guarantees an irredeemable non-place for the racialized, alienized, border-crossing migrant in the United States today" ("Bordering the Civic Imaginary" 59). The body and mind, like the land, therefore, are sites of control, and simply migrating past the physical border does not mean or by any means guarantee one's body and mind are free from border control. Indeed, while one can cross a physical geographical boundary, it is possible that the body and mind as boundaries ultimately prevent successful border crossing.

The familiar saying among activists that "we didn't cross the border, the border crossed us" suggests that borders crossed the bodies of Chicanas/os, even as Chicanas/os crossing the border is typically emphasized. But, more pointedly, the body as a border, also, is always shifting. As DeChaine writes, "Not only do border guards check papers, but since *the alienized subject carries the border on her back,* she is constantly subject to surveillance and search. She may or may not be what she seems; although she is among the community, although she may be naturalized, she is not naturally of the community" ("Bordering the Civic Imaginary" 51; emphasis added).

The body is a site of signification, one that often determines inclusion and exclusion. Emphases of research, particularly after Operation Gatekeeper, understandably have been on bodies at the border. So, for instance, Karl Eschbach, Jacqueline Hagan, Nestor Rodriguez, Ruben Hernandez-Leon, and Stanley Bailey study the dead bodies of migrants along the border, bodies that died from such things as drowning, dehydration, and hypothermia. However, I would argue that hate crimes, mysterious deaths, deaths because of a lack of health care, and even contested deaths of migrants should also figure as "border deaths," despite their proximity (or lack thereof) to the physical location of the national border, and precisely because we need to reorient our understanding of the border to understand its figural meaning.

Even attaining permanent resident status or citizenship is not sufficient for a complete or successful border crossing. If the border signifies a site of contestation over inclusion, access, rights, employment, and a future for one's self and often one's family, the body may serve as a border that prevents these aspirations from being attained. As I have indicated elsewhere, there is such a thing as formal and informal citizenship that very much determines the different kinds of experiences of citizenship one might have over time, within spaces, and in one's life (Ono, "From Nationalism to Migrancy"). Scholars of whiteness studies in communication have suggested that bodies betray identities, whether self-known or not. Bodies and their performances are at the center of the promise of empowerment and privilege. Ruth Frankenberg has shown that the bodies of people of color have functioned as a map of what whiteness is not for white people. Bodies that have crossed geographical borders, literal borders, may be determining of inclusion, access, rights, employment, and one's future.

There is much more to be learned about bodies beyond borders, and hence the way fences on bodies are constructed through discourse. As Flores suggests, "The various characterizations that emerged across these tales constructed Mexican character so that it had no permanent place in the national body" ("Constructing Rhetorical Borders" 380). Hence in her study, Mexicans came to be what DeChaine calls "alienized," but which I also read here as "denationalized"—the process of one being cast outside of the border, even when one is still located physically within the borders of the nation (from which one seeks citizenship).

From the wink of an eye to the tilt of one's head to the lilt in one's voice, bodies may unknowingly reveal bordered identities. The body itself is a readable text, is discursive, and therefore may be understood to have meanings that need to be controlled, disciplined, deported, imprisoned, or discarded. The body performs bordered identities, revealing aspects of identity that can be regulated as on this or that side of a given border. The body is also a site of signification and can and does serve as part of a rationale for the distribution of resources. The degree to which a body can cross, whether in law or in other realms of daily life, even as the first physical border has been crossed, renders it an object of continuing border politics.[11] As much as human migration has always been definitive of humanity, the regulation of the crosser, and what that crossing may mean about future crossings, is powerfully illustrated by seeing the border as a semiotics of the body's signification of to-be-includedness. With processes of bordering bodies always in flux, always shifting, always yet to be determined, there is much work to do.

If borders are not just there physically to separate national lands and people, but in fact the struggle over the border is the struggle over inclusion, just treatment, and the degree of a society's sense of a common humanity, we must think of borders and border crossing beyond where oceans meet land, where rivers divide nations, and where fences stand, and think of borders as potential limitations on what we imagine others and ourselves to be.

Notes

1. The US/Mexico border is the most crossed national border in the world. Nevins notes that approximately 40,000 people each day cross the border for work (6).

2. Joseph Nevins provides an appendix showing the annexation of land over time, from the bottom of Oregon, Idaho, and Wyoming to all of California, Nevada, Utah, Arizona, New Mexico, Texas, and most of Colorado. From 1836 to 1853, the US claim of territory moved dramatically south, and ended more or less where the line currently exists.

3. The juxtaposition of the multitude of crossings for those encouraged to do so against the enforcement preventing crossings for those discouraged from doing so is all the more tragic and ironic.

4. In *Shifting Borders: Rhetoric, Immigration, and California's Proposition 187,* we suggest that discourse shifts borders. Borders come to have meaning and particular effects, depending on how they are discussed and defined. In that study of rhetoric surrounding California's Proposition 187, we contend that discourse figuratively moved the border, rendering undocumented and documented migrants, especially from Mexico, beyond the acceptable boundary of the nation-state.

5. It is in the video *Stuart Hall: Representation and the Media* that Hall argues that "nothing *meaningful* exists outside of discourse."

6. In the video *Stuart Hall: Representation and the Media,* Hall suggests there are two *old* theories of representation: (1) as standing in for, as a politician *represents* a constituency, and (2) reflecting reality, as in documentaries that show us the way things really are. He argues that a third definition, which addresses the incommensurability between material reality and images/discourses, is needed. My thinking adds to this that images/discourses constitute material realities, even when we sometimes initially think this is not something images/discourses could possibly do.

7. Of course, how well such surveillance and control practices work is up for debate. As Audrey Singer and Douglas S. Massey suggest, studies of the clandestine ways migrants cross borders indicate such practices may backfire. They argue that police patrols at the border, attempts to stem the war on drugs, and the apprehension of undocumented workers "only serve . . . to socialize immigrants into the rules of undocumented border crossing" (562).

8. While not perhaps directly about the border or the state, living conditions and psychological trauma experienced by laborers without adequate health, sanitation, or labor conditions produce a border effect. It is also important to note New York State's attempts to prevent undocumented people from driving cars through the regulation of driver's licenses.

9. Ultimately, there is no desire for those who do the work, no interest in their becoming permanent and legitimate members of the society. Rather, those who do the most work do the work that is the least desired and desirable; hence, while their labor may be indispensable, their citizenship and humanity are expendable, indeed deportable.

10. Indeed, immigration and nationhood is a kind of metaphor. I fondly remember Michael McGee asking, "when was the last time you saw a 'people' walking up your driveway?" The conceit of the nation-state is effectively a metaphor, just as the body is a metaphor.

11. The courts have been one site where the arbitration of color has taken place, from laws regulating miscegenation to laws that determine citizenship. Bodies are read; readings of bodies happen. Readings of bodies have material effects.

2
Bordering as Social Practice

Intersectional Identifications and
Coalitional Possibilities

Julia R. Johnson

As sites of cultural contestation and negotiation, borders are material spaces and symbolic constructions that regulate and reflect cultural citizenship and belonging. While borders are frequently conceptualized as geographic spaces, recent scholarship has addressed bordering as social practice, or a performative and rhetorical construction operating in and through law, public discourse, and human interaction. As Anzaldúa argues in *Borderlands/La Frontera,* bordering practices are divisive and reinforce hierarchies of power:

> A border is a dividing line, a narrow strip along a steep edge. A borderland is a vague and underdetermined place created by the emotional residue of an unnatural boundary. It is in a constant state of transition. The prohibited and forbidden are its inhabitants. *Los atravesados* live here: the squint-eyed, the perverse, the queer, the troublesome, the mongrel, the mulato, the half-breed, the half date; in short, those who cross over, pass over, or go through the confines of the "normal." . . . The only "legitimate" inhabitants are those in power, the whites and those who align themselves with whites. Tension grips the inhabitants of the borderlands like a virus. Ambivalence and unrest reside there and death is no stranger. (3–4)

In this chapter, I explore the themes and implications of Anzaldúa's theorizing, including the processes of constructing borders, the differences that are fundamental to bordering practices, and the construction of border(ed) bodies as perverse and beyond normalized citizenship. I approach bordering *as* performance, which allows me to attend to the ongoing activities that create border geographies on the land and also in a nation's social relations. By their very existence and definition, bordering practices involve identity intersections, embodiment, as well as coalitional possibilities.[1]

Identity categories always intersect, although we often engage identity as immutable and categories as natural. Modes of identification[2] and identity categories are inscribed in social interactions, and I contend herein the rhetorics of the US-Mexico border draw on intersectional activities and configurations as a fundamental component of defining national (il)legitimacy. Generally, race, ethnicity, and even social class are foregrounded in discussions of bordering practices. Less prevalent are public considerations of gender, sexual identification, sex, or dis/ability, although we are regularly confronted with "concrete instances of gender-based or gender-motivated violence" (Corona and Domínguez-Ruvalcaba 1) as evidenced by femicides in places such as Ciudad Juárez or violence against persons who are transgender. The bodies of persons who identify as women or gender nonconforming are targets of related, connected, and yet distinctive forms of violence in border zones. For this reason, I focus herein on how identity intersections—particularly sex, gender, nationality, race, and sexuality—are constructed and/or impacted by (other) bordering practices.

Although it is imperative to address the distinctive histories that particular groups face in terms of systematic state oppression and violence, there are three reasons for theorizing intersectionality: At the most basic level, intersectionality is always inscribed in our identifying practices, including bordering. In order to understand the complexity of bordering and its significance in our social imaginary, the act of naming and dissecting constructions of intersectional identifications is imperative. Second, nuanced understandings of the privilege-oppression dialectic are palpable and visible when the dynamic interchange between identifications and identity categories is explored. Finally, and this point is related to the second, if an analysis of bordering practices is designed to promote social change as much as it is intended to be an intellectual exercise, then attending to intersectionality creates the possibility for analyzing how oppression functions as a prelude to disrupting domination. Until we can both respect the important differences that define us as well as build coalitions that resist dominant cultural interests, we will continue to perpetuate the injustices and violence that result from crossing the US-Mexico border or that result from occupying a body targeted and terrorized by the state and normalized citizens.

Herein, I examine the intersectional nature of bordering practices by first exploring bordering as a social process informed by questions of citizenship and belonging. Second, I address the complexity of bordering through scholarship that attends to the interconnectedness of citizenship/migration and constructions of sex, gender, and sexual orientation. Finally, I explore relational practices that offer possibilities for working across lines of difference to transform the normative, oppressive, and violent realities imposed on persons most impacted by border rhetorics and performances.

Border(ing), Citizenship, and Racialization

Borders and bordering are treacherous, precarious, and complicated—and they regulate embodiment and social identifications. Bordering marks social belonging as some people are included and others excluded. In the context of the US–Mexico border, bordering almost always involves state-encouraged physical violence (or threats), sexual assault, policing, and social surveillance by normalized citizens. Although borders are constructed as immutable territories (terror-tories), as Bosniak notes, "borders are neither fixed nor static; what counts as part of the inside or outside is subject to ongoing negotiation and contestation. And whatever the prevailing understanding of their character or location, as a practical matter national borders are very often tested, stretched, permeated, or breached" (7). Borders are, most importantly, rhetorical and relational performances that circulate within and reconstruct the social fabric of civic life. Borders move with the people who cross them (Bosniak; DeChaine, "Bordering the Civic Imaginary") and function as lines of demarcation between and within communities. As DeChaine contends, examining "the rhetorical dimensions of the border requires a shift in focus from borders to bordering, from a consideration of static entities to an analysis of a dynamic practice" (46). When borders are treated as static geographic spaces, peoples' embodiments and identifications are reduced to essentialized identity categories. A performance approach to the study of borders disrupts fixedness because it requires attending to the processes that make borders meaningful. By critically examining the processes or acts that construct border realities, one can attend to the dynamic interplay between the structures that benefit from stasis and the human agency that acts within and on structural forces.

Symbolic processes are always imbued with morality and hierarchy. The rhetorical constructions of nationality and bordering practices illustrate how different nations separated by borders are constructed as existing in different stages of hierarchical development that marks the migrant's body in degrees of "more or less sophisticated" (Brady, *Extinct Lands* 50). Brady continues: "National borders utilize the fantasy that a nation on one side of the border exists in one phase of temporal development while the nation on the other side functions at a different stage. . . . [A] person can be formed in one temporality but when he or she crosses a border that person transmogrifies, as it were, into someone either more or less advanced, more or less modern, more or less sophisticated" (50). Historically, we have ample evidence that some migrants[3] are welcomed more readily than others and allowed to fold seamlessly into the social fabric, while other migrants are always positioned as foreign, subordinate, or dangerous to the nation. As Schmidt Camacho describes, "The migrant [from Mexico to the United States] . . . not only connotes one who moves within and across national boundaries; it also references a subordinate position with respect to that of the citizen" (5). Rhetorical scholars (and migration scholars more generally) have provided significant insight into the how Mexican-ness, Latina-ness, or Chicano-ness are marked as foreign, alien, illegal, pollutants, criminals, and/ or parasites (Chávez, "Embodied Translation"; Flores, "Constructing Rhetorical Borders"; Ono and Sloop). In this volume (and elsewhere), performance scholars like Calafell illustrate how these public bordering practices infiltrate even the most intimate relationships we have with family or ourselves.

The rhetorical process that constructs particular migrants as threats to the nation also draws on the symbolic practices that subjugate people within a national body. Those embodiments dehumanized by dynamics of oppression within the nation-state are the very migrant bodies the government works diligently to exclude.[4] The literal territories of borders extend into the social sphere as a relational politic that defines national belonging, a point that is most clearly demonstrated when "foreigners enter the bounded national territory from the outside and, once present, are assigned the status of alienage. These noncitizen immigrants . . . remain outsiders in a significant sense: The border effectively follows them inside" (Bosniak 4). When the "alien within" (Bosniak) slips beyond the militaristic barriers of a border territory, s/he must contend with the figurative borders operating within the national imaginary. There is a connection between the dominant discourses that are used at geographic borders and the social/relational borders at work within the US nation-state: for example, white supremacy is used to mark some racialized bodies as always foreign and others as intrinsically "American";[5] heterosexual supremacy is used to ensure that gender-conforming, sex-conforming heterosexuals are given access to legal and social rights while persons who are lesbian, gay, or transgender are socially stigmatized and denied entry to the United States or denied legal sanctions; ableism is used to assert the normalcy of particular embodiments and bodily functions while simultaneously pathologizing, institutionalizing, and denying entry to those with disabilities; and so forth.

Bordering practices involve constructions of what constitutes a citizen and who is allowed to perform that role. The rhetoric of citizenship has relied on the systematic privileging of some bodies and systematic exclusion, oppression, and victimization of others. In legal scholarship, citizenship has been conceptualized in a myriad of ways, including as "self-governance," "the entity that both guarantees rights and defines legal status," a "right to decent work," "the assurance of community recognition despite difference, or as recognition of 'the right to be different,'" and the recognition of "social and cultural . . . group identities" (Bosniak 21–23). These definitions of citizenship range in their assumptions, beginning with dominant (positioned as putatively objective, universal, and/or neutral) definitions of "exclusively state-centered conceptions of citizenship" (24) in which "all citizens of a particular nation state are [considered] equal before the law" to those definitions that address the "men of privilege from the rest, second-class citizens and non-citizens" (Rosaldo, "Cultural Citizenship" 253). As critical scholars contend, citizenship has always referenced more than the "objective" definitions of who has legal recognition and sanction. Gaining access to rights has always involved dynamics of privilege and oppression, and specific groups have historically been excluded from both the idea of citizenship as well as its empirical benefits. Immigration rhetorics regularly invoke notions of citizenship, addressing not only who belongs, but also "what kind of member of a society a person will be, what benefits of citizenship will be offered to some and not others, and how those who do not belong and are not members ultimately will be treated" (Ono and Sloop 106). Visual markers of difference have been a primary mechanism for determining people's access to "full democratic participation" (Rosaldo, "Cultural Citizenship" 254) and have been used to justify state-sanctioned bordering acts.

Bordering practices rely on identity constructions and inscriptions for their efficacy and force. Historically, US citizenship has been racialized, a process that has systematically privileged (monied, heterosexual, able-bodied, Protestant) whiteness and systematically oppressed persons of all other colors. It was one of the most prolific scholars of the twentieth century, W. E. B. Du Bois, who contended that blackness and Americanness are positioned in opposition. "The American Negro . . . simply wishes to make it possible for a man to be both a Negro and an American, without being cursed and spit on by his fellows, without having the doors of Opportunity closed roughly in his face" (9). The political efforts of Du Bois permeate contemporary citizenship struggles. Bordering continues to be racialized and bordering practices are directed inward as well as outward—what Bosniak calls the "introjection of borders." National borders are policed through legislation such as Arizona's Senate Bill 1070 and House Bill 2281. SB 1070 gives Arizona police authority to request proof of citizenship/immigration status from someone who "looks like" an "alien." The law makes "the failure to carry immigration documents a crime and give[s] the police broad power to detain anyone suspected of being in the country illegally" (Archibold, "Arizona Enacts"). HB 2281 prohibits Arizona schools from teaching courses in ethnic studies. Of course, the persons profiled by the police or the prohibited studies of ethnicity are not directed to persons who appear or identify as white. They are targeted primarily against Latina/o communities who are constructed as perpetually foreign and threats to the normalcy of white supremacist constructions of race and ethnicity, although racialized bordering is directed at most communities of color. For example, on June 5, 2010, the US Border Patrol and Immigration and Customs Enforcement (ICE) raided the wedding reception of a newly married, interracial, binational Vermont couple, Danielle and Thierno Diallo (Huneke) and requested papers and information about from where guests had traveled (Welch). ICE agents claimed that "someone had called them and said there were people here from all over," although the police department hadn't received any noise complaints or calls. "The Diallos said they wanted to tell their story because racist and anti-immigrant harassment are daily realities for the state's immigrants and racial minorities" (Welch). From the segregation of Native Americans onto reservations, to the internment of Japanese, to the assimilation of most white ethnic groups, to the detention of persons from Haiti, Cuba, Afghanistan, and/or persons described as terrorist (which, in the context of the West, is most often a man perceived to be from Western Asia) in Guantanamo, racialization has defined citizenship and belonging.

Racialized bordering practices—as well as the bordering practices described in the next section—all involve the process of alienization and abjection. A nation-state needs its scapegoats as much as it needs its "legitimate" citizens because belonging is performed through exclusion. In *Imperial Leather,* McClintock contends that imperialism requires the presence of abject subjects, or those persons who "inhabit the impossible edges of modernity" such as slums, ghettos, and garrets. "[S]laves, prostitutes, the colonized, domestic workers, the insane, the unemployed" occupy physical and cultural zones that are "policed with vigor" and whose presence is integral to the construction of the nation (72). The process of rhetorically expunging "undesirable" persons defines who "belongs" within the national territory. The nation knows itself by deflecting and extirpating "interlopers," which preserves a dehumanizing social system. An imperial state must subjugate in order to retain its raison d'être—it creates abject subjects because it cannot do without them, in part because nations like the United States were formed by colonizing and exterminating indigenous people. DeChaine describes the process of rendering "individuals and groups abject and inassimilable—irredeemable others whose putative exclusion from the national body is virtually absolute"—as alienization ("Bordering the Civic Imaginary," 45). Alienization is an affective process that is constantly in flux and that "provides a national community with a repertoire of symbolic resources for naming and thus bringing into being its valuative [liberal democratic] structure" (48). It is a "moralizing discourse" that marks the "border-crossing migrant" as "the social (dis)ease of the US border problem" (49) and that vilifies the "un-American presence from within" (50).

Importantly, the abjection and alienization processes McClintock and DeChaine describe are as mundane as they are extraordinary. They are part of our daily communicative practices and, thus, are foundational to our collective self-knowledge. Furthermore, the symbolic and mundane are material and impact physical reality. As Rosaldo notes, "The physical border has become a line of demarcation enforced by stayed high-tech violence that is no less violent for being symbolic and vice versa—no less suffused with cultural meanings for being lethal and material" ("Cultural Citizenship" 259). Furthermore, Manalansan contends that a focus on the everyday "points to the complexities of various intersections and borderlands of race, gender, class, and sexuality in diasporic and immigrant groups" and is a "crucial 'problematic' and as a site of tactical maneuvers for creating selves and forging relationships for marginalized groups, particularly diasporic queers everywhere" ("Migrancy, Modernity, Mobility" 147). As Goltz and Pérez illustrate in this volume, we are all implicated in bordering practices. They state: "We all do the border, just as the border does each of us."

Bordering Interconnections: Genders, Sexes, and Affectional/Sexual Identifications

Public discourse about the US-Mexico border and bordering practices tends to direct our attention to racialization and often excludes the identifications that are in simultaneous operation. Bordering practices always involve the simultaneous performance of intersectional identifications, even in moments or cases when we can't know or feel the intersectional forces (Johnson, Bhatt, and Patton). As Lister claims in her feminist analysis of citizenship, "exclusionary tendencies are inherently gendered" and "Gendered patterns of exclusion interact with other axes of social division such as class, 'race,' disability, sexuality, and age in ways which can be either multiplicative or contradictory, and which shift over time" (38). Border and migration scholars have affirmed the intersections of identity, particularly the ways "race," class, gender, sexual identification, ability, and sex intersect—or, more to the theoretical point I want to make in this chapter, the ways racialization, classing, gendering, heterosexualizing or queering, ablizing, and/or sexing are interimbricated in bordering practices (Anzaldúa; Chávez, "Border [In]Securities"; Luibhéid, "Introduction"; Manalansan, *Global Divas*). The embodied realities of those who must address multiple forms of oppression prompted theoretically and politically relevant research because "[I]n the United States and elsewhere, citizens who were not white, male, able-bodied, property-owning, and sexually reproductive faced great struggle in becoming formally recognized as full, rights-bearing members of the national community" (Luibhéid, "Introduction" xix).

Performing identity and citizenship in alignment with dominant discourses is a predominant feature of liberal democratic life, both in terms of who and what we learn to value and the subsequent relational engagements this socialization encourages. Importantly, biology and physiology do not determine ideology, so engaging discourses of domination can be done by any *body*. Groups who are structurally oppressed along one axis of identification often use discourses of privilege to address their oppression. Dominant groups regularly uphold their privilege by dehumanizing Others and even blame the oppressed. In his exploration of cultural citizenship, Rosaldo notes that "too often social thought anchors its research in the vantage point of the dominant social group and thus reproduces dominant ideology by studying subordinate groups as a 'problem' rather than as people with agency—with goals, perceptions, and purposes of their own" ("Cultural Citizenship" 260). Certainly the authors in this volume approach the study of borders from "the aspirations and perceptions of people who occupy subordinate social positions" (Rosaldo, "Cultural Citizenship" 260). Additionally, significant scholarship has been dedicated to intersectional explorations of bordering practices, ranging from studies addressing gender violence along the US–Mexico border (Corona and Domínguez-Ruvalcaba), to ethnographic explorations of queer diasporic communities living in New York (Manalansan, *Global Divas*), to the assemblages of identifications central to imperial war machines like the United States (Puar). In what follows, I address two intersectional analyses that complicate our understandings of bordering.

Gender violence is a significant problem along the US–Mexico border, as evidenced by the brutal murders of women in Ciudad Juárez.[6] Persons who are transgender are also targets of violence and surveillance along geographic borders (Castillo, Gómez, and Solís; Solomon), and, as analysis of media coverage demonstrates, gender violence is a dominant theme emerging in coverage of border life (Corona). As Mackie contends, the ideal citizen is expected to be "monosexual," an expectation that corresponds to state interests in regulating each person's reproductive capacity (189). In the United States, the medical and state regulation of reproductive capacity and the sexed body is complex and violent. The very nature of transgressing gender and sex categories invokes logics of belonging and citizenship—when a person is not easily recognized as conforming to a particular gendered identity or in cases in which one is misrecognized (that is, read as a gender or sex other than one with which one identifies), the result is often physical violence, social rejection, and/or the demand for identity confirmation/identity papers. In short, citizenship demands a situating of self within the sex binary, as evidenced by our constrained choices of public restroom, sex markers on state-sanctioned documents, or proof of sex-gender alignment when flying. "For gender-variant bodies, the border at which identity documents are demanded might be located anywhere, in a public toilet . . . on the street, in a bank or a doctor's surgery" (Aizura 290). Aizura continues: "To speak about gender-variant bodies is often to engage in a metaphorical slippage between geography and gender" (289).

For gender nonconforming persons, intersectional identifications further complicate the bordering practices they are forced to address. Transgender sex workers along the US-Mexican border have been used as evidence of an "emblem of menacing excess and indeterminacy" of Mexican migration and posing a kind of doubled threat to US gender and national hierarchies (Solomon 18–19). In a preliminary study of transgender sex workers in Tijuana, Castillo, Gómez, and Solís illustrate the intersecting practices of sex, class, gender, race, and sexual identification. As is most often the case with sex workers, the sex workers they studied enter the profession as a way to earn a living and the sex trade creates a market for sexual commodification. In this case, gay sex tourism enforces a market for transgender sex workers as gay clients "hook up" with gender nonconforming persons when they cross from the United States into Mexico (although the majority of the clients of the persons interviewed in this study were local). As working people who have no social or state-sanctioned protections, transgender sex workers are subject to the violence of state agents and other "citizens": they experience physical beatings and rape from police, they are extorted, and they are frequently raped and then dumped beyond the city limits. The bordering practices Castillo, Gómez, and Solís describe are varied and complex. The workers are desired for their intersecting identifications, including their racialization as Latina/o as well as their gender- and sex-nonconformity. Their availability for consumption is both informed by their agency and the structural processes that make sex work and gender nonconforming bodies (trans)national commodities. Men—self-identified as gay and heterosexual from both Mexico and the United States—perform their own identifications in relationship to the transgender workers, and act with/on the sex workers' bodies to perform racialized, gendered, sexed, sexual, and classed fantasies and identifications.

The intersectional borderings of mainstream lesbian, gay, and bisexual (LGB) communities within the United States further illustrate the complexities of identification and border rhetorics. Mainstream lesbian, gay, bisexual, transgender, intersex (LGBTI) movements in the United States have been "formed on normatively white and national terms" (Morgensen 106) and have tended to mainstream consumptive practices as well as exclude people who identify as people of color, working class or poor, people with disabilities, and those born outside the US. The contemporary analysis of homonationalism, or homonormative nationalism,[7] illustrates this claim well. In *Terrorist Assemblages: Homonationalism in Queer Times,* Puar extends homonormative theorizing to offer a trenchant analysis of the ways mainstream LGBTIQ communities make claims to normalized citizenship that rely on the perversion of and "improperly hetero- and homo-Muslim sexualities" (xxiv). Through her analysis, we are given compelling evidence of the ways that LGBTIQ demands for normative rights are deeply intertwined with the construction of "foreign" and terrorist threats by those constructed as Muslim. For example, Puar assesses the connections between the legalization of sodomy in the United States at a historical moment when " 'gay sex' [was] used as torture at Abu Ghraib," Michael Jackson was on trial for molestation, and Pashtun Afghanis were reported to be pedophilic (117). She illustrates how persons defined as nonnormative enlist claims of queer exceptionalism that are always positioned in contrast to "perverse (Orientalist) *and* repressed (neo-Orientalist human rights discourse)" as in the case of "South Asian queer diasporic subjects" targeted for "sexual, verbal, and physical assaults" as part of a post-9/11 series of hate crimes (168–69). Arondekar elaborates with an example from San Francisco: "A Latino gay man was reportedly beaten up for appearing Middle Eastern by a gang of Latino youngsters . . . while the media quietly ignored the presence of his gay white lover who accompanied him and was also similarly brutalized by the same group of individuals. Such misrecognitions of civil rights have been accompanied by a concurrent and visible remasculinization of American culture as strong, turban-less, aggressively heterosexual, and refueled with a newer, more bellicose version of the colonial *mission civilisatrice*" (242–43). Puar's and Arondekar's analyses of interconnected identifications offer various insights. First, sex, gender, and sexual orientation are always raced and racialization is always sexed, gendered, and sexualized (along with other identifications). Second, the examples the authors offer extend an understanding of how privilege and oppression interact as nondominant groups engage alienizing discourses in their quests for citizenship/belonging. Third, structures of power position historically oppressed groups in opposition through the state's practices that operate beyond any one geographic location or beyond the choices one person can make.

Connective Practices and Alliances

Dismantling the violence inflicted by interpenetrating forces of privilege and oppression requires naming, resistance, and refusal—naming power and how it operates, resisting the impulse to engage one kind of cultural dominance in the name of combating another, and a refusal to gain rights while others are dehumanized. Here, I want to take the opportunity to examine, briefly, two examples of intersectional and coalitional work that illustrate the deep humanity, resistance, and perseverance of those who question dominant constructions of citizenship and exclusionary modes of belonging.

Transgender author-activist Leslie Feinberg has consistently addressed the interconnections of the oppression ze[8] experiences as a white, US-born, Jewish, working-class, gender-nonconforming person. Simultaneously, ze has examined these identifications as relational by regularly analyzing differing positionalities, including hir's positioning in relation to others. Feinberg's novel *Drag King Dreams* (*DKD*) is the story of a racially diverse, transgender, working-class community of friends and activists living in post-9/11 New York City. As the story unfolds, we experience the politically charged, border world of Max Rabinowitz and his immediate community of activist-ally-family members who work in drag bars at night, who split their wages so that all of them can survive, and who persistently face the boundaries of citizenship defined by a structure that systematically seeks to exclude, dehumanize, and do violence against them.

The relationships in the novel prompt the reader to question the politics of belonging and exclusion, particularly as Feinberg constructs the city as a border zone—a trans/national space of interdependent differences that challenge and transform binaries of woman/man, feminine/masculine, home/elsewhere, and us (American)/them (foreign threat). The narrative of the novel is structured around Max Rabinowitz, a working-class, queer-identified, transmasculine[9] person. From the first pages of the novel, ze negotiates physical and rhetorical violence based on individual gender expression and as a member of a multiracial, multiethnic, multi-gendered, and queer-identified[10] community. As the story unfolds, Rabinowitz moves through spaces marked by gender variance (bars, hospital rooms) as well as through im/migrant communities that are part of hir geographic home, such as neighborhoods ("Little India"), celebrations (Navratri), and local businesses (owned by Muslim im/migrants). Within spaces occupied by national and ethnic "Others," Rabinowitz reflects on hir own identities as well as the identity positions occupied, celebrated, and rejected by friends and neighbors. Through these reflections—and through the generous acts of coalition extended to hir by persons also positioned precariously in bordering practices—Rabinowitz forges deeply felt communal alliances with those who differ from hir, which pushes hir to move from a consciousness of "individual" resistance to gender and class oppression into collective action that challenges US imperialism, class supremacy, white supremacy, gender oppression, and xenophobia.

In her essay entitled "Border (In)Securities: Normative and Differential Belonging in LGBTQ and Immigrant Rights Discourse," Chávez illustrates the power of coalitional collaboration. Chávez uses the concept of "differential belonging"[11] to explore how one immigrant rights organization (Coalición de Derechos Humanos) and one LGBT rights organization (Wingspan) work coalitionally to address anti-immigrant and anti-LGBT oppression. She cites the organizations' joint statement constructed to respond, in part, to propositions on the Arizona ballot that "are simply the latest in an ongoing, state- and nationwide campaign of coded racist dehumanization aimed at undocumented migrants and anyone else of color who might fit in the underlying racial profile. We also recognize that proposition 107 is a continuation of homophobic attacks aimed at lesbian, gay, bisexual, and transgender people of all races, ethnicities, and nations. Using an onslaught of initiatives in multiple states, state and federal legislation, and demonizing words and images, these campaigns of dehumanization do great harm to all people" (147). Chávez argues that "to overtly link anti-migrant and anti-queer oppression and to demonstrate solidarity between two seemingly separate communities" (146), the groups illustrate through their statement and work that "they are all implicated in the dehumanization of each other" (147). Both the examples Chávez uses and the nature of her analysis illustrate that identifications are always mutually formative and that solidarity is formed through an investment in challenging interlocking as well as distinct forms of oppression.

Feinberg's book and Chávez's analysis of differential belonging illustrate the importance and the power of combating bordering practices across lines of difference. They move us beyond the "first-person narrative point of view" characteristic of our post-9/11 world (Butler, *Precarious Life*), and they challenge the ways some identifications (i.e., homosexualities and queer-nesses) can both resist and legitimate the interests of a US war machine (Puar). Additionally, they offer examples for theorizing how queerness and transgenderism are intimately intertwined with the histories of colonialism (Richardson, in Currah) and for exploring how borders function as sites of resistance and mourning as well as sites of oppression (Schmidt Camacho).

To clamor for rights using dominant cultural logics may ultimately lead to benefits for aspects of one community, but those rights will always re-quire structural oppression of others. The only chance we have for social justice is through making the oppressions of others our own. We must also employ activisms and rhetorics that rigorously address the intertwined reali-ties of vastly different social groups. The undocumented migrant, the trans-gender worker, and the Imam all have distinct histories and experiences to which we must attend as we correspondingly imagine the rights of one as central to the possibility of belonging to the other.

I read the chapters in this volume as a form of scholarly activism— intellectual and affective interrogations into bordering practices. The authors may not conceive of themselves as activists, but, hopefully, these critiques of rhetorical borders and bordering as performance provide insight and inspira-tion for collective efforts to transform the very rhetorical-material dynam-ics about which we write. Coalitional work is complicated and painful, and it requires constant vigilance to disrupt the conflicting and interrelated his-tories and dynamics of power that position us hierarchically. In spite of our best intentions, we often invoke the oppressions we seek to disrupt. With diligence and through vigilant coalitional engagements, we might trans-form systematic subjugation. I take seriously Freire's contention that our ability to be humanized is interdependent. If one of us is subjugated, dehu-manized, or oppressed, then no one can be fully human.

Notes

1. In this chapter, I focus on bordering practices generally, and address the US-Mexico border in various examples; however, I contend that it is impor-tant to avoid constructing this particular border region as exceptional (Corona and Domínguez-Ruvalcaba). While there is clearly a specific history to US-Mexico bordering policies and practices to which we must carefully attend and that should not be equated with other spaces and processes, bordering dynamics and problems cannot be attributed to any one geographic space, and situating the rhetorics surrounding the US-Mexico border in a broader bordering matrix

will aid in an understanding of the structural forces at work on the lives, bodies, and discourses of human subjects in relation to the nation-state.

2. I use the word "identification" in order to highlight the processual and relational nature of how social categories of identity are navigated and social group memberships are constructed and performed.

3. In this chapter, I refer to "migrants" and "migration." Following Luibhéid, I use "migrants" as an encompassing term that refuses the delineations between different types of migrants because those "distinctions function as technologies of normalization, discipline, and sanctioned dispossession" ("Introduction" xi).

4. Not coincidentally, the very same migrants are included when the economy is strong and inexpensive labor is needed.

5. By American, I mean those persons constructed as "legitimate" citizens of the United States, which is about a social recognition and not about documented citizenship. I realize that persons from South America to Canada are Americans, but am highlighting here the nationalizing process that occurs in the United States only.

6. Since the early 1990s, hundreds of women have been reported missing, have been sexually assaulted, and/or have been found murdered in Ciudad Juárez, the city directly across the border from El Paso, Texas. As stated by Amigos de las Mujeres de Juárez, "Since 1993, more than 550 women have been murdered. . . . Of these deaths, Amnesty International states approximately 130 have been sexual-torture killings of young women, ages 12–19" ("Background"). Other groups, including the Council on Hemispheric Affairs and Amnesty International, project that "more than 800 bodies had been found as of February 2005, and over 3,000 women are still missing" (Sarria). In spite of this horrific violence against women, the US and Mexican governments have done little to resolve the crimes or to protect women in the area.

7. I use the word "homonormativity" to describe the neoliberal politics of gay and lesbian communities that uphold hetero- and gender-normative values and practices. Puar extends an understanding of the term "homonormative" through her use of "homonationalism" "to mark arrangements of US sexual exceptionalism explicitly in relation to the nation" (39).

8. I use the gender-neutral pronouns hir (in place of her or his) and ze (in place of she or he) for two reasons: first, these pronouns reflect Feinberg's identity as gender-nonconforming, and, second, I mean to respect the complexity of gender identities people experience or claim culturally.

9. "Transmasculine" refers to persons assigned the sex of female at birth who identify as male and perform masculinity by their everyday activities (such as dress, patterns of speech, use of the body) and/or through the use of testos-

terone and/or surgery. There are multiple monikers of transmasculinity, some of which include female-to-male, boi, transman, man in transition, Two Spirit, Chican@, gender queer (and more). Some of these identifications, including gender queer and Two Spirit, are also claimed by transfeminine communities. My use of this term assumes that gender is a social construction and is performed on a spectrum that transcends the binary of woman/man, female/male.

10. I use queer to reference persons who avow gender, sex, and sexual identifications that challenge heteronormativity, which includes persons who claim membership on the transgender, lesbian, gay, bisexual, queer, questioning, intersex, and asexual (TLGBQQIA) spectrum as well as heterosexuals who may be gender-conforming but whose relationships defy heterosexual norms (such as polyamory or bondage, discipline, sadism, masochism [BDSM]). "Queer" is not necessarily a synonym for TLGBQQIA.

11. Chávez engages Aimee Carrillo Rowe's exploration of the ways "differently-situated groups" can work together to explore the "causes of interlocking oppressions" and, thus, create transformative social relations ("Border [In]Securities" 137).

3
Border Interventions

The Need to Shift from a Rhetoric of Security
to a Rhetoric of Militarization

Karma R. Chávez

Scholars of rhetoric and performance have opened important terrains in the study of immigration and borders pertaining to subjects such as citizenship, media representation, and migrant identity (Cisneros, "(Re)Bordering the Civic Imaginary"; DeChaine, "Bordering the Civic Imaginary"; McKinnon; Ono and Sloop; Shi). Though a number of scholars in other academic disciplines within the humanities and social sciences have written about border militarization (e.g., Andreas, "Redrawing the Line"; Dunn, *Militarization of the US-Mexico Border;* Nevins), in reviewing rhetoric and communication scholarship pertaining to immigration and borders, with the exception of a few passing mentions (Demo, "Afterimage" and "Sovereignty Discourse; Carrillo Rowe; DeChaine, "Bordering the Civic Imaginary"; Ono and Sloop), an engagement with the rhetoric of border militarization is virtually nonexistent. Instead, in post–September 11, 2001, US America, where the dominant border rhetorics emerge from the so-called War on Terror, discourses of "border security" and "national security" are the parlance of the day for rhetoric scholars (e.g., Dunmire, "9/11 Changed Everything" and "Preempting the Future"; Gales; Ivie; Ivie and Giner; Mirrlees; Ono; Rojecki; Ross). Though many of these analyses offer rigorous critiques of the way security discourses manifest and perpetuate troubling imaginaries of safety and privacy, the problem with the emphasis scholars place on analyses of the rhetoric of security is that it enables state apparatuses and conservative ideology to dictate the framing of discussion and debate. Ono and Sloop argue that discourses construct borders, and I would extend this to say that discourse constitutes the way immigration, generally, is understood. If scholars use the state's conservative ideographs—their ideological building blocks—to talk about matters of public interest (McGee, "'Ideograph'"), conservative ideology continues to frame the broader debate in people's minds. This in turn suggests that the public may be more willing to support problematic state policy and action, for no other terms exist by which to understand important issues.

The issue of framing is especially dire in relation to the US-Mexico border, which has, in the eyes of many politicians, pundits, and citizens alike become the greatest source for *insecurity* in the national imaginary. The discourse of national security intertwines with the War on Terror, the threat of drug smuggling, and the invasion of "illegal aliens" so that militarization of regions of the US-Mexico border seems natural and warranted in order to protect citizens from these supposed threats. Moreover, as scholars increasingly note, "everyday militarization" aptly describes the ways in which "ordinary people" accept the beliefs of militarism and militarization in such a way that upholds state military and militarization policy (Bernazzoli and Flint). Caren Kaplan quips in an essay on how the popularity of technology like Global Positioning Satellites (GPS) can lead to militarized consumers and citizens: "For most people in the United States, war is almost always everywhere" (693). Feminist scholars such as Cynthia Enloe have long called attention to the way that militarization seeps into ordinary lives as a regular part of public discourse (Enloe, *Does Khaki Become You?*, *Globalization and Militarism, Maneuvers*). Because military discourse pervades the everyday, its further expansion in myriad forms proves for many to be commonplace instead of worrisome.

Importantly, militarization of the US-Mexico border has not occurred in response to the War on Terror; instead, it has been in the US government's plan at least since the Reagan administration, and has virtually nothing to do with the events of September 11, 2001 (Dunn, *Militarization of the US-Mexico Border*). As one example, the Immigration and Naturalization Services' (INS's) four-phase "Southwest Border Strategy," implemented post-NAFTA in 1994, strategically planned to militarize the US-Mexico border in order to allegedly deter clandestine crossings (Stana and Rezmovic). The events of September 11, 2001, provided a convenient rationale to heighten these strategies, which had been in motion for decades; yet, a context of "everyday militarization" coupled with the rhetoric of security has obfuscated an urgent need to focus on the devastation of border militarization on border crossers and communities specifically, and privacy and civil liberties more generally.

Gordon Mitchell suggests that rhetoric scholars who study social movements should also enable movement with their work. This chapter will demonstrate the need for border rhetoric scholars to turn the discourse of security toward a discourse of militarization in the hopes of making a civic intervention into the broader national debate. If more people understood how militarization works and the careful way that the rhetoric of security disguises its material impacts, it is likely that the US government would be forced to be more accountable to its people, and rhetoric scholars should lead this charge. I begin this argument by first defining militarization and briefly tracing the increase in border militarization, specifically on the US-Mexico border since the mid- to late 1980s. Next, I outline the severity of the consequences such militarization has had for border communities and border crossers, and what this means for residents of the United States more broadly. I then argue why the language of militarization is so crucial through a brief analysis of *Secure Border Initiative Monthly,* or *SBI Monthly,* produced by the Secure Border Initiative (SBI) Program Management Office (PMO) and designed to provide news and information on the SBI and the now-defunct SBI *net,* two major programs of the Department of Homeland Security (DHS) to augment "border security."[1] These newsletters evidence the ease with which undocumented migration and terrorism are conflated, similarly to how undocumented migration and drug trafficking were conflated decades ago, as a justification for increased militarization. I end by mapping some theoretical and pragmatic interventions rhetoric scholars should make through a shift from an emphasis on border security to border militarization.

Border Militarization

In the broadest sense, militarization "refers to the use of military rhetoric and ideology, as well as military tactics, strategy, technology, equipment, and forces" (Dunn, *Militarization of the US-Mexico Border* 3). More specifically, militarization suggests the intermingling between police and military forces, so much so that police engage in military functions and the military engages in police activity. As Timothy J. Dunn argues, one of the most significant sites of border militarization is the US-Mexico border, as the US Customs and Border Patrol has increasingly teamed up with US military forces in order to deter drug trafficking for the past three decades. As a consequence of this relationship, and because the border is also the stage for concerns over undocumented migration, both migration and drug trafficking have become central to the development and implementation of militarization policies and practices. The intentional development of such policies is more than three decades in the making, beginning with the earliest implementation during the end of US President Carter's administration.

For example, events such as the Mariel boatlift in 1980, which landed tens of thousands of Cuban refugees in the United States, provoked alarmist calls for stricter immigration policies. Dunn explains that as immigration gained salience as a social, political, and economic issue in the United

States, the INS budget and staff also increased (Dunn, *Militarization of the US-Mexico Border* 35). The INS made equipment and technology enhancements, increasing its enforcement capacities, which were designed to ameliorate concerns over national security that emerged particularly following Mariel. While Carter set the ground for increased militarization, President Reagan's administration was most responsible for rolling out the immense infrastructure that would lead to the most drastic border militarization. As Reagan came into office in the United States, the US approach to the US-Mexico border took the characteristic of "low-intensity conflict doctrine" (LIC). Though this approach typically refers to how the US military managed counter-insurgencies internationally, especially in Central America, it also refers to the supposedly low level of military involvement (with significant effects) designed for "maintaining social control over targeted civilian populations" domestically on the US-Mexico border (Dunn, *Militarization of the US-Mexico Border* 35). In other words, the militarization of the US-Mexico border was designed to be relatively minor in the sense that the goal was not to have an overwhelming military-like presence, but rather one that was visible and tactical enough to suggest control.

Spending for the INS, and especially the Border Patrol, grew tremendously as the number of staff increased 90 percent and funding 149 percent (Dunn, *Militarization of the US-Mexico Border* 49). Moreover, the Reagan administration established detention as an appropriate punishment for non-Mexican undocumented migrants (Mexicans could simply be sent back) and for political asylum seekers. Thus, more detention facilities were established, and as is consistent with LIC doctrine, many nongovernmental organizations' housing resources were used for detention (Dunn, *Militarization of the US-Mexico Border* 59). In addition to this growth, the Border Patrol also incorporated increased high-tech equipment ranging from M-14 and M-16 military rifles to extensive sensor and night-vision systems, television surveillance, and airborne infrared radar, to name a few of the new technologies.

By the time George H. W. Bush was elected president, the INS's realm of control had greatly expanded, and most congressional allocations for spending were aimed at the Enforcement Division. The so-called War on Drugs was in full swing by this time, and it functioned as a convenient excuse to exacerbate enforcement measures on the US-Mexico border, while also leading to a close association between "drug trafficker" and "illegal alien" among immigration officials (Dunn, *Militarization of the US-Mexico Border* 87). Additionally, the increased emphasis on targeting "criminal aliens," those immigrants who had committed crimes other than overstaying visas or making a clandestine crossing into the United States (actions which are misdemeanors), further linked immigration and crime. Moreover, the reach of this category was often unclear as immigrants who hadn't committed other crimes were regularly detained alongside so-called criminal aliens at the growing number of detention facilities in the United States.

Under the first Bush administration, reports emerged of systemic human rights abuses at the hands of Border Patrol agents. The INS also waged its largest immigration enforcement crackdown since the infamously named Operation Wetback in 1954 in the Lower Rio Grande Valley in south Texas. The INS's strategy, as outlined in a 1989 internal document titled "Enhancement Plan for the Southern Border," included: (1) rigorous enforcement of immigration laws and detention for those who violated laws; (2) quick and thorough processing of asylum claims; and (3) a media campaign that would work to create "'public understanding and acceptance of the difference between claims [for political asylum] made from a third country and those made after entry [into the United States] without inspection'" (INS Report 2 as cited in Dunn, *Militarization of the US-Mexico Border* 92). The INS's crackdown not only resulted in human rights violations within the United States (and in parts of Mexico and Central America due to related information-seeking missions), but also demonstrated the INS's ability to engage in carefully targeted militarization tactics without disrupting usual business, traffic, and life for most local residents in the area.

The entrenchment of militarization policies and practices undoubtedly existed during the first Bush administration; however, the detrimental impacts on human lives would take a worse turn during President Clinton's administration and in the wake of the North American Free Trade Agreement's passage. NAFTA advocated free trade and open foreign investment at the same time that it more or less promoted closed borders for the movement of people (Johnson, "Free Trade and Closed Borders"). The creation of NAFTA was an impetus to restrictionist attitudes and anti-migrant legislation on the state and federal levels (Johnson, "An Essay on Immigration" 122). For example, the 1993 INS campaign "Operation Blockade/Hold the Line" sought to deter undocumented migration in El Paso, and the 1994 INS campaign "Operation Gatekeeper" aimed to curb migration from Tijuana to San Diego, both of which represented the highest traffic areas for undocumented crossings. These federal initiatives were bookends to California's 1994 ballot initiative, Proposition 187 (Save Our State). At its most basic level, according to the summary prepared by the attorney general, Proposition 187 "makes illegal aliens ineligible for public social services, public health care services (unless emergency under federal law), and public school education" (cited in Ono and Sloop 169). Ultimately, Proposition 187 was deemed unconstitutional, despite passing with 59 percent voter approval. Both the overwhelming support and the extensive campaign surrounding the initiative paved a pathway for additional anti-migrant initiatives and legislative efforts throughout the United States. Operation Gatekeeper came on the tide of the Proposition 187 campaign, and could have even been viewed as a federal response to the proposition (Nevins 92). Clinton's immigration positions were constantly under conservative fire, and Gatekeeper functioned to "restore integrity" of the San Diego-Tijuana border by enforcing the border more stringently (Nevins 3). Gatekeeper was a part of a broader four-stage Southwest Border Strategy that sought to funnel migration out of metropolitan areas and into desolate areas like the Arizona desert as a means of deterring crossers, and in fact, in 2001, a General Accounting Office report suggested that shifting traffic was the primary effect of the strategy (Stana and Rezmovic). The rationale for what the University of Arizona Binational Migration Institute describes as the "funnel effect" was that both the deaths that would undoubtedly occur as well as the danger posed by the desert would be enough to prevent people from making the clandestine journey (Arnoldo García; Rubio-Goldsmith et al.).[2]

Though many earlier militarization strategies overtly suggested that the primary goal of militarization was to enable successes in the War on Drugs, the Southwest Border Strategy expressly states its focus as deterring "illegal aliens" (Stana and Rezmovic 1). This focus led to the Border Patrol's budget being around $1.2 billion in 2001 and, of the 9,096 Border Patrol agents in the United States at that time, 93 percent of them being located in sectors on the Southwest border (5). The "funnel effect," which pushed crossings to the most desolate and dangerous parts of the Arizona desert, also led immigration officials to suggest a need for increased military-like technology in order to find and apprehend border crossers (Rubio-Goldsmith et al.). As of May 2001, around 76 miles of border fence were erected as part of the strategy (Stana and Rezmovic 8). Though the Department of Homeland Security and, more specifically, US Customs and Border Protection suggest that nearly two decades of border militarization strategies are leading to more security on US borders and ports of entry, the human consequences of such strategies are astronomical. The impacts of militarization are most devastating for border crossers. In a 2009 report sponsored by the American Civil Liberties Union and Mexico's National Commission of Human Rights, María Jimenez calculates the numbers of deaths and apprehensions along the Southwest border from fiscal year 1994 to 2008.[3] Compiling data from Mexico's Secretariat of Foreign Relations, the US General Accounting Office, the US Department of Homeland Security Border Safety Initiative, and various news sources, Jimenez reports 23 deaths in 1994, 358 deaths in 1999, and 827 in 2007 (Jimenez 17).[4] On average, between 356 and 529 migrant remains are recovered each year along the Southwest border. Meanwhile, apprehension rates have hovered between 723,840 and 1,643,679, with the two lowest years for apprehensions (2007 and 2008) correlating with the two highest years for remains recovered.

Moreover, as Dunn shows, even as it became clearer that militarization policies and practices were as much, if not more, about immigration as they were about drug trafficking, prevention of drugs was used as a rationale for increasingly bringing members of the military to the Southwest border. In 1989, the military created Joint Task Force-6 (JTF-6), a military operation designed to help patrol the border and collect information for the Border Patrol, largely to prevent drug activity. Because of the intermixing of drug trafficking and immigration, the actions of JTF-6 pose a serious dilemma for human rights on the border, which evidences the grave consequences of militarization. Dunn explains that while police forces such as the Border Patrol are tasked with caring about human and civil rights—though their failures are well documented (see Falcón)—military forces are tasked with diffusing potential hostile situations at virtually any cost. When JTF-6 soldiers and marines do the job of the Border Patrol, interacting with civilian populations and having little training in the Border Patrol's operating procedures, the consequences can be dire (Dunn, "Border Militarization"). Dunn illustrates this situation through examining the case of the "Redford shooting," in which a marine shot an eighteen-year-old US citizen, Esequiel Hernandez, who was tending his goats and carried a single-shot .22 caliber rifle with him to ward off animal predators. Though one might describe the Hernandez murder as an isolated incident, it suggests that militarization practices have been detrimental for citizens and migrants alike.

The War on Terror and Homeland Security

It should be clear by now that border militarization has been in place long before the events of September 11, 2001. As indicated above, the impacts on human life since that time have been increasingly harsh, and the rate of militarization has increased. However, much like the War on Drugs consistently functioned materially and symbolically as a rationale for heightened border militarization in the '80s and '90s, the War on Terror and "homeland security" have functioned as a rationale for augmenting border militarization in the last decade.

Shortly after the attacks of September 11, 2001, conservatives such as Tom Tancredo, former Republican congressman from Colorado, demarcated the US-Mexico border as one of the primary vulnerabilities for a future terrorist attack (Tancredo, "Immigration, Citizenship, and National Security"). This rhetoric about the porous nature of the Southern border wasn't new, and, furthermore, there has never been a documented instance of a terrorist against the United States using the Southern border for entry. The rhetoric pervaded the national imaginary, nevertheless, and the Office of Homeland Security was created in 2001. Ratified in late 2002, the Department of Homeland Security (DHS) took as one of its primary goals the securing of national borders. The Immigration and Naturalization Service was subsumed under DHS, and two new agencies were created: Immigration and Customs Enforcement (ICE) and Citizen and Immigration Services. Moreover, border security, including the Border Patrol, became the responsibility of US Customs and Border Protection (CBP).

In addition to the creation of new agencies, and the expansion of budgets and staff in the name of security, massive border militarization plans also followed. As one example, the budget for DHS in fiscal year (FY) 2004 was $32.6 billion, 64 percent higher than the budget in FY 2002 (*Department of Homeland Security Budget in Brief*). This budget has continued to increase, as have Border Patrol agents; the number has grown from just over 9,000 prior to 2001 to nearly 20,000 in FY 2009. A 2009 brief from the White House Office of Management and Budget boasts an addition of 1,000 new detention beds, bringing the number to 33,000, and an expansion to the controversial 287(g) program, which deputizes local and state law-enforcement officers as federal immigration officers. It also announces $2 billion to support a militarization program called SBI *net* ("Budget FY 2009"). SBI *net* is a branch of the Secure Border Initiative, a program started in November 2005 in order to secure US borders. According to the CBP home page, the SBI has as its mission to:

1. Enhance and improve border security by identifying, designing, developing, deploying, and maintaining border security tools, capabilities, and other systems.
2. Establish a bridge between operational and acquisition elements in CBP to ensure deployed technologies provide the needed capabilities.
3. Provide program management expertise and acquisition competency for

implementing and executing nationally significant border security programs. (Customs and Border Protection)

SBI *net* is a critical part of the SBI, which is designed to enable the CBP to secure the border through a mix of infrastructure, technology, and communications. The first part of SBI *net* is something called Project 28, designed to enhance border security along twenty-eight miles of the border around Sasabe, Arizona, in the Tucson Border Patrol Sector, which is the site of the highest migration traffic (as a result of the "funnel effect") (Stana, *Secure Border Initiative: Observations on the Importance*). The Boeing company was awarded the contract to build "redeployable sensor towers, Unattended Ground Systems (UGS), and upgrades to existing Border Patrol vehicles and communication systems—to increase their communication speed and interoperability" (*SBI Monthly* 1.1). Within three years, what became known as the "virtual fence" project was well over-budget. Additionally, local communities, human rights activists, and environmental rights groups have all challenged the implementation of all parts of the SBI (Archibold, "Scathing Report"). Internal oversight issues, as well as contractual problems, have also stalled the progress of the initiative (Peters; Stana, *Secure Border Initiative: Observations on Selected Aspects;* Stana, *Secure Border Initiative: Observations on the Importance*).

Nonetheless, from the time of its inception, creators and advocates of the SBI within the DHS and the CBP have waged a rhetorical campaign designed to frame what is one of the—if not the—most extensive border militarization plans to date. This rhetoric is all couched within a framework of security and anti-terrorism, as well as a concern for greater communication and environmental responsibility. Additionally, this analysis will demonstrate how the primary mission of the SBI is really about regaining "control" of out-of-control borders. The militarization required to regain control, however, also does not overshadow two additional goals: protecting undocumented border crossers and enacting environmental stewardship. In addition to revealing how this "security" rhetoric operates in a seemingly mundane way by highlighting community interaction and environmental preservation, examining these newsletters also highlights the importance of moving beyond "national security" rhetoric as activist-scholars in order to intervene in militarization practices at the discursive level. Though the SBI program started in late 2005, the newsletter appears to have been produced from December 2006 to March 2008, though all the newsletters have been removed from the CBP website, and the e-mail address to obtain back copies is now defunct.[5]

Illegal Aliens, Terrorists, and Out-of-Control Borders

Many scholars have commented on the way in which out-of-control borders feature in anti-immigrant and nativist discourse in order to bolster the need to regain control that has apparently only recently been lost (e.g., Chavez, *Covering Immigration* and *Latino Threat;* Brady, "Homoerotics of Immigration Control"). Such arguments appear in almost each *SBI Monthly,* and they are often accompanied by language that links "illegal aliens" with terrorism. Each *SBI Monthly* extends two pages long, and other than an occasional note from an SBI administrator, the different pieces in the newsletters do not list authors. The inaugural issue of the newsletter introduces Greg Giddens, the executive director of the SBI. In the last paragraph of the introduction, it is easy to see how the slippage between undocumented migration and terrorism frames the mission of the SBI: "Awareness of the factors causing the flow of illegal immigration to the US is also key to understanding the problem. Those who wish to cause harm to the US must never be allowed to enter. We must protect our citizens, yet remain a welcoming nation" (*SBI Monthly* 1.1). This tension between exclusion and inclusion points to the way that border rhetorics more generally remain fraught with contradictions, as a nation-state wishes to appear tolerant yet tough, without slipping into isolationism and nativism. A similar statement exists in the second newsletter, which introduces Dr. Kirk Evans, SBI *net* program manager. The introduction quips that Evans helped with national security during the Cold War, and "will again assist the US in locating threats to homeland security—illegal border crossers" (*SBI Monthly* 1.2). The next paragraph reminds readers that the program will protect against "terrorists, narcotics, and illegal aliens." Both of these statements link undocumented migrants with terrorism and harm to the United States. The putatively natural linkage is likely intended to justify and normalize the actual militarization practices that the SBI will enact. The same newsletter describes how the contractor, Boeing, will aid in national security: "The Boeing SBI *net* team, under the direction of CBP, will implement a system that notifies CBP of an illegal entry, classifies the entry (number of aliens, armed, animal, etc.), provides a means to efficiently respond to the entry, and brings the illegal entry to the appropriate law enforcement resolution" (*SBI Monthly* 1.2). Such information essentially logs any movement on the border, which poses a potential threat to Native American nations whose national borders span the US-Mexico border, animals that freely cross the border, residents who live near both sides of the border, as well as undocumented crossers. Even with so many affected, because of the emphasis on security, such initiatives can be publicly talked about and seem normal.

Moreover, as the link between terrorism and undocumented immigration is solidified, military-technologies seem more warranted in order to increasingly help law-enforcement officials to regain control of the border. For instance, in talking about a piece of technology called the Common Operating Picture, which is a camera and a key resource for maintaining control, one newsletter offers the following hypothetical scenario of a breach of national security:

> A group of individuals has just entered the US illegally and is on foot. As they make their way across the desert, they are picked up on radar. The radar sounds an alarm at a nearby sector communications center. A Sector Enforcement Specialist identifies the location of the radar hit, and then takes control of a camera in that area. Using the camera's remote capabilities, the Specialist zooms in to get a visual on what triggered the radar. The Specialist identifies the group of illegal aliens.
>
> The Specialist then notifies Border Patrol Agents in the vicinity through voice communications. The responding Agent is then relayed the coordinates of the illegal aliens to their Mobile COP, displayed on their laptop computer mounted in their vehicle. The coordinates allow the Agent the ability to understand where they are in *proximity to the threat*. After confirmation with the Specialist, the Agent goes to intercept the illegal aliens. Moments later, the Agent locates the illegal aliens and makes the apprehensions. (*SBI Monthly* 3.2; emphasis added)

Though this group of hypothetical border crossers is "on foot," it is still "a threat" that must be captured through use of sophisticated tracking and communications technology. These hypothetical crossers and other "real" ones must indeed be a threat, as the deputy commissioner of the SBI, Deborah Spero, states: "Technology and tactical infrastructure are essential to enabling CBP to secure our borders" (*SBI Monthly* 3.2).

The powerful War on Terror discourse and the ease of accepting the importance of "national security" function to allow extreme and expensive "security" measures on the US-Mexico border seem normal and needed. Though earlier instantiations of border militarization enacted during the era of the War on Drugs typically relied on overt links between drug trafficking and undocumented migration, the contemporary rhetoric of the *SBI Monthly* newsletters does not. Likely because of the desensitization of most Americans post–September 11, 2001, to the importance of preserving "national security," some, at least, will accept that any proclaimed "threat" is threat enough to potentially be connected to terrorism.

Protecting Other Interests: Migrants and the Environment

While it is clear that a large portion of the rhetorical agenda of the SBI is to ensure a logical link between terrorism and undocumented migration, another rhetorical move suggests the necessity of militarization in order to protect important interests. These interests include the safety of undocumented migrants as they cross into the United States, as well as the environment, which is said to be both devastated by undocumented migration and important to protect alongside of national security. As stated above, although militarization has funneled the crossing of undocumented migrants into the worst terrain and climate, *SBI Monthly* suggests that a main threat to crossers is that many enter the Barry M. Goldwater Range (BMGR) in southwest Arizona during live military exercises, which is dangerous for them. Moreover, of course, these interruptions cost valuable dollars and training hours, which may impact "military readiness" (*SBI Monthly* 2.2). Clearly, protecting military capacity is also very important here. Project 37 is an SBI program designed to control the thirty-seven miles of border in the BMGR, and it is touted as necessary since 8,600 migrants were apprehended in the BMGR during 2006 alone. In addition to protecting migrants and military capacity, protecting the environment also seems to be an important part of border militarization projects.

A relatively unknown feature of the 2005 REAL ID Act allows the secretary of the DHS to bypass any environmental law if it is in the name of homeland security. Though the secretary at the time, Michael Chertoff, assured legislators that this provision would never likely need to be used, waivers have occurred to ensure the successful implementation of the SBI. In the same newsletter article that states that projects will not be undertaken without consideration of environmental concerns, there are further indications that "certain" environmental laws will be waived so as not to impede the SBI. The section then goes on to say that the SBI will deter border crossings and "reduce the environmental damage caused by such activities" (*SBI Monthly* 2.2). The newsletter does not report that, among others, the Federal Water Pollution Control Act, the Endangered Species Act, and the National Environmental Policy Act (NEPA) were all circumvented (Associated Press). A few months later, the importance of "minimizing and mitigating adverse effects" on the environment appears again after SBI officials met with concerned residents about the plans to militarize the border (*SBI*

Monthly 7.2). Residents in some locations in Arizona, however, were only given four days to view the Environmental Assessment that the SBI created, and two of those days were weekends, so the local library where the plan was available, was closed. Organizations and collectives of people in towns all along the US-Mexico border came out to question the impacts of fences, virtual fences, as well as infrared sensors and radar for animals and humans that live along the Southwest border (Moreno). Additional meetings with locals were held in Texas as plans moved east, and hundreds of people also attended these in order to offer their opinions about environmental impacts (*SBI Monthly* 12.2). Nevertheless, repeated references to environmental stewardship and mitigating environmental impacts proliferate on the pages of the newsletter. In fact, after reporting about the SBI's neglect of environmental laws, including NEPA, the November 2007 newsletter assures that the CBP abides by NEPA and the National Historic Preservation Act (*SBI Monthly* 11.2). In addition to suggesting that the SBI's environmental impacts will be "minimal," and highlighting all of the agencies being consulted about environmental impacts, the newsletter also includes images of border fences in the BMGR that have holes in them every one hundred feet, designed "to allow the safe passage of small migratory animals, such as the Flat-tailed Horned Lizard." Such rhetoric mitigates concerns people might have about environmental impacts, and provides assurances that the environment is a priority within the larger thinking about "border security." More sinisterly, this rhetoric also privileges considerations for animal migration at the same time that human migrants are dehumanized, and featured only as threats.

From a Discourse of Security to a Discourse of Militarization

The word "militarization" is, unsurprisingly, not in any of the SBI newsletters or in any SBI rhetoric at all. In the twelve newsletters analyzed here (a total of twenty-four pages of text), the word "security," on the other hand, shows up well over forty times. Additionally, words such as "secure" and "protection" pervade SBI rhetoric. A resonance can be seen between this and public immigration discourse which is also dominated by the rhetoric of security. "Security" functions as an important ideograph in these contemporary times (McGee, "'Ideograph'"), as it is a significant way in which the entire anti-immigrant, anti-terrorist, and protectionist ideology is upheld. This ideograph and its various manifestations (i.e., national security, border security, and homeland security) certainly deserve attention to understand how they function. Nevertheless, when rhetoric scholars who study issues of security, borders, terrorism, and immigration maintain a strict focus on and usage of "security" rhetoric, we do a disservice to our readers and to the political communities with whom many of us intend to be allied. The fact remains that for more than three decades, the US federal government, with the compliance of state and local governments in Southwest border states, has increasingly militarized the US-Mexico border (and slowly plans to do so on the US-Canada border, though one imagines this is less inflected by racialized discourses, and perhaps functions to minimize the connections between militarization of the Southern border and racism). Such militarization occurs in the name of border security, and as a necessary part of the War on Drugs, and now the War on Terror. But no matter what war Washington claims we are waging, the main victims continue to be undocumented border crossers, residents on the US-Mexico border, and the environment. Moreover, no research indicates that our national security interests have been preserved or protected due to militarization. Instead, border regions are continually disrupted, and in some instances destroyed at US taxpayer expense, while deaths along the border rise or remain stagnant. The question becomes: Whose security is being preserved?

As feminist scholars have long documented, for example, violence against women, particularly rape, has always been associated with militarization (Falcón; Enloe, *Does Khaki Become You, Globalization and Militarism, Maneuvers*; Ochoa O'Leary). Following the work of Enloe, Falcón explains that four conditions of militarization for which rape is likely to happen exist on the US-Mexico border:

1. A regime is preoccupied with "national security";
2. A majority of civilians believes that security is best understood as a military problem;
3. The making of national security is left to a largely masculinized political elite; and
4. The police and military security apparatuses are male-dominated. (Enloe, *Maneuvers* 124, as cited in Falcón 33)

Not only do these conditions exist, but many migrant women have reported being raped under the conditions of militarization for reasons that would not exist if not for militarization (see also DiBranco; Frosch; Ochoa O'Leary). For example, women report being raped in order to have falsified documents returned to them, or as "payment" for being taken across the border by various actors, including federal immigration officials. As Falcón concludes based on her extensive field and interview data, these incidents are not isolated, but rather they are systemic. In this sense, heightened "border security" makes the border far less secure for migrant women (and some men) because of the conditions of militarization. Rhetoric scholars should not call attention to these and related systemic forms of violence in the name of protecting women; instead, we should see these as strong *human* reasons to shift the nature of security discourse toward militarization.

Finally, consider that local communities in the far corners of the United States, in places thousands of miles from the US-Mexico border such as Iowa, Nebraska, and New York, have felt the squeeze of militarization through raids on meat-packing plants facilitated in part through CBP and ICE relations with local law-enforcement agencies due to provision 287(g) of the Immigration and Nationality Act (Forrestal and Moreano; Sanchez, House, and Moulton; Hendricks). Activists on the US-Mexico border, people with whom I have worked closely, have long indicated that the militarization they have experienced will continue to move inward until the border is no longer just a distant place in the sand (Chávez, "Coalitional Politics"). One wonders when rhetoric scholars may take the lead in calling militarization what it is, in refusing to see it as a necessary evil in the plight to protect "national security," and in being a progressive and vital civic voice in the preservation and protection of a host of human rights that currently and essentially do not exist within the conditions of border militarization.

Notes

1. In January 2011, DHS secretary Janet Napolitano reported that SBI *net* was "costing too much and achieving too little" (Wagner). As a result the administration shut down the program.

2. Former INS commissioner Doris Meissner even said as much overtly.

3. Though this report uses the word "death," it mentions, and I agree, that it is more accurate to suggest that these numbers refer to remains or bodies recovered, as it is hard to determine actual numbers of deaths in desolate areas like the Arizona desert. I am appreciative of activists at Coalición de Derechos Humanos in Tucson, Arizona, for teaching me to acknowledge this distinction.

4. The Department of Homeland Security numbers taken alone are, for the most part, much lower than those taken from the combination of sources.

5. Prior to their removal, I fortunately created and/or downloaded PDF copies of the newsletters for this research project, of which I retain possession.

II
Historical Consequences

4

A Dispensational Rhetoric in "The Mexican Question in the Southwest"

Michelle A. Holling

Suppression of cultural rights, calls for deportation of immigrants, poor working conditions of agricultural workers, and citizen and state patrols of the border are all contested issues in the public sphere, in congressional debates, and in national protests that have occurred in recent years. Some have gone so far as to characterize the issues as provoked by "the Hispanic challenge" (Huntington). This "challenge" refers mainly to Mexicans, yet broadly accuses "Hispanics" of taking jobs from US Americans, depleting social resources that belong to those citizens, posing a threat to national security, and colonizing and bifurcating the country to the extent that two peoples, cultures, and languages will exist, consequently diminishing the national identity of the United States. The challenge was made all the more clear when national demographic shifts revealed that Latina/os, or Hispanics, became the largest ethnic "minority" group in the country. Thus, in the twenty-first century, challenges—cultural, political, economic, national—perceptibly brought about by and attributed to the increased presence of "Hispanics" function as one anxiety confronting the United States.

However, the supposed "Hispanic challenge," along with the issues identified above, is not new. A look back to the late 1920s reveals a parallel national concern with a "Mexican problem" in which the presence of Mexican (Americans)[1] in the United States was perceived increasingly as a problem. Challenging the political and ideological positioning of Mexican (Americans) was a political document entitled "The Mexican Question in the Southwest" by Emma Tenayuca and Homer Brooks. Its contents detail the social status of Mexican (Americans) beginning with a historical overview of Mexican (Americans') experiences, while also drawing parallels to the plight of African Americans in the South, delineating the social and political demands sought by different Mexican (American) struggles, and outlining a path that sought to secure the rights of Mexican (Americans). As noted by Calderón and Zamora, Tenayuca[2] offers "the most lucid and accurate analysis of Mexican people ever produced by a Communist party representative" (34–35). Surprisingly, scholars have paid scant attention to "The Mexican Question in the Southwest." Some offer a summation or excerpts of "The Mexican Question in the Southwest" while others merely mention its existence (Acuña; Calderón and Zamora; Gabriela González; Gutiérrez; Kanellos; Meier and Ribera; Vachon; Vargas, "Tejana Radical," "Emma Tenayuca," and "'Do You'"). Continued neglect of such a document misses its rhetorical dynamics and the conditions characterizing the United States. In the years leading up to and during World War II, there were "crisis moments," including Hitler's embodiment of communism and food production–labor shortage concerns (Flores, "Constructing Citizens"), whereas in recent years, there are discriminatory acts and policies impacting Mexican (Americans).

Critically examining "The Mexican Question in the Southwest" reveals a "dispensational rhetoric," a discursive process supplementing individuals' and ethnic groups' efforts to rectify the position of an oppressed national group through "rearticulation."[3] A rhetoric of dispensation counters hegemonic positionings and/or narratives of a subjugated citizenry in an effort to secure rights (e.g., cultural or political) granted, but not honored. Such an undertaking in the case of "The Mexican Question in the Southwest" requires that Tenayuca counteract prevailing social tendencies and attitudes that positioned Mexican (Americans) as a "problem," through a series of arguments that render visible potential and existing racial-economic relationships, in order to rearticulate their identity as a *Mexican people*. Doing so functions as a basis from which to argue for Mexican (Americans') rights and inclusion within the nation-state that date to the ratification of the Treaty of Guadalupe Hidalgo, which ended the Mexican-American War of 1846–1848. Of least concern is whether the ideas advocated by Tenayuca were effective or enacted.[4] As Vargas notes, "The Mexican Question in the Southwest" "was printed in the *Communist,* a journal devoted principally to addressing the finer theoretical points of party strategy for an intellectual audience well versed in Marxist philosophy. It is doubtful that large numbers of Mexicans had access" ("'Do You'" 145). Furthermore, assessing any accrued benefits or material gains stemming from what was advocated in the political plan is to partake in a spirit of a capitalist-economic attitude of gains and losses that runs contradictory to Tenayuca's politics. More important to recognize is a dispensational rhetoric that encouraged "transborder solidarity" (Schmidt Camacho) and nation-state unification that enhances our understanding of Mexican (Americans') discursive struggles for social justice.

To facilitate the analysis of "The Mexican Question in the Southwest," I structure this chapter in four parts. I situate the political document by first discussing briefly who Emma Tenayuca is, given her pivotal role in authoring the document. Second, I position "The Mexican Question in the Southwest" as a political treatise exemplifying "localized rhetoric," thereby shedding light on its significance, historically and theoretically. Following this I theorize a "rhetoric of dispensation" that works at the intersection of critical-cultural rhetorical studies and Chicana/o-Latina/o studies, which involves tracing the process of rearticulation of a Mexican people against the political, social, and economic context of the time. Finally, in the discussion section, I sketch out the relevance of a dispensational rhetoric to contemporary conditions surrounding Mexican (Americans) or "Hispanics."

La Pasionaria [The Passionate One]

La Pasionaria we called her
because she was our passion,
because she was our corazón [heart]
defendiendo as los pobres [defending the poor], speaking out
at a time when neither Mexicans nor
women were expected to speak out at all.[5]

I had a basic underlying faith in the American idea of freedom and fairness. (Tenayuca, in Rips 9)

The honorific title "La Pasionaria" derives from and pays homage to Tenayuca's assigned role as strike leader during the Pecan Shellers Strike in San Antonio, Texas, in 1938. Tenayuca's life is a demonstration of her commitment to speaking out against social injustice and to acting in the service of social justice. While the focus of this essay is on advancing a dispensational rhetoric communicated in "The Mexican Question in the Southwest," equally vital is offering insight on Tenayuca[6] that not only contextualizes the content advanced in the document but also elucidates why some consider her a precursor to Chicana feminism.

Tenayuca's legacy demonstrates a heritage of Chicana feminism often neglected in "herstories." Preeminent scholar Marta Cotera criticizes several collections of herstories that claim to reflect women's contributions and activism, all the while remaining blind to the contributions of Mexican American women who were active throughout the southwest in the early twentieth century (Cotera, "Our Feminist Heritage" and "Among the Feminists"; Ruiz, *From out of the Shadows*). As a labor and civil rights advocate, Tenayuca credits a number of influences with informing her political activism: her grandfather and moral lessons learned from him, Catholicism and its emphasis on "championing the cause of the poor," attendance at political rallies, and a broad education based on extensive reading and learned from public conversations occurring in open plazas prominent in San Antonio during her early years (Calderón and Zamora; Rips; Tenayuca; Vargas, "'Do You'"). The plazas were spaces in which she became exposed to the radicalism of the Flores Magón brothers and their publication *Regeneración,* as well as the Wobblies, while also witnessing the effects of the Great Depression on her family and the Mexican (American) community (Gabriela González; Rips; Vargas, "'Do You'"). In the years preceding publication of "The Mexican Question in the Southwest," Tenayuca was visible in the arena of labor rights struggles wherein she demonstrated leadership through her membership in a trade union protest with unemployed workers, participated in the Finck cigar strike of 1932–1933, and organized Mexican American unemployed workers to join the Workers Alliance of America in 1934. In that year Tenayuca joined the Communist Party of the USA (CPUSA), which she believed was concerned with Mexican (Americans) and offered "the best avenue for social change."[7] By age twenty-one, Tenayuca's activities led to her surveillance by local police officials, blacklisting by the House of Representatives Un-American Activities Committee, and denunciation by the League of United Latin American Citizens (LULAC) (Acuña; Hardy; Vachon). Finally, in 1938 she was elected as head of the Pecan Shellers Strike, initially receiving backing from the United Cannery, Agricultural, Packing, and Allied Workers of America, a Congress of Industrial Organizations union. However, later she was removed as strike leader by the CIO union who voiced concern about her communist influence (Hardy; Ruiz, *From out of the Shadows*). Even so, Tenayuca is responsible for leading twelve thousand workers (composed mainly of women) off their jobs in protest of low pay exacerbated by subsequent wage reductions and poor working conditions. During the three-month period, strikers were arrested, teargassed, and physically abused, as well as obstructed in their right to demonstrate and, once jailed in "overcrowded conditions," had fire hoses turned on them by their jailers for protesting such conditions (Blackwelder; Gabriela González; Vargas, "Tejana Radical").

Her efforts to improve the lot of Mexican (American) community members, particularly female workers, led a few scholars to view Tenayuca's work as contributing to a heritage of Chicana feminism that predates contemporary Chicana feminism (Cotera, "Among the Feminists" and "Our Feminist Heritage"; NietoGomez). Tenayuca's recognition of and challenges to a classist-racist-sexist system that impacted the lives of Mexican (American) women in various labor industries, coupled with her zeal to protect

Mexican workers' right "to unionize without fear of deportation" (Vargas, "Emma Tenayuca" 175), do lend credence to the designation of her politics as feminist; they also exceed gender politics. That is, ways that Mexican (American) women's labor was underpaid, exploited by labor industries, and used to advance capitalist interests throughout San Antonio culminate in Tenayuca's abilities to theorize similar linkages between oppressive social conditions and the plight of a people that manifest in "The Mexican Question in the Southwest." Concomitantly, the document pursues issues of social, political, economic, and cultural inequities deriving from a historical legacy of colonialism that work against Mexican (Americans') complete incorporation into the state replete with citizenship rights. The political treatise predates similar theorizing by contemporary Chicana feminists Gloria Anzaldúa and Cherríe Moraga. While a thoroughgoing treatment of their ideas is beyond the scope of this chapter, suffice it to say that each of them has addressed the ways in which the "nation"—be it the United States or Aztlán—has excluded Chicana/os (queer and/or straight), and exacted practices that maintain racism, (hetero)sexism, and classism. As each of their projects seeks to unify individuals and reform the nation, so too did Tenayuca's. As such, recovering her—a Mestiza's[8]—contributions and words merit attention, for the instances in which scholars extend attention to public address by Mestizas, Chicanas, or Latinas are indeed rare within rhetorical studies (see Enoch; Flores, "Creating Discursive Space"; Palczewski; Sowards).

Accessing audio records of Tenayuca's speaking style has proven difficult; however, her oratorical style is quoted as "incendiary," and she is described as a "fine speaker" who possesses a "fiery eloquence" (Blackwelder 195; Vargas, "Emma Tenayuca"; Berson 249; Hardy). Such elements of her style are approximated in "The Mexican Question in the Southwest." It illustrates her acumen and her commitment to issues of equity, fairness, and justice as she is credited with conceiving and writing the document during the Pecan Shellers Strike, only later coauthoring it with her then-husband, Homer Brooks (Gutiérrez; Vargas, " 'Do You' "). It is likely that her activism throughout the strike served as inspiration for the arguments contained in "The Mexican Question in the Southwest."

The Mexican Question in the Southwest

"The Mexican Question in the Southwest" is a "ground-breaking effort" that drew upon Marxist principles to examine Mexican (Americans') situation and "one of the first political treatises written by a Mexican American in English to argue for the rights and status of Mexicans [(Americans)] in the United States" (Kanellos 156). I critically examine "The Mexican Question in the Southwest" as an instantiation of "localized rhetoric" (Rigsby), thus offering an opportunity to rectify past omissions by excavating a localized text.

"Localized rhetoric" (Rigsby) privileges texts produced by localized community actors as a means of elucidating the rhetorical meanings and impacts brought about by *historical and discursive events,* as well as meanings that may be missed when examining only the rhetoric of prominent leaders. In the context of Texas, Tenayuca was a local community actor who established ties to and worked on behalf of her San Antonio community. Contemporarily, she would be (and is) considered a "prominent leader," but within Tenayuca's localized arena her prominence was based on her designation as an agitator by local officials, a "communist" due to her membership in the CPUSA, and an exiled citizen from San Antonio, Texas, due to the death threats she received following the Pecan Shellers Strike.[9] Dedicating critical attention to "The Mexican Question in the Southwest" as an instance of localized rhetoric contains "the potential to inform rhetorical studies historically, critically, and theoretically" (Rigsby 195). In all three areas, there remain significant gaps in understanding the ways that Mexican (Americans), individually or communally, responded rhetorically to their social condition *following* programs such as the repatriation program (aka "Operation Deportation") during the early 1930s, and *preceding* the activism of the Chicano movement during the 1960s–1970s. The former is explored from the perspective of dominant mediated discussions about Mexican (American) immigrants (Flores, "Constructing Rhetorical Borders" and "Constructing Citizens"), whereas the oratory of Chicano leaders is well documented (Jensen and Hammerback).

The intervening years between the 1930s and 1960s are often neglected by scholars not only in the field of history, as claimed by Mario García, but also in rhetorical or Chicana/o-Latina/o communication studies. As I argue elsewhere, "scholarly examinations of Chicana/os' rhetorical history have not ventured into what precedes the emergence of 'Chicana/o' as a signifier of identity, cultural pride, and anti-assimilation. There is a rich legacy to be pursued when one considers the work of . . . activists in the early twentieth century" (Holling, "Retrospective" 303). Scholars recognize the 1930s–1960s as the "Mexican-American era," the period during which Tenayuca authored "The Mexican Question in the Southwest," when she also served as state chairman and Brooks as state secretary in the CPUSA. During this era, an array of political groups such as LULAC, social organizations, and fraternal orders developed not only as support networks but as a means through which rights were sought. In particular, Mario García calls attention to what he names a "Mexican American generation" who demanded first-class citizenship. Leaders of this generation sought both inclusion and reforms from the state on behalf of Mexican (Americans), and worked on different class and ideological fronts (middle- to working-class, and liberal to radical) in an effort "to wage protracted struggles for change in the Mexican communities and . . . a rightful place for Mexican Americans in US society" (Mario García 16).

"The Mexican Question in the Southwest" contributes to intellectual and political understandings of the "Mexican American generation" and later Chicana/os' struggles for self-determination by formulating nation-state unification ideologically on a class alliance that sought transborder solidarity. In so doing, "The Mexican Question in the Southwest" both compares to and contrasts with other political discourse produced by Mexican Americans and Chicanos.[10] "The Mexican Question in the Southwest" shares a commitment to liberating oppressed and dispossessed groups and recognizing cultural differences of Mexican (Americans) that uniquely situate them socially. Yet, absent in "The Mexican Question in the Southwest" are calls for insurrection and reconquest, or ideological organizing on the basis of race-ethnic separatism; also missing are the signs of "otherness" reverberating in political discourse by Mexican Americans.

The consciousness structuring "The Mexican Question in the Southwest" is one that located class as a central force intertwined with ethnicity that shaped the lives and predicament of Mexican (Americans). Visible is the indictment of capitalism (e.g., Tenayuca points out capitalist farmers' desire for a cheap labor force), a particular nomenclature (e.g., "Anglo bourgeoisie" or "super-exploited wage workers"), and quotations from Joseph Stalin and Frederick Engels that Tenayuca uses to exemplify the class dimension. As she elucidates the ways the working class became the "working class," she locates this process in an oppressor/oppressed relationship that resulted in a conquered status among Mexican (Americans), whose sovereignty was ripped from them by the United States' disregard for their rights as guaranteed by the Treaty of Guadalupe Hidalgo. Such disregard variously manifests, but Tenayuca hones in on the overtaking of lands by speculators and Anglo settlers that was pivotal to shaping a subjugated status for Mexican (Americans). From this act followed an oppressed economic condition that was continually exacerbated by a dual wage system, exclusion from and/or relegation to particular labor industries, transformation of small family-owned farming into corporate-owned farming, and employment discrimination. The possibility of the Mexican (American) working class overcoming their economic oppression was severely hampered through the absence of a political voice due to imposed poll taxes, for example, that disenfranchised Mexican (Americans), consequently allowing for political control by Anglo Americans. Such control, asserts Tenayuca, resulted in poor health conditions, inferior educational opportunities, and suppressed cultural rights for Mexican (Americans) that begged for alteration.

Tenayuca's call to action for retrieval of citizenship rights due Mexican (Americans) is radical for its time. Vargas comments that "not since 1915, when the irredentism program, El Plan de San Diego, was drawn up, had a member of the Spanish-speaking community of the Southwest raised the issue of nationhood in a radical form" ("'Do You'" 144). Vargas's statement begs the question: what are the ways in which Tenayuca argued for nationhood when such claims would rely upon rhetoric? Given that the nation-state involves a people, or citizens within whom rights inhere, on what grounds does Tenayuca argue for the rights of and advance an understanding of the status of Mexican (Americans)?

A Rhetoric of Dispensation

The content of "The Mexican Question in the Southwest" proffers what I advance here as a dispensational rhetoric. Working in tandem with advocacy efforts circulating socially is a counter-hegemonic discursive attempt to rectify the position of an oppressed national group involving rearticulation to counteract prevailing social ideas that hamper a retrieval of rights. Inhabiting a dispensational rhetoric is a systematic agenda to understand, remedy, and advance the position of a "people" in order to promote a political myth of nation-state unification. Dispensational rhetoric further illuminates extant understandings of constitutive rhetoric (Charland; McGee, "In Search of 'The People'"). A rhetoric of dispensation searches for and desires inclusion in the state (rather than pursuing sovereignty or separation from the state, as Charland argues) based on the existence of a collective being (rather than coming to be, as McGee maintains), and on the existence (rather than creation, as both Charland and McGee argue) of a national and political identity. In sum, a dispensational rhetoric seeks for a society to *dispense with* dominant narratives that hinder recognition of existing citizen-subjects while simultaneously calling for a *dispensing of* political rights.

The dispensational rhetoric of "The Mexican Question in the Southwest" aims to set right the position of an oppressed national group such as a *Mexican people* through a rearticulation of their identity to work against prevailing ideas of Mexican (Americans) in an effort to have rights and protections distributed in accordance with and delineated in the Treaty of Guadalupe Hidalgo. That treaty importantly acknowledges and establishes a political identity, being, and rights of Mexican (Americans) as citizens. In "The Mexican Question in the Southwest," Tenayuca historicizes Mexican (Americans') experiences, critiques state actions that have exacerbated their position, and delineates a methodological approach by which civil rights need to be restored. Seeking the implementation of rights for a "people" requires that they be perceived and accepted as such. For Tenayuca, that became the first objective.

Contextualizing the "Mexican (People) Problem"

A relatively axiomatic argument in rhetorical studies is that "the people" is not an objective entity, not a mere manifestation of living, individuated subjects, and not to be equated with an "audience." Nor is "the people" simply a mob. Rather, the production of "the people" has to be and is conjured up rhetorically in the name of the state (McGee, "In Search of 'The People'"). Constituting "the people" is noted as a process (re)produced continually by a rhetor, leader, or vernacular community through an ideology (or ideologies), political myths, a "fictive ethnicity," or a state force that collectivizes a body of individuals. Thus rhetorically materialized, "the people" may function as an apparatus of the state, serve as warrant for establishing a sovereign nation, or function as a national space by and for Chicana/os who assert a group identity and sense of community (Balibar; Delgado; Flores and Hasian; McGee, "In Search of 'The People'"). What becomes apparent from published scholarship is that "the people" are to be understood as state formulations (i.e., top-down, presumably absent the identities shaped by race, ethnicity, class, gender, etc.) or as vernacular instantiations (i.e., separate from, yet living within, the state albeit marginalized along the lines of race-ethnicity). Consequently, undercut are the possibilities of "the people" operating and existing in between those polarities. Speaking to this dilemma is Tenayuca's advancement of a "Mexican people," whom she seeks to collectivize on the basis of already *being* a nation-state; "being" is one of three possible stages of the collectivization process—coming to be, being, and ceasing to be (McGee, "In Search of 'The People'"). That Mexican (Americans) exist in a corporeal sense is stating the obvious, but less certain is the extent to which, within the United States, they have been recognized as citizen-subjects rather than as a "problem," replete with a history, rights to be protected, and a place within the national imaginary. Historical disregard for the Treaty of Guadalupe Hidalgo, practices such as the repatriation program, and political positionings of Mexican (Americans) as a "problem" belie the US government's and its citizenry's treatment of Mexican (Americans). Even so, Tenayuca seeks *not* to disassociate as a separate nation or create a sovereign state. Rather, she pursues the possibilities of unifying the nation-state of Mexican (Americans) and the state.

Invoked at both national and state levels, the "Mexican problem" emerged in the 1920s and reflected the view that the presence of Mexican (Americans) in the United States was increasingly a problem to the nation's identity that required supposed immediate attention. Today, as in the past, responses to the "Mexican (or Hispanic) problem" include pronouncements for more restrictive immigration policies, worker programs, and/or repatriation. Today, as in the past, political debates ensue over whether and how to offer pathways toward citizenship. Today, as in the past, discussions proceed about extending social, political, civil, and economic rights to Mexican (Americans). Implied are the internal struggles of the United States to solidify its identity and its citizenry. For example, formal inquiries[11] commenced in 1924 at both state and national levels to understand the "Mexican problem" in order to address the question of what to do with Mexican (Americans). Characterizing the "Mexican problem" were social anxieties about Mexican (Americans) as an "unassimilable" group. Implicitly, then, Mexican (Americans) mimic a "fictive ethnicity," racially produced by the state as a means of forming a distinctive population who are "ethnicized—that is, represented in the past or in the future *as if* they formed a natural community" (Balibar 223–24). Mexican (Americans) were thought to be "an economic and social threat"; language deficient; lacking in morals, sanitation, and intelligence; and thus unable to fit within the social system (Mario García 26; Gutiérrez). More to the point, Mexican (Americans) were uneasily placed in a racial social system that was structured as a black-white binary. As Montejano writes, "In short, the Mexican problem . . . was a question of locating another inferior race in American society. There was general agreement, in Texas and elsewhere, that Mexicans were not a legitimate citizenry of the United States. They were outside the civic order, and references to American national integrity . . . were often ill-disguised claims of Anglo supremacy" (181). As such, prevailing discourses of the time often characterized Mexican (Americans) as a race that was in a state of limbo; they were neither white nor black.

Explaining further the "Mexican problem" were the economic and political conditions coalescing during the 1930s within the United States that placed Mexican (Americans) in a tenuous position. There was, for instance, the Great Depression, as well as the increase in unemployment rates and the decrease of wages, both of which amplified the continued prejudice and discrimination experienced by Mexican (Americans). During this time, Mexican (Americans) were blamed for causing unemployment, depressing wages, and draining welfare rolls (Meier and Ribera 151; Mirandé 116). In short, their presence lent them to being easy scapegoats. Yet, in the decades preceding the Great Depression, Mexican nationals were often courted to enter the United States to perform various types of labor, most specifically in the areas of transportation and agriculture. But the Depression turned the tide against Mexican (Americans) and nativism surged (or, perhaps re-surged), after which immigration reform followed.

Understanding the hypocritical stances taken on immigration reform from one decade to the next is to recognize the interplay between political and economic forces that variously position Mexican (Americans). Policies passed by Congress such as the Immigration Act of 1921 and its stronger version in 1924 tended to exclude Mexican (Americans) while targeting other immigrant groups. Some claim that these immigration policies were not only nativist, but also racist in that they were to ensure an American identity as white (Acuña; Gutiérrez; Montejano). That Mexican (Americans) were excluded from the immigration acts had more to do with po-litical interests and opposing positions and hence less to do with any sense of responsibility on the part of the US government to care for a portion of its citizenry in adherence to the Treaty of Guadalupe Hidalgo. Nonethe-less, debates about immigration split between the restrictionists and anti-restrictionists (Gutiérrez; Montejano). From the perspective of agribusiness and railroad executives (i.e., anti-restrictionists), an open border was advo-cated in order to recruit Mexican (American) workers, who were consid-ered an exploitable and cheap labor force. From the perspective of small farmers, labor unionists, and eugenicists (i.e., restrictionists), tighter con-trols on immigration were necessary in order to maintain the integrity of the United States and control the growing population of Mexican (Ameri-cans). Operating from an assumption that "American" equated with white persons, restrictionists argued that Mexican (Americans) were an "inferior race," responsible for the economic decline, who deprived Americans of jobs (Gutiérrez; Meier and Ribera).

The solution to the "Mexican problem" decidedly was Operation De-portation, or the euphemistic "repatriation" (that is, returning to one's coun-try of birth). Perceived as the solution to the economic ills the United States was experiencing, repatriating Mexican immigrant workers began in 1930 and ended in 1937, once no longer deemed an economic necessity. Repatria-tion was but one of several efforts[12] advanced, condoned, and carried out by local, state, and federal government officials along with companies such as Ford Motor and the Southern Pacific Railroad. The INS and the Secretary of Labor, in cooperation with local authorities, initiated the repatriation program as a means of providing labor for unemployed Americans by deporting "employed illegal aliens" (Mirandé 116). The program was rationalized with the argument that Mexicans retained an "inclination" to return to Mexico and, if the US government paid for their transportation, they would willingly leave (Meier and Ribera). Such a rationale, of course, glosses over how officials would distinguish a Mexican national from a Mexican (American) possessing US citizenship, thus leading to the repatriation of US citizens. Implicitly the state not only envisioned citizenship on the basis of race, but conceived of it on the basis of economics and political determinants, thus advancing imperialistic desires to the negation of extant rights and protections constitutionally guaranteed.[13]

The "problem of the Mexican" is one that Tenayuca implicitly addresses, but from an alternate vantage point. Most often, the Mexican problem assumed that Mexican (Americans) were the problem within the context of the United States; hence, the issue that followed was what to do with them. As concluded by Gutiérrez, "The so-called Mexican problem was only a problem insofar as Americans refused to take responsibility for their actions" (116). In that vein, Tenayuca reverses the issue from contemplating the "Mexican problem" to pursuing the problems encountered by and confronting Mexican (Americans) in order to advance ideas about what to do with/for them. Central to that endeavor is understanding the processes by which Tenayuca rearticulated Mexican (Americans). Doing so required that she craft such an existence discursively. She repositioned Mexican (Americans') experiences as historically embedded in and integral to the building of the state, subsequently making visible a *Mexican people*.

Considered the work of public intellectuals, *rearticulation* is a process by which political interests, identities, and/or ideological themes that already resonate within society are discursively redefined, reorganized, or reinterpreted to produce new or unrecognized meanings or coherence (Omi and Winant). The rearticulation of a people is premised on the simultaneity of reorganizing the identity of Mexican (Americans) and reinterpreting their political interests in order to highlight the two groups, Mexican nationals and Mexican (Americans) born in the United States, as multiply bound historically, culturally, linguistically, politically, and socially.

Throughout "The Mexican Question in the Southwest," Tenayuca makes no symbolic distinction between Mexican nationals and Mexican (Americans) born in the United States through her referents of "Mexican" or "the

Mexican." This is not to say that she fails to recognize any actual differences between the two groups. Rather, her strategic emphasis on a singular ethnic label facilitates acknowledgment of the shared condition of both groups. Tenayuca does in fact underscore the historical material reality forming the two populations—there are Mexican (Americans) who resided in the United States prior to Mexico's annexation of the southwestern states, and there are Mexican nationals who migrated during a second wave of immigration.[14] With respect to the latter group, Tenayuca rightly points out that US companies desiring "a source of cheap labor" sought Mexican nationals' migration (257). Irrespective of Mexican (Americans') positionality, Tenayuca asserts that "no sharp distinction" exists between the two groups when considering their social condition (e.g., mortality rates, both adult and infant; illiteracy; types of labor performed; educational discrimination; and disenfranchisement) (258–61). Moreover, Anglo[15] treatment of Mexican (Americans) underscores the absence of any distinction made between both groups given that they contend with wage differentials and were "segregated into colonies" (259). In short, combining "the unequal treatment that the Mexican people suffer . . . in all phases of life" with Mexican (Americans') cultural ties based on language, and an avowed identity of Mexican, makes them "one people" (261; 258). The collectivization process of being a Mexican people hinges on Tenayuca's assertion that "the Mexican population of the Southwest is closely bound together by historical, political and cultural ties" (258). A status of "a conquered people" suffuses Mexican (Americans') experiences, consequently contextualizing their plight.

Tenayuca's rearticulation of a *Mexican people,* wherein differences based on nationality and/or legal status are subordinated, signals a transborder composition that is progressive in light of prevailing politics during the 1930s. For comparison, consider the difference between *mutualistas* and LULAC. Each sought to empower Mexican (Americans) during the same era as that of Tenayuca, albeit quite differently. *Mutualistas* were mutual aid organizations formed throughout the Southwest that united middle- and working-class Mexican (Americans) and "served both American citizens *and* immigrants of Mexican descent" by offering legal assistance, providing life insurance, as well as performing other charitable acts (Gutíerrez 96, emphasis added; Ruiz 86–87). By comparison, LULAC was explicitly oriented toward serving Mexican Americans.[16] To its members, LULAC advocated fitting into the United States and stressed "Americanization" (in other words, embracing English as the dominant language, acculturation, national loyalty, social and cultural assimilation, and exclusion of Mexican nationals from membership) in their constitution, code, and political activism (Mario García 29–34; Gutiérrez 74–92; see also Flores and Villarreal in this volume).[17] Functioning behind the emphasis on Americanization is the ideological positioning of whiteness that framed LULAC's politics (see Flores and Villarreal in this volume). In essence, LULAC wanted to present a "clean, middle-class, patriotic image" (Berson 258).

Tenayuca, based on a steadfast commitment to attaining social and cultural equity, did not view the socioeconomic position of Mexican (Americans) as being rectified through an avenue of assimilation. In implying that Mexican (Americans) are an internal colony, she takes a position at odds with that advocated by LULAC, which did not view Mexican Americans as a "colonized people" (Mario García 46). Tenayuca writes, "the Mexicans have been practically segregated into colonies"; as such, little if any distinction will be made by society to differentiate between populations (259). Whether one has always resided in or has migrated to the United States, both groups are caught up in the politics of colonization; therefore, individualized political interests that may have formulated around nationality demonstrated via assimilation need to be eschewed. In lieu of assimilation, Tenayuca emphasizes the establishment of a unified *Mexican people* who participate in a larger democratic front—namely, a "people's movement." Once the author has discursively rearticulated a *Mexican people,* the audience to whom the political myth of nation-state unification would appeal becomes more complex. Tenayuca is directing her rhetoric not only to Mexican (Americans) and the CPUSA, but also to a larger audience, including African Americans and Anglo Americans supportive of the political myth. The political interests of "the people"—Mexican and otherwise—are resituated in a wider context that lends support to the political myth underpinning a dispensational rhetoric.

Seeking Rights and Unification

The establishment of a "Mexican people" for whom a rhetoric of dispensation speaks is the process of putting right their position, beginning with, first, historicizing the people's experiences and, second, critiquing state actions that have exacerbated the people's position. Those arguments span the southwest region, subsequently illuminating the scope and magnitude of problems confronting Mexican (Americans). Undeniable are the social, political, and economic struggles that emanated from historical legacies and actions that continued to beleaguer Mexican (Americans). And, third, Tenayuca delineates a methodological approach by which civil rights need to be implemented, which in lieu of a leader to enact social change calls for a "people's movement" that is broadly inclusive to encourage a transborder solidarity.

The rhetoric is informed by the Marxist concern with "the national question," which draws ideas from colonialism in order to understand racial dynamics that carry forward and influence national oppression, and which resulted in the "Negro Question" and the "Mexican Question" (Omi and Winant). Although the latter "remained a low priority" and in "the shadow" of the "Negro Question" for the CPUSA (Buelna), Tenayuca's "The Mexican Question in the Southwest" played an important role in directing attention to the plight of Mexican (Americans). In pursuit of the national question, Tenayuca offers Stalin's definition of a *nation:* "A nation is a historically evolved, stable community of language, territory, economic life and psychological make-up manifested in a community of culture" (262). The definition opens the space for Tenayuca to assert that Mexican (Americans) are "an oppressed national group" in that they lack "territorial and economic community" (262). However, she steers clear from positioning Mexican (Americans) as a "race" or more noticeably as a separate nation.[18] Instead, she affirms that a *Mexican people* has lived side by side with the "Anglo-American population" in which both communities' "economic life" has been "inextricably connect[ed]" (262). As such, she makes the following argument, which is worth quoting at length: "Should the conclusion, therefore, be drawn that the *Mexican people* in the Southwest constitute a nation—or that they form a segment of the Mexican nation? . . . Our view is no. . . . We must accordingly regard the *Mexican people* in the Southwest as part of the American nation, who however, have not been so accepted heretofore by the American bourgeoisie" (262; emphasis added). By claiming that a *Mexican people* are a part of the "American nation," Tenayuca retains the ability to generate widespread identification and support for nation-state unification.

Toward that end, Tenayuca historicizes the experiences of a *Mexican people,* the first component of a rhetoric of dispensation. Doing so materially grounds a population's experience as a result of territorial and economic struggles and thus fosters understanding of a people's plight. She begins by referencing the annexation of Mexican territory based on the Treaty of Guadalupe Hidalgo, which allows for emphasizing the colonized-conquered position of a *Mexican people.* She then progresses to the period of "expansion and industrialization that followed the Civil War" through "the development of capitalist farming" in a few of the southwestern states, an era that ended in the 1930s. Across these periods, Tenayuca suggests that the nation-state lacks unity due to the exploitation and oppression permeating the lives of a *Mexican people*. Such a move enables her to establish a link between the historical events defining Mexican (Americans) and their "present social status" (259–61). Yet, Tenayuca intimates that because of the ways Anglo society has responded to a *Mexican people*—ranging from conquering to acts of land-grabbing to labor exploitation—they are responsible for the social conditions in which a *Mexican people* exist.

Remedying the position of Mexican (Americans) so that the political myth of nation-state unity may prosper is not to be effected by way of repatriation or assimilation. Instead, the author suggests here the second component of a rhetoric of dispensation, which involves a critique of prior actions taken by the state. Critique functions to identify and expose the limits of proposed remedies by the state or others that would maintain the subordinated status of a particular population, and then argues against such remedies. For instance, one remedy critiqued is assimilation, as advocated by LULAC and opposed by Tenayuca. Implicitly adopting a route of assimilation would not redress the class and racial discrimination experienced by Mexican (Americans); moreover, it contained the potential to fracture a Mexican people, as assimilation was tied to a US national status subsequently dividing Mexican (Americans) and Mexican nationals. With respect to repatriation, the government's use of this method belies its impetus, the importation of workers to feed capitalist interests. Tenayuca suggests that the United States has created the problem (that is, the presence of Mexican [Americans] associated with and attached to a *Mexican people*); subsequently, favoring repatriation simply displaces problems onto Mexico. Emphatically, she writes, "No, the solution to the problem of the Mexicans and Spanish Americans lies in the Southwest and not in Mexico" (266). Furthermore, although "liberal Anglo-Americans" view repatriation as "an economic necessity," it does not rectify the problems that Mexican (Americans) continued to encounter. Thus, she recommends that "barriers to employment of Mexicans" be removed along with making possible "the cultural development of the Mexican people," both of which attenuate the social and economic condition of Mexican (Americans) as "unskilled workers" (266).

Thus, in lieu of remedies such as repatriation and assimilation, she proposes a methodological approach by which civil rights are to be implemented, which relies upon a "people's movement" that simultaneously remedies and advances Mexican (Americans') position. As Tenayuca notes, "It [Mexican unification] is a people's movement, uniting the interests of large and important sections of the population . . . who, in alliance with the country's democratic forces . . . can free themselves from the special oppression and discrimination in all its phases that have existed for almost a century" (264).

As the third component of the rhetoric, the method requires lifting social and legal restrictions that curtail the exercise of rights. Who may be involved and what needs to occur are explicated with clarity in an effort to claim guaranteed rights based on a platform pursuing unification. Tenayuca focuses specifically on four areas: the eradication of economic discrimination, particularly in regard to employment; the promotion of educational and cultural equality so that there is an emphasis on bilingual education at primary and secondary levels; the elimination of social oppression, specifically legally sanctioned and de facto segregation; and the elimination of political repression, referring to enforcing citizenship rights for Mexican (Americans) and to democratizing federal regulations for permanent residents (264–65). Tenayuca's espousal of political rights, and enfranchisement in particular, is understandable in light of the poll taxes enacted in Texas. Beginning in 1902 and continuing until the 1960s, Texas enacted a poll tax that was "designed expressly to limit voting," which lessened the political participation of and diminished the rights of Mexican (Americans) (Berson 252; Mario García 41). Tenayuca's own family struggled to exercise their voting rights amid economic hardships, yet continued to do so (Blackwelder 192). Overall, emphasizing civil rights beckons not only Mexican (Americans) to the movement, but any and all groups whose position may be implicated in the aforementioned four areas.

The "people's movement" advocated is a broad-based alliance deriving from diverse populations and constituents that encouraged a "transborder solidarity," one that acknowledges but seeks to transgress the limits imposed by national lines and identifications in an effort to protect and honor the labor of individuals that benefited the state. Foremost is "the proletarian base of the Mexican population," who would lead based on a demonstrated commitment to contesting the violation of labor and union rights (265), and whose political, cultural, and economic rights had been denied them. The author also considered as an ally "El Congreso del Pueblo de Habla Española [the Spanish Speaking Congress]," maintaining a labor and working-class orientation.[19] Yet, Tenayuca expresses reluctance to confine the "people's movement" to labor concerns, conveying that strong relations and alliances with other populations and groups are needed. Recognizing that the "American bourgeoisie" is not a monolith, she speculates that "the labor and democratic forces in the Anglo-American population of the southwest" may be supportive of a *Mexican people*'s efforts based on intersecting concerns about exploitation (265–66). There are also possibilities with "Negros" [*sic*] in the South,[20] who share similar conditions such as wage differentials, discrimination, and disenfranchisement with Mexican (Americans) (260). Hence, ending the exploitation of a Mexican people, which is "in many respects, simply a continuation of the special exploitation and oppression to which the Negro people in the South have been subjected . . . will be a blow for the freedom of both" (267). Finally, she also identifies LULAC as a potential ally, whose mention is specious. Early in Tenayuca's career, she was a supporter of LULAC, though she grew to be disaffected by its politics and withdrew her support (Gabriela González 210). Later, during the height of the Pecan Shellers Strike, LULAC denounced Tenayuca and her role as strike leader because of her communist affiliation (Berson 257). Within "The Mexican Question in the Southwest" Tenayuca characterizes LULAC's approach as a "sterile path" due to its assimilationist stance and the support lent to US deportation/repatriation policies that splintered Mexican communities on both sides of the border (265–66). However, Tenayuca opines that LULAC has "undergone significant changes" in its politics that make it a welcome presence in securing support of Mexican middle-class persons (266).

The implications of the steps advocated by a rhetoric of dispensation bear on the improved status not only of a *Mexican people* via restoration of their rights, but also on all oppressed individuals within the state. Inflected in the rhetoric is an emphasis on all peoples' ability to live humanely and free from discrimination and degradation, to have dignity in who they are and what they do, to have their cultural rights preserved, to be active participants in the civic realm absent legal or social infringements, and, finally, to have their constitutional rights protected rather than violated. The dispensational rhetoric of "The Mexican Question in the Southwest" suggests that maintaining domestic or "national unification of the American people" (268) is integrally connected to international relations. In the conclusion, Tenayuca underscores that the integrity of and commitment to the "Good Neighbor" policy hinges on the ability of the United States to manifest it within the nation-state, which ultimately is of great import in the fight against "Nazi influence."

Discussion

The rhetoric of dispensation inhering in "The Mexican Question in the Southwest" relies upon the rearticulation of an Othered "people" in order to ameliorate its position by historicizing its plight, critiquing state actions, and advancing a four-pronged agenda to implement and/or restore rights. In particular, the four areas that Tenayuca sought to redress—economic discrimination, educational and cultural equity, social oppression, and political repression—remain ever-present challenges in contemporary society, thus underscoring the instructive nature of both "The Mexican Question in the Southwest" and a rhetoric of dispensation to scholars interested in studying border rhetorics.

Implicitly, "The Mexican Question in the Southwest" calls for transgressing the multiplicity of borders (perhaps even including the "figural borders" Ono discusses in his chapter in this volume) that aid in the separation of groups on the basis of nationality, class, and racialized ethnic identities while also detailing a pathway for uniting across class borders. Predicated on a transborder solidarity, a rhetoric of dispensation seeks to enable a civic identity by naming points of common cause across "peoples," simultaneously enacting a reclamation of citizenship denied. Doing so, however, becomes fiercely complicated when considering, for example, recent legislation in the state of Arizona. Two pieces of legislation bear mentioning: (1) House Bill 2281, signed into law in May 2010, which eliminates ethnic studies courses at secondary-level educational institutions, and (2) Proposition 203 passed in November 2000, which eliminated bilingual education. At the heart of these legislative acts is educational equity, a right advocated by Tenayuca. However, these legislative acts undermine the ways in which educational equity may be enacted in Arizona. Educational equity instead morphs into curriculum that all but erases already neglected and marginalized histories, chips away at youths' understanding of self and Other as relational and instead reinforces understandings of racialized-ethnic youth as Other, and inhibits the possibilities of students' development of a civic identity in all of its complexities. Arizona's legislation in effect exemplifies the retrenchment of a civic identity that all but seeks to exclude on the basis of racial-ethnic borders and raises the question: to what extent has a Mexican (American) peoples' educational standing been redressed since 1939?

Dispensational rhetoric also bears on border rhetorics that centralize immigration. In contrast to completed work regarding constructions of Mexican immigrants in dominant media discourses (Ono and Sloop), what is known about immigration rhetoric from immigrant activists themselves? What dispensational rhetorics do activists invoke in order to advocate for the rights of (un)documented immigrants? These questions could be pursued by examining the discourse following national protests in response to the passage of either Arizona's Senate Bill 1070 (the "Support Our Law Enforcement and Safe Neighborhoods Act"), or House Bill 4437 (the "Border Protection, Anti-Terrorism, and Illegal Immigration Control Act of 2005"). Does immigration activist rhetoric proceed in parallel ways to the rhetoric of dispensation in "The Mexican Question in the Southwest"? More importantly, where Tenayuca advocated for a "people's movement," is there such a discursive construction among immigration activists? In closing, continued work is needed on past and present rhetorics of dispensation as a means of evaluating the distribution of rights within the nation-state.

Notes

Earlier versions of this chapter were presented at the National Communication Association Convention (November 2005) and at the Association for Borderland Studies Conference (April 2006).

1. From here forward, I cite Mexican (Americans) as such because, throughout the first half of the twentieth century, little to no distinction was made in political or social discourses to differentiate Mexican nationals, who may or may not have become naturalized, from Mexicans born in the United States. The collapsing of "legal" distinctions was especially acute in the state of Texas (Blackwelder; Gutiérrez).

2. The published form of "The Mexican Question in the Southwest" gives coauthorship to both Tenayuca and Brooks. But, by all accounts the political document is often associated with and credited to Tenayuca (Gutiérrez; Vargas, "'Do You'"); therefore, throughout this chapter I cite only Tenayuca.

3. The work of Omi and Winant is most influential in my thinking about rearticulation.

4. Assessing the circulation of "The Mexican Question in the Southwest" would illuminate its impact; regrettably such information is unavailable in extant periodical directories (Library of Congress, personal communication, August 5, 2009).

5. The poem "La Pasionaria para Emma Tenayuca" was delivered by renowned poet Carmen Tafolla, who eulogized the labor activist's life in 1999.

6. For additional biographic reading, refer to Berson; Blackwelder; Calderón and Zamora; *La Voz de Esperanza;* Gabriela González; Hardy; Rips; and Vachon.

7. She later withdrew from the CPUSA with the signing of the Nazi-Soviet pact (Gabriela González 219; Vargas, "Emma Tenayuca" 180).

8. In an interview, Tenayuca voices her identity as a Mestiza, born of Spanish and Texan Indian parentage (Rips; Vargas, "Emma Tenayuca").

9. Tenayuca's "prominence," for example, was formally recognized at a tribute in her honor by the National Association for Chicano Studies (Calderón and Zamora).

10. Refer to critical essays by Delgado, Hammerback and Jensen, and Torres-Saillant.

11. Examples of the inquiries included President Hoover's Committee on Social Trends, the state of Texas' Educational Survey, and California's Mexican Fact Finding Committee (Acuña 187, 202–210; Meier and Ribera 123, 157).

12. The first of such efforts was the New Deal, which was aimed at stimulating the economy. Included within it were the three R's: recovery, reform, and relief. However, many Mexican (Americans) at the time were unable to receive assistance due to legislative restrictions. Complicating Mexican (Americans') ability to secure assistance was the "public charge" stereotype developing during this time. Arising from a combination of factors including underemployment, low wages, the inability to maintain a savings, and dependence on local and state relief, the stereotype was racialized and made applicable only to Mexican (Americans) (Meier and Ribera 151–52).

13. For specifics about constitutional violations, consult Mirandé 116–20.

14. The first wave of migration from Mexico to the United States occurred in the wake of Mexico's 1910 revolution; following it was a second wave of migration that spanned 1914–1930, which was provoked by multiple push-pull factors in both Mexico and the United States (Acuña; Meier and Ribera).

15. On this point of wage and labor concerns, Tenayuca is pointed in her identification of Anglos, referring to an Anglo bourgeoisie.

16. I do not place "Americans" in parentheses because LULAC distinguished itself and its members as being explicitly for Mexican-Americans.

17. Additionally, Mario García notes that "Americanization for LULAC revolved around the following issues: (1) adjustment to American values and culture, (2) political socialization, (3) cultural pluralism, (4) desegregation, and (5) education" (35).

18. A case in point is the Communist Party's examination of the position of African Americans in the "southern region known as the Black Belt" in the United States, who the party argued "constituted a nation and were therefore entitled to 'self-determination'" (Omi and Winant 43).

19. For an in-depth treatment of El Congreso, see Mario García.

20. Although the label "Negro" is no longer part of contemporary parlance, at the time of "The Mexican Question in the Southwest" it was the label invoked by Tenayuca.

5
Mobilizing for National Inclusion

The Discursivity of Whiteness among Texas Mexicans' Arguments for Desegregation

Lisa A. Flores and Mary Ann Villarreal

In January of 1948, Texas Mexican communities joined together, in Delgado v. Bastrop Independent School District (B.I.S.D.), to fight the segregation of students of "Mexican extraction" in Texas schools, a battle they expected would have to be fought all the way to the Supreme Court. A short six months later, a federal court in Austin ruled that the segregation of children of "Mexican extraction" was indeed unconstitutional. The ruling, which followed a similar California-based struggle, was based on the argument that segregation "within one of the great races" and by "national origin" was in violation of the Fourteenth Amendment's protections of the rights of citizenship (Allsup). Not surprisingly, the victory was heralded as an instrumental moment in Texas Mexican history. For instance, community leaders Joe Garza, retiring vice president general of the League of United Latin American Citizens (LULAC), and Hector de Pena, president of the Corpus Christi LULAC, described the ruling as "a great step forward for the Latin American people" (quoted in "Segregation Ban" 1). In practice, the victory had less impact than was hoped for, as schools across Texas managed to circumvent the ruling in a variety of ways (Quiroz 49).

Delgado v. B.I.S.D. was one of several significant struggles against the segregation of Mexican American students. Ruiz notes that the various cases, though often missing from public histories, paved the way for the landmark Brown decision, despite the various maneuverings following each case that enabled such segregation to continue ("South by Southwest" 26–27). We turn to the discourse surrounding Delgado v. B.I.S.D. not for its lessons in legal strategies and successes, but for what it tells us about the negotiations of whiteness and citizenship. In particular, we track the public discourse in and around Corpus Christi, Texas, a community that mobilized in large part because of sustained commitment to the legal struggle. Though the specific suit was filed against the Bastrop Independent School District, located outside of Austin and thus perhaps closer to central Texas, the suit generated considerable support among communities as far south as

Corpus Christi. Indeed, South Texas was instrumental in the suit, in part perhaps because the two organizations leading it, LULAC and the American G.I. Forum (AGIF), originated in Corpus Christi.

For six months, from the announcement of the suit to publication of the victory, the battle to desegregate students of "Mexican extraction" dominated the public discourse of the community. On the front page and in the editorials, as well as across the pages of the *Sentinel,* community leaders and residents in Corpus Christi and in nearby towns and communities commented regularly on the importance of the lawsuit as well as on the need for continued community-wide support of it. From their conversations, we gain important insight into the complex negotiation of whiteness and citizenship. Interestingly, the arguments offered rarely made specific reference to race but instead were mobilized around a discourse of descent and citizenship in which Texas Mexicans crafted an identity that positioned them within whiteness but did not directly claim whiteness nor disavow Mexicanness. It is in this careful dance around the borders of whiteness that we witness its strategic potential.

In her assessment of the status of whiteness studies, Shome identifies significant questions for whiteness studies scholars, including "How does whiteness function as an organizing social principle in society? How does it secure its hegemonic everydayness, its violent normativity, its power to be everything, to be everywhere, disguised under facile values of individualism and meritocracy?" ("Outing Whiteness" 367). These questions guide our analysis of the discourse surrounding the desegregation of Mexican American students. We explore this discourse to uncover the mobility and maneuverability of whiteness. We argue that this moment reveals how Mexican Americans situated themselves "in between" white and "colored" in ways that enabled them to claim citizenship (and whiteness) while still retaining "difference." To make this argument, we begin by examining the workings of whiteness, paying particular attention to its intersections with citizenship and mobility. We then identify key strategies at play in the discourse against segregation. We conclude by reflecting on the lessons of whiteness that emerge.

Moving into Whiteness

Identifying whiteness as a "social analytic," Garner argues that the study of whiteness exceeds the study of race and can perhaps be better conceived of as the study of a process of mobilization that entails race along with class, nation, gender, and sexuality. This perspective on whiteness asks, or perhaps requires, that we think of whiteness as a complex matrix through which social and cultural practices—legal, historic, embodied, and mundane— converge. Institutionalized and systemic, as Shome rightly notes, whiteness is dynamic, able to maintain its center while also always shifting and moving ("Outing Whiteness" 367).

Crucial to the workings of whiteness is that it draws much of its own identity, so to speak, via contrast. Whiteness exists as a conceptual category through its oppositional relationships. That is, whiteness is the opposite of, for instance, "color." Captured most dramatically and familiarly in what has come to be known as the black/white binary, whiteness exists because we have understandings of blackness and racial difference. Attributed or explained often through its invisibility (Rasmussen et al. 8–10), this dynamic of whiteness functions both to secure more strongly its seemingly unshakeable hold on dominance as it also enables whiteness's adaptability. Through its ephemeral quality and its almost intangibility, whiteness morphs and changes, adapting to a range of circumstances and contexts.

Attending to this changeability, scholars have drawn attention to what we might think of as the mobility of whiteness. This work has identified a range of affiliations and/or intersections crucial to who and what is included in "white." Consider, for instance, the importance of geography, or what Shome identifies as the "politics of location" ("Whiteness and the Politics" 108). Considerable work has illustrated that one's nearness to whiteness is linked, in part, to the racial matrix of where one lives. In a compelling historic example, Foley draws attention to "Mexican Jim" (23). Firmly situated as Mexican, and thus nonwhite in central Texas, Mexican Jim moved closer to whiteness simply by traveling from central Texas to Georgia, where the black/white racial logic had less investment in the racialization of Mexican Americans. There, in Georgia, Mexican Jim created some racial confusion, illustrated in the comments his body evoked: "He is as white as anybody" and "Mama, is Mexican Jim sure enough white?" (qtd. in Foley 23). In a more contemporary example, Shome notes that her experiences of and with whiteness as a child in India were located in between the privilege afforded her due to her education and class status and the social and cultural denigration evoked by her darker skin ("Whiteness and the Politics" 119). Though her position within whiteness in India was ambivalent at best, her relocation to the United States quickly meant that she was more firmly positioned as racial "other": "because of class privileges, whiteness/Anglocentricity in India does not mark me as 'other' in the ways that the forces of racism and white anti-immigrant sentiments 'other' me in the United States" (Shome, "Whiteness and the Politics" 119).

Across these examples is clear indication both that what is defined as white occurs in part via some sort of contrast grounded in a racial matrix and logic and that the standard against which that contrast occurs is not always fixed. "Mexican Jim" moved closer to whiteness in the US "South," where the polarity of black and white was so firmly entrenched that his body became ambiguous. Not yet or not quite white, he was also not Black.[1] Yet outside of that specific racial logic, his identity differed. Foley explains that, at least for Mexican Jim and other Mexican Americans, "in Texas, unlike other parts of the South, whiteness meant not only not black but also not Mexican" (5). Geography is of course not the only mediating factor. As Shome's example indicates, class too intersects in defining ways with whiteness.

If race is, as Matthew Frye Jacobson argues, "a theory of who is who," then who we are appears to be in part what we "do," what we "have," or what we are seen as "having" ("Becoming Caucasian" 88.) In other words, our access and affiliation to whiteness are quite clearly connected with our perceived social class (Moon and Rolison). Wray notes, for instance, that poor whites or "white trash" exist along what he identifies as the "boundaries" of whiteness (22–24). Naming poor whites in the title of his book *Not Quite White,* Wray argues that poor whites' lack of whiteness indicates that whiteness is more than just race. It is perceived as social fitness, which has, both historically and contemporarily, been linked with assumed intelligence, cleanliness, and hard work, all traits that poor whites allegedly lack (Wray 139–40). Indeed social class and labor have been important barometers of whiteness. Foley and Wray both argue that poor whites' exclusion from whiteness was indelibly linked to their perceived inability to maintain employment and/or to the degradation linked to the kinds of labor in which they engaged (Foley 65; Wray 97). Arguing similarly, Goldstein, Ignatiev, and Roediger (*Wages of Whiteness*) have all demonstrated that new immigrants, including Italians and Irish, effectively negotiated their access to whiteness in part via their ability to move out of what were commonly considered Black jobs. In the process, Roediger explains, new immigrants "often existed between nonwhiteness and full inclusion as whites, not just between black and white" (*Working* 13).

A key lesson to be learned from the connections between class/labor and whiteness is the importance of the performativity of whiteness. The work that we do with our bodies and the ways that our bodies "perform" class, through such things as dress, nonverbals, and language, are key social markers used culturally to locate us within the racial matrix (Moon 182–95). As Skeggs notes, "Class is always coded through bodily dispositions—the body is the most ubiquitous signifier of class" (83). Warren links this performativity to embodiment and argues that whiteness is produced "through a repetition of mundane and extraordinary acts that continually make and remake whiteness, all while eluding scrutiny and detection" (92). His argument draws attention to the often invisible everydayness of the performance of whiteness and/or of race. Illustrative of this invisible everydayness, Moss recalls instances in which his voice and language marked him within whiteness to such a degree that when he would meet his interviewees in person for the first time, they were surprised to learn he was Black. In contrast, Moon and Rolison detail how white skin is insufficient to grant its bearer membership within whiteness if the body within that white skin is unable to "do" whiteness adequately. Across this attention to the bodily enactments of race and whiteness, what again becomes clear is that movement into and out of it occurs and is not necessarily linked to what we might commonly think of as race.

Importantly, however, such racial movement or ambiguity should not be overstated. That some might escape the rigidity of the classification of "Black" does not mean that they have become white or at least that their whiteness is equivalent to a hegemonic whiteness. Instead, Guglielmo complicates contemporary understandings of race and whiteness by drawing attention to a crucial distinction between race and "color." Drawing on his extensive study of the arrival of Italian immigrants in the early twentieth century, Guglielmo concludes that "race was more than black and white. If Italians' status as whites was relatively secure, they still suffered . . . from extensive racial discrimination and prejudice as Italians, South Italians, Latins, and so on" (7). He argues that upon their arrival within the United States Italian immigrants were white, and they remained so while they were also often considered "racially inferior" (10).

What Guglielmo's project provocatively suggests is that there is an interesting simultaneity of inclusion and exclusion from whiteness. For those populations who have been and perhaps continue to be "not quite white," "inbetween peoples," "intermediate" races, or "other" whites,[2] membership within whiteness is contingent, contextual, and often relational. That is, one is able to move closer to whiteness in particular times and places, dependent in part on the larger racial logic at play as well as on one's specific bodily performances. This contingent access may occur at one level, such as legal or social, but be denied at a second level, such as political or educational. Still, in the mobility, we gain insight into the parameters of race and whiteness, uncovering the complexities and contradictions that impact all of us in our everyday negotiations of race and social location. For Texas

Mexicans battling educational desegregation, attempts at movement into whiteness also reveal the discursivity of whiteness and race.

Race, Education, and Social Class: Learning the Lessons of Whiteness

Led by the leaders of Corpus Christi's LULAC and AGIF, chief instigators of the lawsuit against the Bastrop Independent School District, Texas Mexican residents of Corpus Christi and the surrounding areas engaged in a vigorous discussion about the importance of supporting it. Their conversation filled the pages of the *Sentinel,* Corpus Christi's main Mexican American newspaper. The *Sentinel* provides important insight into what we might think of as the everyday discourse of Texas Mexicans surrounding the issue of education. Although considerable work has been done on the legal issues and strategies of cases arguing for desegregation and for other issues of due process and equal protection, the voices of Texas Mexicans have been under-investigated (Gross 201; S. H. Wilson, "Tracking" 211). Here, in the pages of this newspaper, we find those voices. We chose the *Sentinel* for various reasons. First, as we note above, both LULAC and the AGIF are crucial to this lawsuit. Indeed, without the efforts of LULAC, it is possible that the suit would not have been filed. Both organizations originated in Corpus Christi, with the AGIF emerging in March of 1948, just two months after the suit had been filed ("GI Forum" 1). The voices and vision of Corpus Christi leaders helped shape the lawsuit and the support of it. Second, residents of Corpus Christi and the surrounding towns and rural areas were some of the most active participants in what became a community-wide campaign for desegregation. Their fund-raising efforts, for instance, generated considerable funds for the lawsuit. Finally, the *Sentinel* was, for Texas Mexicans, one of the most widely read newspapers in South Texas. Thus, it served as a key public space through which community members participated in the building and developing of arguments about education and desegregation, which, we will argue, were also arguments about race and identity.

In the pages of this newspaper Texas Mexicans identified themselves as both a distinct community disadvantaged by prejudice and discrimination as well as members of a larger nation, of proud Americans. Their negotiation of their place in the social/racial hierarchy relied on several key strategies: a containment of race to heritage and descent, a commitment to education as the path to whiteness and inclusion, and a belief in the power of community to organize on behalf of its "people."

We might imagine that an argument against segregation would turn on the explicit language of race. However, at least across South Texas, the language of race was almost completely absent. Instead racial/ethnic "difference" was contained in a discourse that positioned it as a remnant or legacy of the past. This is most pronounced in a discourse of "extraction" and "descent." Almost without exclusion, when referring to themselves, organization leaders and everyday citizens identify as being of "Mexican extraction," Mexican descent, Latin American descent, and/or as Spanish-surnamed. Consider, for instance, LULAC, the League of United Latin American Citizens, the oldest and one of the most active Mexican American voluntary organizations of the time, both then and now (Orozco 1). Originally named the Order of Sons of America, when LULAC was formed in Corpus Christi, Texas, in 1929, its naming of itself was neither incidental nor accidental. Instead, as Orozco explains, the choices of "Latin American" and of "citizen" were careful and deliberative, designed to reference connections to Mexico and nations south, to exclude immigrants, and to emphasize US citizenship (153–57). This seemingly strategic emphasis on roots was prominent and virtually univocal in the discourse surrounding the segregation lawsuit. One article commented, for instance, that the lawsuit is designed to counter "alleged segregation of school children solely on the basis of parentage" ("Canvassing" 1). A second news article, addressing the larger issue of segregation and discrimination, reported a complaint that "persons of Mexican extraction were not permitted to use recreation facilities in the state park at Mathis" ("Mathis" 4). The announcement of the legal victory continues in this vein: "The victory . . . gives children of Mexican extraction the same educational opportunities as any other group" ("Same Educational" 1). Parents and everyday citizens also adopted this strategy of containment, as evident in a letter to the editor in which a parent states, "My two daughters are fortunate to be able to attend one of the better schools. They are about the only two with a Mexican name in the class rooms" (A.G.L. 2). Another parent also participated in this discourse: "Few parents of Latin extraction take an interest in such things as Parent-Teacher Association meetings" (De Los Santos 2).

This rhetorical containment of race to heritage and descent is not unique to this particular case. Instead, Steven H. Wilson identifies it as part of a larger legal/racial practice and perhaps strategy through which Texas Mexicans as well as other Mexican American populations positioned themselves within whiteness as they also maintained their cultural difference ("Brown" 146). Naming themselves as an "other white" via this containment, Mexican Americans laid legal and cultural claim to a racial in-betweenness that they hoped would garner them cultural and legal distance from Blacks. As in the intentional naming of LULAC that Orozco details, what we see occurring here is a considered choice to be a (distinct) part of a larger population as well as a careful distancing of themselves from the negative associations with "Mexican." That is, these children were not racial beings. Instead, their difference was situated in ways that we see today with references to Irish grandparents or Italian ancestry. Yet for all their careful distancing of themselves from being "Mexican," the language of "Mexican" does appear.

Though Texas Mexicans rely on extraction and descent to name themselves and contain their racial position, they appear well aware that a larger discourse exists in which they are reduced to a denigrated racial/ethnic status. In several instances, community members refer to moments in which they are named, seemingly by Anglo Americans, as "just Mexicans." For instance, in one editorial, a writer comments, "Should people of Spanish extraction in the future be looked upon as true Americans rather [than] the now popular view of 'just Mesicans,' the citizens who are today taking part in the struggle for equal educational opportunities will be looked upon as heroes and pioneers for posterity" (Editorial, 12 March 1948, 2). Here, the phrase "just Mesicans" appears in quotes and Mexican is seemingly deliberately spelled to approximate the common Texas pejorative pronunciation. A similar moment occurs in an article protesting segregation practices at a local state park. Allegedly, students tried to rent skates at a roller rink operated at the park but were told that they could not use the rink because they were "Mexicans" ("Mathis" 4). Again "Mexican" appears in quotes. In contrast, when the various citizens and authors writing in these many articles and editorials reference descent or parentage, in terms such as Mexican extraction, quotes are not used. The use of quotes noted above with "Mesican" and "Mexican" suggests that community members were well aware of the differences and were deliberately choosing to identify themselves differently. They were NOT Mexican. They were of Mexican descent. The language of Mexican occurs differently when linked to cultural practices, where it was neither problematized nor questioned. For instance, fund-raisers for the lawsuit were regularly staged. Many such fund-raisers were named "Mexican fiestas," but the term "Mexican" was not marked by quotes but was seemingly used as an unproblematized label (e.g., "Barbecue" 1).

In these different uses of the same term, "Mexican," we begin to see part of the strategy through which Texas Mexicans positioned themselves within whiteness. Their pervasive and almost univocal adoption of the language of descent contrasts sharply with the notations of instances in which they were "just Mexicans." This contrast suggests that the strategy of containment is a deliberate one. Moreover, in the unproblematized terms of "Mexican extraction," "Spanish parentage," and even "Mexican fiesta," "Mexican" and "Spanish," as well as "Latin American," function as adjectives describing a kind of noun. The phrase "just Mexican," however, uses "Mexican" as a noun. While there is no clear rhetorical evidence of deliberate grammatical strategy, the grammatical difference is significant. Adjectives name a type of noun; thus they show gradations among a larger shared category. Nouns are the category. The distinction is important, for what Texas Mexicans did was refuse to become the category Mexican and instead insisted upon being a type of American or a type of citizen. They formed the League of Latin American citizens, and they were American citizens of Mexican descent. The occasional naming of whites by Texas Mexicans demonstrates the parallel process, for Texas Mexicans referred to whites as Anglo Americans, again, a particular type of a shared larger category. This practice counters the more common reductionist usage of "Mexican" as noun and thus as the category. Detailing the racial arguments made for legal purposes in Texas school desegregation cases, Steven Wilson identifies an important question: "Did the legal regime of whiteness [that Texas Mexicans appealed to in this and other cases] have any larger significance?" He then answers that question, "yes, gradations of whiteness mattered even to the lay public" ("Tracking" 211). Here, in naming themselves at the intersections of descent and race, and yet simultaneously avoiding almost all explicit language of race, Texas Mexicans could engage in rhetorical movement toward whiteness.

That movement into whiteness required more than a rhetorical naming of Texas Mexicans. It entailed as well a clear mobilization around the intersection of race and class, most vividly evident in arguments about the importance of education. Granted legal access to whiteness via a historic process, Texas Mexicans often claimed their whiteness even as Anglo Americans denied them that status. Though the battle over whether or not Texas Mexicans were "really" white played out, and continues to do so, across a number of fronts, including the physicality of the body, the proximity of the US/Mexico border, the number of immigrants coming into the United States, and of course the larger racial logic that encompasses all of this and more, the success with which Texas Mexicans in South Texas negotiated their access to whiteness varied in part by class. Indeed, the community leaders of both LULAC and the AGIF, who were often successful doctors, lawyers, and other professionals, were not necessarily trying to guarantee access to white schools for their own children, who were often already attending the better schools (S. H. Wilson, "Tracking" 212). Instead, school desegregation promised that more Texas Mexicans could rise into the professional class and, in doing so, disrupt prevalent stereotypes that "Mexicans" were intellectually and socially inferior, thus perhaps showing that such attributes were characteristics that could be changed.

Across this discourse, education was situated as a key means through which Texas Mexicans could change their social location. In part, this discourse emerged through an emphasis on the problem of being undereducated. For instance, one editorial writer commented that "of the total number of our scholastics who start in the junior school, only about 50 per cent enroll in the high school three years later. Of this 50 per cent, only about 20 per cent ever get a diploma from the local high school. Apparently something is wrong and action should be taken to correct that situation" (Editorial, 23 April 1948, 2). More commonly, however, the discussion centered on the larger importance of education, particularly for social mobility. A news article emphasized the need to fight segregated schools "if we are ever to improve our standing in society" ("LULAC Attorney" 6), while an editorial proclaimed that "it [segregation in schools] is a pressing problem and it must be brought to a successful end. Segregation must end and equal educational opportunities must prevail" (Editorial, 5 March 1948, 2). A second editorial perhaps captured the larger sentiment more completely: "This fight has been brewing for more than 100 years. A hundred years is too long to wait. Imagine how much better off this generation would be if our forefathers had put their foot down on this practice when Texas became a member of the United States. A century of equal education opportunities and the inevitable rise in social and economic standing would have obliterated racial distinction such as prevails today" (Editorial, 12 March 1948, 2). Across these and other comments, the link that appears—explicitly in this final example—between education, race, and socioeconomic status is made clear. Education was the means through which Texas Mexicans could better their social status and escape racial discrimination.

This connection between race and class offers important insight into the ways that race is made and remade or, to borrow from Butler's language in *Undoing Gender,* perhaps into the ways that race is done and undone. That is, "equal" education is important here because of what it offered in terms of social mobility. It is likely not coincidental that the strongest voices and leaders in Corpus Christi were the voices of educated professionals (S. H. Wilson, "Tracking" 212). Doctors, lawyers, and dentists, who owned businesses and sought and held local political offices and occupied a space on the racial matrix between white and Black, wanted to change the social positioning of the larger community of Texas Mexicans, many, if not most, of whom were undereducated and underemployed and were thus, to Anglo Americans, more firmly nonwhite (Quiroz 50–51).[3] Perhaps they also wanted to secure their own status, and perhaps large numbers of under- and uneducated "Mesicans" were a threat. Jacobson argues that race is "made" between the perceptual and the conceptual (*Whiteness*). We come to know, understand, and "see" race, he explains, by attaching thoughts about what a particular body seemingly conveys to what it "means." If he is correct, and we suspect he is, then there is some logic to the emphasis on education in this discourse. Though Mexican Americans across the United States had been legally white since the mid-1800s, that legal whiteness was not sufficient to grant them either perceptual or conceptual whiteness, at least not without conditions. Within the racial logic of Texas, Mexicans, like Blacks, were "colored" (Foley 113). But some Texas Mexicans, particularly those with middle-class status and its accompaniments, such as language skill, education, income, employment, and deportment, could, at the very least, escape some of the race-related discrimination and prejudice that surrounded many Texas Mexicans (Steven H. Wilson, "Tracking the Shifting Racial Identity" 212). Class, then, provided a perceptual scheme that partially undid the conceptual one, enabling some Texas Mexican bodies to perform a racial identity that was not fully "colored."

Added to arguments about education and class was a clear emphasis across the discourse that Texas Mexicans were citizens, they were Americans. Moreover, Texas Mexicans consistently argued that they were dedicated citizens who believed in and identified with the "greatness" of the United States. Consider, for instance, the public report of LULAC's participation in the local "I am an American day" celebration ("Am an American" 1). Note, as well, the strong declarations made by community members about the importance of holding the United States accountable for its great democratic potential: "If the United States of America, the greatest nation on earth, hopes to pattern democracy in all the corners of the globe she should commence here in the Lone Star State. She should put her house in order first, then the neighbors!" (J. G. Rodriguez 2); "Fighting for one's rights is traditional in America and the very existence of our great country is due to the spirit of freedom and equal opportunity that beat in the hearts of the early pioneers" (Editorial, 12 March 1948, 2); and "The decision rendered . . . in the school segregation issue is one of the foremost decisions rendered in this state. . . . People all over the world . . . will now have a greater faith in a 'True Democratic United States of America.' We have defended our country in the last two wars and we are ready to defend it again if necessary. We will do it with a feeling of equality and clearness knowing that we are fighting for the same ideals and privileges given other groups" ("One of the Foremost" 1). These proclamations of the nation's greatness evince an interesting border themselves; these citizens of "Mexican extraction" were loudly voicing both their commitment to nation and their expectations of it. They were, perhaps, enacting citizenship in the vein of informed advocate. Akin to what Hahner identifies as markers of national belonging, for Texas Mexicans the simultaneous identification with the nation and challenge of it served as a discourse of citizenship (115).

This performance of national belonging was extended in the heightened attention throughout the community discourse on civic responsibility. That is, Texas Mexicans exhorted each other to enact their civic duty, as individuals and as shared members of the subset of the larger population, American citizens of Mexican descent, as they also praised others for doing so. Members of LULAC and the AGIF expected their members to be vigilant in the fight. Consider this call to the AGIF: "All members [of the AGIF] should get behind the orgnization [sic] and work as hard to weld a better community, city and country as they did to win in the Great Struggle; to weld as a great and democractic [sic] country as they dreamed of when they were in the service" (Editorial, 2 April 1948, 2). The *Sentinel* regularly announced fund-raising efforts and the amounts raised, thereby demonstrating larger community participation in the protest of the lawsuit. In a different vein, a letter writer, seemingly responding to arguments that community support of the lawsuit and other instances of discrimination went against the nation, claimed that their actions were the very constitution of civic duty, stating, "Is that [public protest and organizing] un-Texan or un-American? Heck no! It is democracy as it was taught to us while in the service of our country" (Joe G. Rodriguez 2). Finally, another editorial draws attention to the important work done for desegregation by young people's organizations: "It's a good sign that the new generation appears to take on the 'in union there is strength' attitude. It smacks of better citizens, versed in the ideas of democracy and determined that what can't be gained by individuals can be gained by parliamentary power" (Editorial, 5 March 1948, 2).

Like the emphasis on education, these invocations of citizenship serve to move Texas Mexicans toward whiteness. They may well be the discursive link between the rhetorical containment of difference that emerges in the language of extraction and the arguments for social mobility through education. Both Jacobson (*Whiteness*) and Roediger (*Working* 153–55) argue that social and cultural ideas and ideals of "fitness for citizenship" have long structured informal boundaries about who gets to be included in the notion of "America" and who is excluded from it. Noting that criteria for fitness are complex and span such intangibles as moral character, intelligence, work ethic, and one's ability to participate rigorously in a republican government, Roediger and Jacobson both argue that "fitness for citizenship" has been a flexible construct—relying on stereotypes about immigrants, race, and class—that has served historically to cast doubt on the place of many immigrant and nonwhite populations, including Mexicans and Mexican Americans. Yet here, what emerges is a discourse of fitness. In their simultaneous declarations of the nation's greatness and their call to the nation to live up to its promises of democracy and equality, Texas Mexicans enact the very ideal of republican government. They do so by locating their claims on grounds of morality, or perhaps the immorality of the two-tiered school system that marginalizes and fails their children.

In their determined efforts to battle a social and cultural issue, school desegregation of their children, Texas Mexicans mobilized around arguments of descent, education, and citizenship. Their arguments come together through the discursivity of whiteness such that what they were claiming, in effect, was more than just their children's rights to better schooling. They were arguing that they were white, and that, as white, they belong.

Conclusion

In January of 1948, Raul Cortez, governor of the Texas chapter of LULAC, proclaimed, "We believe that the case will go to the Supreme Court before we can gain a favorable verdict; we must fight until we win" (qtd. in "LULAC Attorney" 1). To the surprise of Texas Mexicans, the Texas courts ruled in their favor, and in June of 1948, Bastrop I.S.D. was directed that segregation of students of Mexican extraction was prohibited unless deemed pedagogically necessary.[4] Deemed a landmark case and a victory for Texas Mexicans, the ruling, to many, was an important step toward social change. Yet, as Quiroz notes, little changed as school systems across the state found ways to circumvent the ruling (49). Perhaps this lived reality—that Texas Mexicans, particularly poor, rural, and migrant children, continued to be contained to underfunded schools that offered little real educational help—should be the marker of the significance of this cultural moment. Yet for rhetorical scholars invested in border rhetorics and the dynamics of whiteness, there is much more to be learned here.

What occurs rhetorically across this discourse is a direct claim to belonging that belies any "probationary" status that might be accorded to Texas Mexicans. Historically within the United States, access to whiteness for some, including Irish, Italians, and Jews, has been conditional and contingent, granted in differential degrees based in part on perceptions of one's "fitness" for citizenship. Here, Texas Mexicans assert their fitness for citizenship through a complex argument of belonging that begins with historic precursors to what we might now call their "hyphenated" identity. In other words, it is possible that the terms of rhetorical containment, such as "of Mexican extraction," functioned in ways akin to what "Mexican-American" and "Asian-American" try to do today—assert a particularized belonging. In discussing the communicative function of the hyphen in identity, Pathak asserts that "it is both a subversive response to *and* a product of the race matrix in the US" (187). Though discussing the contemporary identity negotiations of Indian-Americans, her argument is insightful in unpacking the rhetorical moves at place in South Texas in 1948. Roediger states that "to argue for inbetweenness necessarily involves a willingness to keep both similarity and difference at play" (*Working* 12). In part, it is this tension, or fine line, that the discourse of containment attempts. Texas Mexicans were often highly aware that they occupied legal status as white, and yet their cultural racialization as "just Mesican" was also vivid and difficult, if not impossible, to ignore.

Amidst this glaring contradiction lay the possibilities of class. The cultural leaders whose voices dominated this public conversation, demanding equal educational opportunities and proclaiming their citizenship while naming their discontent, mobilized a whiteness grounded in citizenship and class. This particular nexus has significance for our understanding of the possibilities of whiteness, for it enables several rhetorical moves. First, by relying on rhetorical containment, via their self-naming, Texas Mexicans disrupt the racial matrix of Texas in which, as Foley argues, whiteness meant not only not Black but also not Mexican (5). But what happens if Texas Mexicans refuse that identity and instead retain but contain their cultural difference? The language of extraction that permeates this discourse established an identity position within, or at least closer to, whiteness. Second, in their insistence on desegregation, Texas Mexicans built this argument of whiteness. In his discussion of the legal strategies at play in Texas Mexican arguments about desegregation, Wilson identifies a crucial difference between the arguments advanced by Mexican Americans, which relied on due process, and those made by Blacks, maintaining equal protection ("Tracking" 148). The distinction is crucial, for due process arguments begin by assuming shared racial identity, while equal protection assumes racial difference. Thus, by focusing their efforts on education and grounding their arguments in what they, as whites, should be accorded by law, Texas Mexicans assumed a racial identity, in a move not available to Blacks. Moreover, their emphasis on education emerged from and through arguments that educational advancement would result in social equity. Classroom learning provides social class privilege. Thus, Texas Mexicans could be schooled into whiteness. And yet, as Wilson notes, arguments by equal protection would ultimately yield the kinds of structural and institutional changes of Brown v. Board, while those made here by Mexican Americans would not. In claiming whiteness and attempting to use it for their own gain, Mexican Americans participated in the reinscription of a racialized educational system that would ultimately continue to segregate them.

Finally, in asserting their citizenship and national belonging, Texas Mexicans lay claim to the nation and to their rightful place within it. Performing their "fitness for citizenship" via arguments about democracy and national commitment, Texas Mexicans challenged historical assumptions, which reflect both class and color prejudices, that they were not fit for citizenship.

Though we would be hard-pressed to argue that the rhetorical strategies at play here had significant effect, and that Mexicans, Mexican Americans, and Latinos/as more broadly are now widely regarded as white, perhaps that is not the underlying issue. Instead, perhaps our critical attention should be directed toward the larger possibilities and boundaries. That is, what emerges here of critical significance for rhetoricians and whiteness scholars is insight into the ways that whiteness works. As Shome ("Outing Whiteness") and others note, whiteness is not a static concept, but a dynamic, slippery one. It is perhaps held and lost simultaneously.

Notes

1. We capitalize Black when it is our usage and it references people.

2. The range of terms used to account for this ambivalent and insecure relationship to whiteness is considerable and too large to account for adequately here. See Barrett and Roediger, Guglielmo, and Matthew Frye Jacobson (*Whiteness*) for greater discussion.

3. Quiroz relays a childhood memory in which a white school friend invited him to join the family on a weekend trip to the lake house. When Quiroz followed up on the invitation, asking when they would go, his friend had to explain that his father didn't want any "niggers" in their house. Though both young boys knew that Quiroz was Mexican, not Black, and though the young friend tried to explain that to his father, to the father there was no difference.

4. Schools were still able to provide separate schooling for students whose English language proficiency was not deemed sufficient (Allsup).

III
Legal Acts

6

The Attempted Legitimation of the Vigilante Civil Border Patrols, the Militarization of the Mexican-US Border, and the Law of Unintended Consequences

Marouf Hasian Jr. and George F. McHendry Jr.

> In April 2005, 1,200 rugged American individualists converged on the Arizona/Mexico border for 30 consecutive days and successfully conducted the largest minuteman assembly since the Revolutionary War. . . . The Project effectively deterred illegal entry in the United States.
>
> —Jim Gilchrist, "An Essay by Jim Gilchrist"

> [T]he "Prevention Through Deterrence" strategy has pushed unauthorized migration away from population centers. . . . This policy has had . . . unintended consequences.
>
> —Nuñez-Neto, *Border Security: The Role of the US Border Patrol*

Vigilante justice seems to have always been a key part of some of the genealogical histories of various populist movements that are associated with democratic governance (Abrahams; Yoxall; Walker), and elite and vernacular communities have participated in heated debates about the merits of citizen activism and the heterodox policing of many imaged borders.[1] Between 2002 and 2007, there would be several organizations—including Chris Simcox's Minuteman Civil Defense Corps (MCDC) and James Gilchrist's Minuteman Project (MMP)—that would garner the attention of millions of viewers (Smith and Waugh; DeChaine, "Bordering the Civic Imaginary"). We are convinced that in many ways the words and deeds of the members of these organizations served as key symbolic markers in the cultural and legal wars that were fought in the name of all sorts of border "deterrence."

As we argue below in our extension of the work of Giorgio Agamben (*Homo Sacer; State of Exception*), the demarcated Mexican-US border has been configured as the norm, while unrestricted flows of human populations have been treated as aberrant and illegal exceptions. The rise of the Minutemen helped develop a populist and legal sense of governmental failure, where oaths were said to have been broken, and where porous boundaries threatened the welfare of the biopolitics of the mythic American nation.[2] To heal these wounds, members of the George W. Bush presidential administration and other decision-makers had to make choices about whether they were going to align with the MMP or dissociate their activities from legitimate border patrols. This debate led to the infusion of billions of dollars and what we argue has been the militarization of the Mexican-US border. Long after US president Bill Clinton pushed through Operation Gatekeeper in 1994—by which an experimental ten-foot wall was placed along a fourteen-mile stretch of the California-Mexico border—the Security Fence Act was passed in 2006 that extended this work for hundreds of miles (Walker 144). Embarrassed officials who witnessed the rise of these civilian volunteer organizations declared several state emergencies, wrote about the importance of the National Guard, and tinkered with the idea of creating surveillance communities that would bring together local citizen groups and military patrols. Detention camps had to be expanded and cleaned up, amnesty plans had to be abandoned, new "virtual" zones of surveillance were created, and a host of organizations fought for credit in the immigration restriction wars.

It is our contention that at the heart of all of these public and elite debates over the nature and scope of immigration restriction were questions regarding the legitimacy of the Minutemen Projects. California governor Arnold Schwarzenegger perhaps spoke for many restrictionists when he argued in April of 2005 that the private "Minuteman" campaign had "cut down the crossing of illegal immigrants a huge percentage," to the point where the MMP showed that "it works when you go and make an effort and when you work hard" (qtd. in Nicholas and Salladay). As Doty noted in 2007, the MMP members may have been unofficial if we evaluate them using formalistic legal criteria, but they were not always operating illegally as they patrolled the borders that in their minds should have been adequately patrolled by the federal government. Using what Yoxall has called a "passive" strategy of claiming to avoid interactions with suspected undocumented immigrants, the members of the MCDC pride themselves on reporting violations to members of the Border Patrol while trying to maintain adherence to "no contact" rules as they approach "Mexicans" (Egan).

We argue in this chapter that debates over the legitimacy of the Minuteman Project did more than just signpost some of the potential infrastructural problematics of the US Border Patrol's policies that preceded the inauguration of the "Prevention through Deterrence" program. It forced ranchers, citizens in San Diego and El Paso, Bush administrators, social activists, and others to seriously contemplate the advantages that might come from militarizing the US-Mexico border.

Rob DeChaine has noted how the image of the alien invader has been used to arouse the patriotism of those who would like to fence out a whole host of foreign interlopers ("Bordering the Civic Imaginary" 52–59), and the elite and public circulation of these mobile signifiers of "illegal alien" and "citizen vigilante" wreaked havoc for the heavily funded United States Border Patrol (USBP). While there is little question that some members of the Border Patrol welcomed some of this voluntary help, other officials complained that the MMP were tripping sensors, making extravagant claims about the success of their efforts, circulating controversial statements about "alien invasions," and complaining before Congress that priorities needed to be changed. Even those who might have agreed about the need to keep out the illegal "other" vociferously disagreed about the social agents and the legality of the various tactics that were deployed by vigilantes at the California, Arizona, New Mexico, or Texas borders. At the same time, there is little question that some of the populist threads that were a part of these vigilante tapestries of ideas resonated with audiences. Debates about deportation, the existence of jobs in places like New York City, and the importance of spending for National Guard units were all symbolically tethered together in a nationalistic universe where the Minuteman played a key characterological role.

Other interdisciplinary scholars have done a masterful job of explaining some of the rhetorical features of the MMP and press coverage of these vigilante groups, but we are convinced that researchers also need to be investigating the rhetorical tactics used to gain legal legitimacy as members of the volunteer civilian border patrols.

We contend that a critical analysis of contested imaginary legal borders illustrates that at various points in time between 2002 and 2007 the MMP and other civilian border patrol organizations gained and lost legitimacy. Sometimes this legitimation came in the form of shared goals, while at other times these conversations moved into matters of specific strategies and tactics. We of course would argue that it is no coincidence that these debates about the MMP were taking place at the same time that state and federal authorities mulled over the question of how best to use Department of Homeland Security resources.

When the members of the MMP were viewed *abstractly* as private citizens who aided state and federal causes, they were welcomed by a few authorities and ordinary citizens, but over time revelations about some of their *concrete* activities created a situation where they lost some of their ethos as they were reconfigured as interlopers. For example, when the G. W. Bush administration spent billions of dollars on revamping the Border Patrol and the creation of various walls and other projects, the political void that had been temporarily filled by ever-vigilant Minutemen was now occupied by thousands of new members of the USBP and other federal agents. But when decision-makers in Washington, DC, or members of the USBP actually acted on some of these volunteers' own suggestions for change, this frustrated the members of the MMP or the MCDC. As private citizens, they could only do so much without running into problems regarding the carrying of arms, the detention of potential deportees, and the dangers of civil suits.

One of the key issues, of course, is whether the law of unintended consequences came into play as these debates about the legitimacy of the MMP also impacted the contours of *militarized* borders. Vigilance had to be maintained, but now it would be thousands of new uniforms who would be protecting *Pax Americana*.

In the first portion of the chapter, we provide a theoretical discussion of the roles that imaginary borders play in the way that we think about space, land, law, and lawlessness. The second portion of the chapter then shifts the reader's gaze so that we can see how various audiences once viewed the MMP (especially during 2005). Here, we briefly contextualize some of the mass-mediated representations that seemed to have aided the cause of those who believe that the MMP offered a legitimate form of vigilante justice. The third part of the chapter augments this commentary with an ideological critique of how the MMP started to become delegitimized or co-opted as various agents began talking about other, more "legal" ways of providing deterrence and population mobilization. In the concluding section, we comment on how the law of unintended consequences seemed to come into play as new "Prevention as Deterrence" programs only complicated matters for those who were trying to provide justice for so many "others."

Geographic Imaginaries and Border Politics

Rosencrantz: Not even England. I don't believe in it anyway.
Guildenstern: What?
Rosencrantz: England.
Guildenstern: Just a conspiracy of cartographers, you mean? (Stoppard 107)

What does one make of borders in the contemporary moment? This central question animates much of the theoretical and critical aspirations we bring to bear in our analysis of the MMP. Has the MMP played some key role in the way that we think about what characters are supposed to help with the patrolling of a border where some 350 million people cross "legally every year" while millions of others cross illegally (Yoxall 519)?

On the one hand, the border is a material place of danger, hostility, and death—in a sense *real*. On the other hand, borders are rhetorical in the ways that we decide to epistemically map this ontological reality. The ways that we configure these borders as adequately guarded or unguarded, porous or contained, impacts the ways that we think about cultural relationships, global conditions, work situations, and imaginary communities. Instead of operating from some imagined dialectical tension between the material and rhetorical border, we seek to collapse such distinctions as a theoretical basis for understanding the border (as an imagined fixed object) and "frontier" borderlands (spaces of indiscriminate and undefined lawlessness). Our contention that the border is a collapsed material and rhetorical space aligns significantly with Kent A. Ono's chapter early in this volume. As Ono argues, a discursive conception of the border insists that "the border is socially constructed" (23). Ono elaborates by noting that the "US/Mexico border is the effect and aftereffect of war, but it is also an outcome of policy, and of law, which means it is the product of discourse" (23). It is at the eventual horizon of enforcement that the border finds its material effect, and for Ono we are obliged "to consider where the border is enforced" (24). Hence, we consider the controversy over border enforcement by non-state actors.

Giorgio Agamben's work on the state of exception has informed the ways that we think about border biopolitics, and in a host of ways the perceptual complaints about the lack of enforcement at the US-Mexico border is based on the politics of fear and indecision that Agamben argues marks times of emergency and violence. Drawing directly from the work of Walter Benjamin, Carl Schmitt, and others who began to explore the state of exception in the early 1940s (*State of Exception* 6–7), Agamben, who would write about the dialectical tension that existed between states of normality and states of exception since World War II, emphasizes the point that it matters a great deal who gets to be the arbiter doing the boundary-work between these two zones. In theory, times of emergency created public perceptions of exigencies which in turn legitimated activities that were supposed to return us to the norm. This state, for Agamben, has transformed from using temporary extra-constitutional measures into one that engages in "a technique of government [that] threatens to radically alter—in fact, has already altered—the structure and meaning of the traditional distinction between constitutional forms" (*State of Exception* 2).

Agamben's genealogical reading of the historiography provides examples of how various polities have commented on necessity and abuse (*State of Exception* 11). While Agamben admits that some of these concepts had evolved over time, he is nevertheless convinced that the contemporary moment was marked by "global civil war" that has justified a "state of exception" unbounded by temporality (*State of Exception* 40; see also Hardt and Negri 4). Ultimately, "the state of exception marks a threshold at which logic and praxis blur with each other and a pure violence without *logos* claims to realize an enunciation without any real reference" (*State of Exception* 40).

The MMP's quest for legal legitimacy therefore takes place during a time of exception in which the securitization of the border is linked to trepidation, existential gaps, and juridical absences. These feelings of voids have to be filled by those who can engage in a biopolitics that promises that certain actions will return the body politic to a time of normality, where the rule of law can return from predatory states of nature. The MMP's claims are clearly emblematic of a rhetoric that shifts border protection from the metaphor of security to that of militarization. Karma R. Chávez adeptly explores this line of thinking in this volume. Chávez argues that "framing is especially dire in relation to the US-Mexico border, which has, in the eyes of many politicians, pundits, and citizens alike become the greatest source for *insecurity* in the national imaginary" (49). The MMP in part takes up the posture as a gap-filler between the failure to secure the border and the desire to militarize the border.

Beyond just the political regimes of "War on Terror" America, the difficult discursive practices and spatial politics of the porous-imaginary-real border between the United States and Mexico served as a state sign of exceptionalism, where fissures created problems for the state.

While critics of anti-immigration policies might point out that our border histories are filled with tales of openness as normality, the members of the MMP are tapping into populist rhetorics that have different notions of what it means to have order, regimentation, and the instantiation of the rule of law. Obviously what constitutes human or inhuman activities in the negotiation of normal and exceptional "states" involves an array of national identities, problems, and solutions. J. David Cisneros argues, "The metaphor of immigrant as pollutant articulated in popular discourse is significant for the ways in which it constructs immigrants, through racial and xenophobic stereotypes, as objects, aberrations, and dangers" ("Contaminated Communities" 591).

The metaphors of pollution are figured as a specific threat to health of the body and require the politics of immigration to take on an urgency to protect the white-American body. Such a danger is reinforced by the relationship of immigration policies and the sovereign body. Anne Demo has argued that studies "of the US/Mexico border are no longer limited to the realm of geopolitics but include the figurative boundaries that separate citizen and other" ("Sovereignty Discourse" 291). Demo argues this connection legitimizes, and even makes mundane, the militarization of the border ("Sovereignty Discourse" 291). However, when such activity fails to produce the desired results of a pure border, then extra-state actors engage in gap filling. As Jacques Derrida argues, "The City's body *proper* thus reconstitutes its unity, closes around the security of its inner courts, gives back to itself the world that links it with itself within the confines of the agora, by violently excluding from its territory the representative of an external threat or aggression" (133).

These medical metaphors of immigrants as pollutants are potent by themselves, but they gain in magnitude when they are tethered to other metaphoric clusters associated with securitization and criminality rhetorics. The decisions that are made by members of the Border Patrol or the MMP thus become the micro-politics which build those states of exception that create the perceptual need for vigilantes. They can hide their own potential extra-judicial behavior behind the pursuit of the true "illegals" who threaten the American body. The MMP, for example, can participate in the process of redefining this national body by attempting to defend it under the dangerous guise of the state of exception.

The Rise of the MMP and Its Temporary Legitimacy

As Margaret Smith and Linda Waugh explained in 2008, the members of the Minuteman Project use the World Wide Web to invite visitors to perceive the MMP as a "lawful, fair and diplomatic organization" that is populated by "knowledgeable" citizens who know a great deal "about current events concerning immigration problems and reform" (144). As Chris Simcox, one of the leaders of these volunteer border organizations, explained in his outlining of the "Standard Operating Procedure for Minuteman Project," the members of this organization are supposed to "observe, report and direct" the border patrol or other "appropriate emergency or law enforcement agencies to suspected Illegal Aliens or Illegal Activities" (qtd. in Yoxall 555).

In order to try to convince visitors to his blog site that they need to join this type of organization, Simcox specifically links the situation at the

Mexico-US border with a host of other socially responsible movements and initiatives:

> You are reading this because you believe that you can actively partici-
> pate in one of the most important, socially responsible, and peaceful
> movements for justice since the civil rights movement of the 1960s. . . .
> You have debated, you have begged, you have pleaded with your gov-
> ernment officials—public servants whom you trusted to stand by the
> oath that they took when sworn into office to protect the United
> States from invasion by enemies foreign and domestic. The human
> flood breaching our Homeland Defense is not necessarily the enemy
> per se; drug dealers, criminals, and potential terrorists are, and they
> should be the source of any ire you may be experiencing . . . (qtd. in
> Yoxall 555–57)

Note the suturing together of several different types of supposedly analo-
gous situations. The historically nonviolent protests of the 1960s are tethered to the civilian border patrol members' quests to provide more "public
servants." The commentary on the "human flood" magnifies the state of
exception, inviting us to believe in the necessity of this type of civic engagement. The credibility and authority of the MMP are crafted by juxtapos-
ing the efforts of this noble organization with the border crossers who are
"dangerous, threatening, predatory, barbaric, alien, numerous, unstoppable,
vengeful, and generally unpleasant and disagreeable" (Smith and Waugh 144).

Although there have been other volunteer groups that have organized
themselves and tried to gain the media spotlight—including Chris Simcox's
"Civil Homeland Defense" organization—the Minuteman Project founded
by retired California businessman James Gilchrist has become one of the
key organizations that garnered attention for those who wanted rigorous
immigration enforcement.[3] During the fall of 2004 and the winter of 2005,
Gilchrist and his supporters put together the logistical materials that they
would need for the voluntary patrolling of a sixty-four-mile stretch of Arizona desert (Viña, Nuñez-Neto, and Weir 9). Some four months before this
scheduled event, Gilchrist would be interviewed by Sean Hannity and Alan
Colmes of *Fox News,* and he explained just why this needed to be thought
of as a major breakthrough in enforcement measures: "We will be recording.
We'll chronicle all these reporters that are going to Border Patrol [*sic*] from
our outposts and our foot patrols and our air wing. We will record whether
the Border Patrol is reacting or not, whether there has been an interception
or not" (qtd. in Hannity and Colmes). This statement invited listeners to

think of these volunteers as dedicated chroniclers of events who had a form of tacit knowledge that could only be gained by staying in the region and walking the grounds. At the same time, the Border Patrol is configured as an organization that needed to be monitored and tracked, so that the public would have accurate records of actual deterrence.

By April of 2005, some nine hundred volunteers had arrived to assist the MMP in their quest, and writers for newspapers, journals, political tracts, and governmental reports let readers know that these volunteers were trying to get across the message that an increase in manpower could reduce the number of illegal "aliens" who were coming into the country. As Stephen Viña, Blas Nuñez-Neto, and Alyssa Weir have pointed out, some of these volunteers carried rifles and firearms and they were told that their mission was to "assist" the USBP agents who were patrolling the border. As a part of the exercise, they were not supposed to do anything other than alert the proper authorities to the presence of illegal "aliens" (Viña, Nuñez-Neto, and Weir 10). The "Standard Operating Procedure" on the MMP website indicated that these volunteers were told that they were to "abide by the rules of no contact and no engagement," so that they would not actually confront the illegal aliens. In theory, the weapons were simply there for "self-defense," and they had to comply with the laws of the state of Arizona. According to Chris Simcox, this project had "assisted" with locating some 349 "aliens" who were illegally entering the country (Viña, Nuñez-Neto, and Weir 10). Official documents repeated these claims, and on April 21, 2005, a reporter for the *Washington Times* would tell readers that Mr. Gilchrist had reported that the "number of aliens crossing where Minuteman volunteers had set up observation posts dropped from an average of 64,000 a month to an expected 5,000 this month" (Seper, "Minutemen Join"). Jim Gilchrist would later tell some of Georgetown's law professors and students that "in a span of two years, with a paltry purse of public donations, the Minuteman Project has brought more attention to the illegal alien crisis than many larger and longer-established immigration law advocacy groups have done in 25 years with aggregate donations of an estimated $20 million" (Gilchrist 416).

In some political and legal commentaries on the need for border reform, hagiographic pictures were used to portray the MMP as organizations that underscored the distance that purportedly existed between legislators in Washington, DC, and "immigration and border security problems." Congressman Thomas Tancredo, for example, claimed that although US president G. W. Bush had been proposing "comprehensive immigration reform" since January of 2004, federal authorities seemed to be confused by all of

the talk of "illegal immigrants" or the middle ground that might exist between "mass deportation and amnesty" ("A New Strategy").[4] Tancredo
claimed that if readers would just pay attention to some of the arguments
of ordinary citizens we would have to conclude that anyone who entered
the country unlawfully needed to be officially designated "an illegal alien,
not an illegal immigrant." Tancredo was very clear when he talked about
which organizations needed to be given credit: "The Minutemen patrol on
the Arizona-Mexico border during the full month of April in 2005 demonstrated to the entire world that the flow of illegal aliens across the border
can be controlled by the physical presence on the border." Tancredo argued
that "security borders" could be achieved within a month if the nation was
serious about the use of "the military," but he complained that some reform programs were only avoiding the prevention of "all illegal entry into
the country" ("A New Strategy").

There were dozens of other congressional leaders who also referenced
the contributions of the MMP and similar volunteer organizations, and
some studies indicate that during 2005 more than 1,700 stories appeared
in the mainstream press on the activities of the organization. Moreover,
popular TV shows, including *Law and Order* and *The West Wing,* provided
even more media exposure for the vigilante groups that "fought to protect
America" (Walker 138).

These organizations could have been marginalized and ignored if officials believed in the stabilization of the borders. Eventually, however, the
nation's commander in chief felt pressured to come up with his plans for
dealing with the immigration "problem." During an address to the nation
that aired on May 15, 2006, US president G. W. Bush averred: "For decades,
the United States has not always been in complete control of its borders. . . .
We're a nation of laws, and we must enforce our laws. We are also a nation
of immigrants, and we must uphold that tradition, which has strengthened
our country in so many ways. These are not contradictory goals. America
can be a lawful society and a welcoming society at the same time." Bush's
argument, of course, assumed that the nation needed "complete control."
The US president's plans included calls for securing the borders, creating a
temporary work program, holding employers accountable, and honoring the
"Melting Pot," but by the end of 2006 increased securitization also meant
the addition of six thousand National Guardsmen at the border.

Some members of the legal sphere harped on the jurisprudential contributions that were being made by social agents who seemed to have some
tacit knowledge of "immigration and national security" law. Take, for example, the way professor Jan Ting wrote about the efforts of the Minutemen

during the winter of 2006: "The Minuteman Project, an anti-immigration group of volunteers, had conducted a one-month patrolling campaign in April, and Washington did not want the number of arrests to show an increase after it ceased. While it will be difficult to secure our entire 2,000 mile southern border. . . . we can put more people at the border, either using volunteers like the Minutemen, or using the US Army Reserve and the border states' National Guards" (48).[5] Within this particular rendition of the state of exception, there shouldn't be any question that we needed to "secure" the border—the key questions were supposed to revolve around whether we want "volunteers" or the militarization of the border. Ting thus promoted the idea that the members of the MMP were public servants who had made meaningful contributions that could be empirically quantified.

State, Federal, and Public Critiques of the MMP

Interestingly enough, the MMP may have helped raise awareness about the perceived dangers of having "alien" enemies massed at the borders, but this success may have contributed to the delegitimation of these same organizations. State and federal authorities could accept some MMP members' idea that more militant action or regimentation needed to be taken at the borders, but this very position could be co-opted by those who could then say that this type of drastic action needed to be carried out by members of the USBP, the INS, or other state or federal agencies. In other words, if enforcement was simply going to be a question of manpower, then the average citizen needed to be protected by professionals and not by amateurs.

The growing power of the MMP in the court of public opinion also gained the attention of those who found that they needed to politically *distance* themselves from these American volunteers. The biopolitics of the border had many defenders of immigration registration that marched under many different banners, and one could identify with the need for change without admitting that the vigilantes were the answer to the conundrums that plagued the borderlands. US president G. W. Bush, for example, commented on some of the MMP practices in 2005 as he stood beside Mexican president Vincente Fox and Canadian prime minister Paul Martin during a news conference in Waco, Texas. "I'm against vigilantes in the United States," noted President Bush, but he was for "enforcing law in a rational way." As far as he was concerned, it was the "Border Patrol" that "ought to be in charge of enforcing the border" (Bush, "President's News Conference" 509). If the nation was living in exceptional times involving terrorist emergencies, then there was no reason to believe that federal authorities couldn't provide these "rational" solutions.

Discursive synergies developed as critics of the MMP noticed that some of those who were in a hurry to participate in citizens' arrests of potential illegal detainees were forgetting about the Fourth Amendment and other rights of both citizens and noncitizens. Stephen Viña, for example, pointed out some of the legal complications: "The Minuteman Project could raise a number of legal issues due to its law enforcement nature. For instance, issues of liability and authority might arise should a volunteer harm another person or conduct an unlawful activity. . . . For example, should the Border Patrol start directing and controlling the volunteers in their operations, it might be argued that the Minuteman Project volunteers are acting as 'agents' or 'instruments' of the Border Patrol" (18). The very activities that Gilchrist and the other leaders claimed had cut down on immigration rates were the same performative acts that could contribute to their delegitimation.

From a rhetorical vantage point, this dissociation involved beautiful strategies that allowed space for some of the more militant actions of state and federal agencies to seem moderate in comparison with the discourse that had been circulated by the MMP. The dangerous signifiers of the "alien" invaders remained, but the militarization of the border was now being cloaked in legalistic rhetorics, US presidential lexicons, and military terminologies that altered the geopolitical landscape. State or federal forces took the place of amateurs, thousands of new state and federal agents were hired, and now the American nation could let the vigilantes go back to their other jobs.

Obviously, these types of critiques that came from some border patrol members were not the only reasons for the demise of these civil border organizations. Many strong pro-immigration countermovements attacked the supposed "multi-ethnic" labeling of the MMP, and turmoil over financial allegations must have had a chilling effect on the donor pools (Geis). During 2007, several Minuteman organizations planned thirty-day operations so that they could watch over the "country's most popular alien- and drug-smuggling corridor," near Palominas, Arizona (Seper, "Ex-Minuteman Members"), but few mainstream outlets carried any extensive stories on these developments.[6] There were even times when volunteer factions began criticizing the plans of rival groups. For example, a fence-building project supposed to build six-foot trenches and coils of concertina wire backed by steel-mesh fence posts had lackluster results. When MCDC volunteers erected over two miles of five-strand barbed wire that was attached to short metal posts, Glenn Spencer of the American Border Patrol commented that it "wouldn't stop a tricycle" (Holthouse).

To this day, a number of divergent communities disagree about the number of illegal residents who live on the American side of the border and the deterrent effect that some of the "comprehensive" immigration reform programs actually have on the biopolitics of the region. Sadly, the temporary rise of the civilian border patrol organizations may have signaled the public acceptance of states of exception that add new layers of dangers and emergencies brought by the rhetorical construction of "the alien" other.

Conclusion: Strategies and the Law of Unintended Consequences

Wayne Cornelius has been warning policy-makers and local activists of the "unintended consequences" that have so often brought death and destruction to the US-Mexico border. As he once noted, during the INS years under Clinton the nation moved away from policing models that focused on apprehending illegal immigrants through inspections and toward "Prevention through Deterrence" policies. While many observers who keep track of the effectiveness of these techniques often claim that they have cut down on the number of apprehensions being made by the Border Patrol along the Southwest border with Mexico, what they often fail to focus on are the recidivist rates (Cornelius 664), the motivations of smugglers (*coyotes*), differential wages, and the other cultural, economic, and political factors that need to become a part of the complex biopolitics of the border (Cornelius and Salehyan).

In spite of the fact that Jim Gilchrist and other leaders of various civilian border patrol organizations are occasionally asked to present their views in legal venues, these particular groups have nowhere near the public visibility that they had during 2005–2006. Their place has been taken by high-tech surveillance towers that were made by Boeing for almost $1 billion, secure border initiatives, hundreds of miles of expensive fencing, and the quadrupling of the size of the Border Patrol. Add to this new fleets of drones, countless sensors, scopes, and new vehicles, and you have a militarized cottage industry that prepares for the new "aliens" who will come at the end of the current recession.

In this chapter we have argued that the ontological gap between spatial border zones and their epistemological construction in the metanarratives of US exceptionalism created the need to discursively construct a state of exception to deal with immigration. In this gap the MMP projects took root to deal with what they perceived to be governmental failures. At the same time, their ability to embarrass public officials with tales of their success and assurances that enforcement was possible with more patrolling bodies led to the dissolution of their own legitimacy. The government continued a decades-long militarization of the border, using new technologies to attempt to create a panoptic space of self-policing, and meanwhile the MMP became a dangerous pseudo-state regime that threatened immigrant populations and the state alike.

Notes

1. For some helpful historical overviews on the imaginations that have been linked to the US-Mexico border, see Nevins.

2. Agamben refers to biopolitics as "the growing inclusion of man's natural life in the mechanisms and calculations of power" (*Homo Sacer* 76). We take biopolitics to be the relations of power that flow throughout social strata and at every turn always already implicate the body of those who experience the flux of that power.

3. The MMP is made up of numerous entities, many loosely organized and/or semi-autonomous, that together mobilize under the signifier MMP.

4. For a critique of other of Tancredo's claims, see Cisneros, "Contaminated Communities."

5. See also Seper, "Border Patrol."

6. For a rare exception, see Seper, "Ex-Minuteman Members."

7
Shot in the Back

Articulating the Ideologies of the Minutemen through a Political Trial

Zach Justus

> This is a day of shame for America. It is every bit of the sickness I felt
> as a teenager after the assassination of JFK. It is the sickness I still feel
> when I think about that day. It is that horrible feeling you got after
> 9-11. It is the destruction of America as a free country . . . with laws
> and gosh forbid, justice for all.
>
> —CTHELIGHT, a participant in the Minuteman
> Civil Defense Corps' online public forum

On February 17, 2005, Texas Border Patrol agents Ignacio Ramos and Alonso
Compean pursued and shot drug-trafficking suspect Osvaldo Aldrete-Davila.
Davila was given full immunity for his testimony against the border agents
despite the fact that agents confiscated one million dollars' worth of mari-
juana that he ditched while running from them (Seper, "Gonzales"). The
agents did not follow procedural guidelines in that they failed to report
the incident to their superiors (Gilot). In the next two years, US attorney
Johnny Sutton brought the agents to trial and oversaw their prosecution and
conviction (Serrano).

In this chapter I explore how the trial was appropriated by the nativist
organization the Minuteman Civil Defense Corps (MCDC), within their
online forum, and what the trial meant to this particular group. The analysis
sheds light on how the "battle" over the border spilled onto the bodies and
stories of salient parties. The rhetoric within the forums highlighted the
existing tensions between the group and different components of the government. The other discursive implication of the episode is that it allowed
the Minutemen to "side" with specific Hispanic-Americans (the agents) and
hence complicate the typical charge of racism leveled against them.

The fact that there was even a trial of Ramos and Compean implies that
at least some facts were disputed. That being said, certain points have been
widely agreed on. Seper reported on some of the generally understood specifics after the verdict had come down:

Records show that after Mr. Aldrete-Davila was spotted in his van near the Rio Grande, Ramos gave chase while Compean circled around to head off the suspect. When Mr. Aldrete-Davila jumped out of the van and ran south to the river, he was confronted by Compean, who was thrown to the ground as the two men fought. Ramos said that when he arrived, he saw Compean on the ground and chased Mr. Aldrete-Davila to the river, where the suspect suddenly turned toward him and pointed what looked like a gun. Ramos said he did not think the suspect was hit. He said Mr. Aldrete-Davila ran through the bush, jumped into an awaiting van in Mexico and sped off. An investigator from the Department of Homeland Security's Office of Inspector General found Mr. Aldrete-Davila in Mexico, where he was offered immunity in exchange for testimony. ("Gonzales")

After their conviction on the grounds of assault with a deadly weapon among other charges, Ramos and Compean were sentenced to eleven and twelve years, respectively, in prison.

The trial, conviction, and sentencing all served as points of concern for many lawmakers. Seper reported, "Dana Rohrabacher yesterday asked Attorney General Alberto R. Gonzales to investigate what he called 'the exceedingly harsh prosecution' of two US Border Patrol agents now facing 20 years in prison" ("Gonzales"). Even Dianne Feinstein remarked that, "undue prosecution of Border Patrol agents could have a chilling effect on their ability to carry out their duties" (Seper, "Gonzales"). These fragments of commentary are only a precursor to the reactions from the MCDC. The Minutemen were almost universally outraged that Border Patrol agents were being sent to prison for the mistreatment of a drug smuggler. Before delving further into the controversy, some background information on the group is warranted.

The Minuteman Civil Defense Corps

The MCDC is an anti-illegal immigration organization founded in Arizona. The group's stated goal is "to see the borders and coastal boundaries of the United States secured against the unlawful and unauthorized entry of all individuals, contraband, and foreign military. We will employ all means of civil protest, demonstration, and political lobbying to accomplish this goal" (Declaration Alliance). The MCDC is well known for the tactics alluded to in its statement of purpose. For instance, MCDC volunteers conduct regular border "operations" in which individuals watch over the border and report any activity to the US Border Patrol. The Minutemen also engage in public protests at sites where day laborers congregate ("Mesa Day Labor Protests") and near locations of institutional power, such as the state capitol of Arizona.

The organization maintains relevance by leveraging media outlets through the use of its sensationalized tactics. DeChaine explains, "Its continued media presence and its often infamous appearances on college campuses have helped the MCDC to maintain a significant profile in the public conversation on immigration reform, while contributing to its ethos as a controversial activist group" ("Bordering the Civic Imaginary" 52). Part of the media attraction to the Minutemen stems from their emphasis on the physical and sociological border between the United States and Mexico. DeChaine argues that emphasizing the "broken border" codes racism in the form of what he terms "alienization." This coding makes the racism of the Minutemen more socially acceptable and allows for the integration of post-9/11 fear into border rhetoric.

The physical border also presents its own set of problems that go hand in hand with alternative rhetorical coding. In a legalistic analysis, Yoxall expressed concern over the border operations of the Minutemen because "the embedded racism of the MCDC alongside its gun-slinging nature provides a dangerous combination in light of the inherent violent nature and history of the border" (646). In this respect, even critical analysis like the kind provided by Yoxall falls victim to the characterizations of borders as violent and broken. This, of course, validates DeChaine's argument and rhetorically positions the MCDC even as it is being criticized in the vein of Yoxall. Characterizing the border as lawless serves a dual purpose for the MCDC. First, it legitimates what the group is doing because there is no law to break. Second, it positions members of the group as lawmakers bringing justice to a wild land.

Another trend when characterizing the MCDC is to contextualize its activities in a history of nativism (Buchanan and Holthouse). However, Yoxall has located a key point of divergence between the MCDC and other nativist movements. He concludes that the widespread ideological organization of the MCDC represents a kind of threat that is different from other vigilante groups that have checkered America's past. Yoxall notes, "the MCDC represents a new prospective threat distinct from the localized threat of past vigilante border groups and is in fact more akin to the national threat of the KKK" (551).

The combination of xenophobia, a motivated base, and new media savvy make the controversial organization worthy of study. Its responses to the trial of Ramos and Compean, as analyzed through the written commentary of participants in the MCDC online forums, yield considerable insight into how the group is ideologically constituted beyond the name calling of the popular press. In order to understand the MCDC's ideological footing and trajectory, we must first identify a set of appropriate tools.

Articulation Theory

Understanding the trial of Ramos and Compean in relation to the ideological structure of the MCDC is aided by what Ernesto Laclau and Chantal Mouffe have termed articulation theory. Stemming from a lack of theory explaining how people organize, dissolve, and reconfigure beyond traditional class politics, Laclau and Mouffe proposed articulation theory as an explanation for dynamic social organizing. The multiple intersections of unstable identities within border politics (see Johnson, this volume) necessitate a theoretical framework that accounts for unstable identities even as groups like the Minutemen attempt to render those identities static. The Minutemen themselves are a nonhomogenous group of people concerned with security, national identity, law and order, and a variety of other issues. In light of their unique formation, articulation theory provides a useful tool for understanding the limits that were identified and exposed by the trial of Ramos and Compean.

According to Laclau and Mouffe, an articulation is "any practice establishing a relation among elements such that their identity is modified as a result of the articulatory practice" (105). Put another way, articulation theory is a mechanism for understanding how identities and ideologies are co-produced. The forming of connections and temporary alliances can reveal a great deal about the capability of groups, both in their current form and as they emerge from crisis. Hall explains, "a theory of articulation is both a way of understanding how ideological elements come, under certain conditions, to cohere together within a discourse, and a way of asking how they do or do not become articulated, at specific conjunctures, to certain political subjects" ("On Postmodernism" 53). The unstable nature of an articulation helps the critic to understand the ideological position of what Laclau and Mouffe call a "moment" (105), a brief ideological window into a larger constellation. Analysis of articulation is critical because it can assist the critic in discerning what sort of future is possible for a group, cluster, or ideology.

Within the framework of articulation theory, Kevin DeLuca explains several concepts that prove especially useful in the analysis of the trial of Ramos and Compean. Following from Laclau and Mouffe, DeLuca identifies "antagonisms" as central to articulation theory. As he explains, "Antagonisms point to the limit of a discourse. An antagonism occurs at the point of the relation of the discourse to the surrounding life world and shows the impossibility of the discourse constituting a permanently closed or sutured totality" (336). Analyzing antagonisms helps the critic understand the limits of a relationship. For as articulations are by their nature unnecessary, they most commonly come with a breaking point that damages the relationship while keeping the formerly connected parties intact.[1] The passage above also references the third critical concept, along with articulation and antagonism, for the investigation of coalitions: "suturing." Suturing can be conceptualized as an attempt to establish or reestablish the connection between coalitions. Sutures can reveal how valuable the relationships between parties are, for there is always the alternative of simply severing the relationship. These concepts prove useful in examining where the Minutemen believed the trial represented an antagonism with different social units, and identifying possible points of suture where antagonism can be limited.

Approach

The forum section of the MCDC website has been identified by Buchanan and Holthouse as "the single largest nativist extremist organization in the country." As of early 2008, the forum had been operational for about two years but already boasted a community of almost 2,000 members and over 50,000 postings. In December 2007, I searched the forum for the terms "Ramos and Compean." The search returned 443 threads, some containing up to eighty-nine relevant posts, dating back to August 2006. I limited the data set to December 2006 through February 2007, because the most vibrant and widespread activity on the forum occurred in the month leading up to, and the time immediately after, the verdict. In terms of analyzing how members of the MCDC made sense of the verdict, this was the most important time because the information was fresh and emerging.

Every forum entry was analyzed using the following criteria. First, entries that were copy-and-paste articles from news sources were excluded. Second, every post that suggested a causal relationship between the trial and an attitude change or action was separated. This data set (111 pages total) was the focus of the subsequent thematic analysis in which forum entries were grouped generating "high-inference categories," as explained by

Lindlof and Taylor (215). These themes that suggest a causal relationship between the trial and the attitudes or behaviors of the poster are the subject of the following analysis.

Analysis

The analysis revealed six pervasive themes in forum responses to the trial of Ramos and Compean. The first three themes—centered around former US president George W. Bush, the judiciary, and the state—are identifications of antagonisms within particular MCDC relationships. The last three themes—political action, direct action, and supportive action—deal with proposed actions and yield insight as to whether the antagonisms previously identified should be seen as permanent ruptures in an articulated ideological constellation or breaks needing suture.

Antagonism: Bush

The MCDC has had a checkered relationship with US president George W. Bush.[2] While the group espouses a reactionary agenda with a focus on securitization that would seem to line up nicely with Bush's perspective, this did not always match his record, which included an amnesty program for illegal immigrants. This rocky relationship was further exacerbated by the trial of Ramos and Compean. Many forum participants blamed Bush for what they perceived as the unjust persecution of the Texas Border Patrol agents. JAMESW62 remarked that "its [sic] a sad day in America when the commander in chief does not stand up for the law enforcement community of this nation." In a similar vein, MANAWA wrote, "I hold Bush directly responsible for punishing BP Agents Ramos and Compean for doing their jobs." For these participants, the trial exposed an antagonism between the MCDC and President Bush. The episode exposed a long-harbored resentment of Bush, and/or the MCDC Forum participants automatically associated any action of the government with the president.[3]

In addition to associating the trial with Bush, many forum participants identified the trial as *the* breaking point for their relationship with the Bush administration. As THE SENTINEL aptly noted, "Ramos & Compean are the straw that broke the camel's back." A large number of MCDC Forum participants used the Ramos and Compean threads as a platform to publicly air their guilt over supporting Bush. In the context of a Ramos and Compean discussion, BALDWIN828 remarked, "I have stood behind Bush through all of the stupid things he has done, but this is it. The man is a moron!" LUCKY expressed a similar sentiment by posting, "A horrified and ashamed former Conservative Republican who contributed to and voted for George Bush 41 and George Bush 43 twice." Several posters characterized Bush's actions as treasonous. CITIZENGRANNY identified a "trend" in the MCDC movement, writing, "I noticed the impeach bush signs at the rally yesterday. I do not believe I have seen them before. People are sick and tired of this jerk in the white house."

The direct association of President Bush with the trial of Ramos and Compean led many of the MCDC participants to some interesting conclusions. For some, it was the final proof that Bush did not have the nation's interest in mind; for others, it was the confirmation of a long-held belief and the grounds for impeachment. For both groups the antagonism of the trial dissolved whatever remaining articulation there seemed to be between Bush's policies of securitization and their agenda. This antagonism was obviously significant for the members of the MCDC, but there is a broader argument here too regarding securitization. Insofar as President Bush was characterized as weak on border policies, he was also seen as weak on the broader issue of security, which was of course *the* significant issue of his presidency. While this theme was certainly prevalent, it was only one of three pervasive interpretations of the antagonisms exposed by the trial of Ramos and Compean.

Antagonism: The Judiciary

The most common target of animosity among forum participants was members of the prosecution. ANNA commented on a series of public interviews in which lead attorney Johnny Sutton was participating: "Sutton is hitting the talk shows to drum up support for his actions in light of the fact that congressional hearings are being sought on this case, and he doesn't want the REAL truth to come out." MANAWA focused his or her attacks on the other lead attorney, noting, "Jose Compean is on the John and Ken show. He said the prosecutor, Debra Kanoff, lied throughout the trial. I'll believe Jose Compean over that piece of sub-human garbage. Yes, she needs to be prosecuted and sent TO A MEN'S PRISON as part of her sensitivity training. Tha [sic] rancid b/witch aided and abetted a drug dealer." The focus on Kanoff's physical body continued as JAMESW62 commented, "EEEWW-WWWW have you seen pictures of that woman. i wouldnt even touch that trash." This rhetorical turn focused attention on the judicial branch representatives as corrupt people. Such a move broadens the scope of the criticism levied by the forum participants beyond the trial itself.

Several forum participants did not stop their attacks with the prosecution team, but rather, perceived a chain of impropriety that ran throughout the judiciary. JAMES62 was concerned that the mailings from the MCDC in support of Ramos and Compean were not reaching the appropriate parties, noting, "too bad that that atty general has probably lied about getting the mails that have been sent to him before because he does not want to have anything to do with the case." SHREDDER took a somewhat more skeptical view and also commented on the ethnicity of Attorney General Gonzales, stating, "The Anchor[4] General will not help them." Forum participant USA TODAY implicated the entire structure of the judiciary, writing, "The first order of business is to get our guys out of jail, after that this needs to be tracked all the way up to as high as it goes starting with sutton, the other b!tch, the judge and up to gonzales and maybe up to bush, conspiracy is still a crime in this country also."

The Minutemen as an organization are ostensibly committed to law and order despite their own marginally legal status (see Hasian and McHendry, this volume). The exposure of antagonism with the judicial branch of government understandably erodes this tenuous articulation. The second critical point regarding this section is that the trial created and exposed an antagonism with(in) the entire judicial branch of government rather than with just the parties involved. Contextualizing the story within a larger narrative of judicial malpractice gave the forum participants license to disregard the judicial branch. It is not difficult to make a connection between this antagonism (a rift with the judicial branch) and the increased possibility of violence. The efforts within the theme of judiciary, aimed at identifying who was to blame or exposing the trial process, all indicate that while there may be bad parts of the state system, there are salvageable parts, too. This may seem to be an insignificant point; however, given the subsequent theme of antagonism, such remarks are relatively moderate.

Antagonism: The State

A certain segment of the MCDC Forum participants seemed to believe that the trial of Ramos and Compean was reflective of, or exposed, a thoroughly corrupt United States government. The Ramos and Compean story has either been appropriated as part of a larger conspiracy narrative or is some sort of critical case study that invalidates the entire state apparatus.

Several posters to the forum were especially concerned with the legal problems that the Ramos and Compean case exposed, but in a much larger sense than those concerns articulated under the judicial antagonism. NATIVE AMERICAN suggested that the Texas Border Patrol agents should not report for jail time: "I say they [Ramos and Compean] should run, this government has already made it their policy that the whole 'rule of law thing' is subjective, all these guys would be doing by running is showing the hypocrisy of the governments policies." JTCOYOTE was even more skeptical, identifying what Agamben would call "lacunas," or gaps throughout the US legal code.[5] JTCOYOTE believed that this was not a problem of interpretation, but that the legal code of the United States was written in a particular way so as to allow abuses like the ones committed against Ramos and Compean. JTCOYOTE wrote, "This type of legal ambiguity is the kind of destructive shenanigans that have been engaged in over the last 80 years in earnest, by errant Congress." Other more radical participants seemed convinced that the trial was proof of an international globalist conspiracy in which Mexican interests were prioritized.

The conspiracy theorists tended to fall into two groups. The first conspiracy group was typified by KROAKER911, who commented that the Ramos and Compean trial was "another case of the mexican masters playing marionette with the 'most powerful nation on earth.' It's a shame the nation doesn't extol that power for the benefit of its citizens!" Similarly, MAGGIEB wrote, "No WONDER Bush will not pardon Ramos and Compean. He is under orders from the President! The real president. The President of mexico . . . It seems that we have allowed mexico to usurp so many governmental functions of the United States, that our own elected government is nothing but a puppet with mexico city pulling the strings." It is never clear in the posters' comments how Mexican forces have taken so much control over the United States. Forum participant STRING believed the conspiracy had yet to come to full fruition, but noted, "once we have a mexican president all appointed office's will be given to mexicans to make them unstoppable in government down to the police on the beat." In any case, it is clear that those who believed in a Mexican conspiracy also believed that the trial of Ramos and Compean was proof of a profound antagonism between "patriots" like members of the MCDC and the Mexican/US government.

The second group of conspiracy theorists held that the invisible forces behind both the trial and the demise of the United States in general were somewhat more diffuse. TARDOVIT painted an ominous picture of the near future, writing, "It feels like all of us may be in a concentration camp in the near future. If we try to protect our country, we are the criminals?" ONEMORECAPTAINSMAST was even more cryptic: "The 'evil money cult' in Washington D.C. is dragging many down with it, as it goes to the depths below." Ambiguous references to the "evil money cult" aligned closely with somewhat more traditional notions of conspiracy. For instance, RAMBLINRAVEN remarked, "The Bush Administration is working for the Globalists introducing their New World Order Agenda." While this theme appears to be the most fragmented, there is unification around the antagonism that the United States government as a whole is corrupt and untenable. In any case, the notion of groups like the MCDC as separatists certainly seems more plausible given this antagonism.[6]

The implicitly articulated relationship between the Minutemen (as defenders of the nation) and the government of the United States is tested by this antagonism. The clear theme throughout the antagonisms is that corruption (at different levels of governance) is rampant and that officials are not acting in the best interest of the people. The variations among the explanations of the antagonisms represent differing interpretations of the pervasiveness of corruption. The differences within the antagonisms are thrown into even sharper relief in the following section, as they are coupled with potential strategies for action that comprise the next three themes.

Calls for Political Action

Political action is a category of response that reflects a desire to take steps within an existing political framework. Working within the conceptual framework of articulation theory, political action does not represent an antagonism, nor is it necessarily a suture. The possibility of suture exists, but only if the political actions suggested and/or enacted articulate a non-necessary relationship linking one group with another. Simply put, within this theme there were two categories of political action—writing letters/making calls and public protest.

The most common form of political action suggested and apparently enacted by the MCDC Forum participants was the contacting and harassing of politicians. Clearly, the choices made regarding whom to contact are reflective of either an opinion about who is to blame, and/or who has the power to do something now. AUNTIE M urged fellow posters to "Close down the phone lines! Flood the White House with 'Free The Border Patrol Agents,' calls today!" After a report was released stating that Agent Ramos had been beaten in prison, JAMESW62 posted, "CALL SUTTONS OFFICE and tell him that Ramos blood is all over his hands because of what happened to Ramos over the weekend. ive called twice and left very obscene tirades."

The other form of direct action discussed in the forum was traditional public protest. ZORRO urged fellow posters to deviate from their normal routines of posting on the message boards. ZORRO commented, "This is something worth getting out of your computer chair for and by showing up EN MASSE at all these Federal buildings it will get a lot of attention."

After the protest, several members posted pictures on the forum. Reception of the photos was universally positive, but some of the most interesting posts were in response to the counter-protesters. Poster LADYMAD noted, "the counter protesters were all the same color (brown). The little, latina, al queda squadron, I like to call them." The perceived linkage between being nonwhite and terrorism is obviously in tension with the support of the nonwhite Border Patrol agents. However, this tension is overlooked in favor of a broad and problematic characterization of the perceived enemies of the Minutemen.

Another commenter, USA TODAY, concurred with LADYMAD's comment, lauding the diversity of the MCDC and proclaiming a contrast to the perceived homogeneity of the counter-protesters: "It seems our group is a cross section of real American patriots." These somewhat traditional political tactics are not out of the ordinary for any political group. While the Minutemen might have been labeled "vigilantes" by President Bush and many political commentators, there was a significant faction within the group that was primarily interested in relatively peaceful and traditional political action. Thus, although the racism and seeping hatred in the postings are obviously problematic, the proposed actions were, at least, not physically violent in the classical vigilante sense.

Calls for Direct Action

This theme represents the worst-case scenario of the MCDC. The allegations of vigilante justice made by a variety of commentators resonated strongly with MCDC Forum participants who called for direct action. Most of the direct action suggested by these posters is violent and intersects with a seemingly widely articulated link between the MCDC and the idea that firearms can be used to solve problems.

Many of the posts in this section advocated that violent action be taken against specific individuals involved in the Ramos and Compean trial. In reference to Aldrete-Davila, the smuggler who testified against Ramos and Compean, PUBLIUS suggested, "someone needs to find him and off him!" LANDWARRIOR directed some proposed violence toward prosecutor Johnny Sutton, commenting, "Sounds to me like a few patriots need to pull Mr. Sutton from his office, tar and feather him before running him out of town on a rail . . . to the first oak tree that is found outside the city limits . . . where a noose awaits." This is precisely the strain of vigilante/frontier justice that has institutions like the Southern Poverty Law Center so concerned over the radical ideology and apparently vast network of the MCDC.

Among advocates for direct action there seemed to be a spillover effect from the Ramos and Compean trial to other issues. Several posters used discussions of the trial to advocate a more violent approach to illegal immigration, even as it is unrelated to the trial itself. One participant, BALDWIN828, wrote, "It's time for the killing to start, all the words in the world don't say as much as 1 well placed bullet." Aside from these quippy and perhaps less-than-serious comments, one poster proposed a well-thought-out plan for expanding the powers of the MCDC to include a citizen's arrest patrol that would physically apprehend illegal immigrants. JCWATSON explained, "I am sure we could do it legally by having people obtain bounty hunting lic." This theme was not as prevalent as the call to political action, but there was a definitive constituency that was making the call for increased vigilance and violence within the MCDC; at the very least, the Ramos and Compean trial appears to have served as a vehicle for that articulation.

Calls for Supportive Action

The last theme is comprised of proposals to directly aid the families of Ramos and Compean. While all of the actions taken can be seen, from a certain perspective, as supportive of the agents, this theme deals with direct support. Perhaps the most illustrative notation on this issue came from MANAWA, who agreed with a suggestion he or she had heard earlier that "when the Republican Party sends mail asking for contributions, send the mail back in their prepaid envelopes with a note saying, 'I'm sending my campaign contribution to Ramos and Compean instead.'" There were many other posters who expressed the same, or virtually the same, sentiment.

Beyond the general desire to support the agents, supportive action is the theme by which the discrepancy between the agents becomes the most visible. Family members of Ramos have openly embraced organizations like the MCDC and have appeared at events, giving speeches and talking about Ramos. Compean's family has not been as interested in associating with the MCDC or related organizations. This comes to light in a post by CITIZENGRANNY, who wrote, "I will send a letter tomorrow along with a check to help Monica out. Let her know we all support her. Would like to do the same for Compean's wife." CITIZENGRANNY's last sentence is critical because it implies that Compean is missing out on the support network provided by the MCDC and related organizations. In all, the theme of supportive action provides strong evidence that the MCDC Forum participants did, in some ways, support the agents, but that they would have liked the ties to be even stronger.

Articulation, Antagonism, and Suture

Several threads pull together the emergent themes from this data set. The trial of Ramos and Compean was used by MCDC Forum participants as a tool to expose existing or new antagonisms that complicate existing articulations with President Bush, the judiciary, and the state. The antagonism with Bush is especially striking, as it seems to rupture an existing articulated relationship between border politics and Bush's particular brand of conservatism. President Bush was generally recognized as a strong national security advocate, even if the policies themselves were controversial. However, for many of the Minutemen, his perceived negligence in this one area was sufficient to convince them that he did not see the security of the nation as a high priority. The revelation of the three antagonisms can alternately be seen as an attempt to suture relations with the Border Patrol by aligning support with specific members, even if it comes at the cost of alienating different components of the state apparatus. Support was both indirect, via the presence of Ramos and Compean signs at MCDC rallies, and direct, via calls to politicians urging them to pardon Ramos and Compean. The critical aspect of this antagonism/suture relationship is that the suture (support of Ramos and Compean) came hand in hand with emerging antagonisms with different state apparatuses. Obviously, the Border Patrol *is* an extension of the state, meaning that the sutured connection between the MCDC and the Border Patrol can be tenuous at best. After all, the government still writes the paychecks for the Border Patrol.

The analysis of responses by MCDC Forum participants to the Ramos and Compean trial also helps us to understand different ideological tendencies within the MCDC Forum community. They are most visible in the articulation of different antagonisms. A sense of civic skepticism undergirds the antagonisms with the judiciary and President Bush, while a radical separation of the MCDC from the entire state apparatus is the outcome of the third antagonism. The implications of these different ideological positions become even more visible when considering the appropriate actions that issue from these assumptions. In the case of civic skepticism, the proper action would be to call representatives and engage in public protest. However, for the individuals for whom the Ramos and Compean trial revealed deep flaws in the entire structure of the United States, a direct and violent advocacy results. The implications of this divide could become more visible in the long term.

Within the context of this volume on rhetoric and the border, this chapter serves the purpose of exploring how the border is written onto the bodies and ideologies of individuals. What is evident from the analysis is that the "border" as a concept has been extended to the agents themselves and that defending the agents is necessary to defending the border. This argument is not unusual in the context of border rhetoric discussions. What sets this study apart is that the border, as represented by Ramos and Compean, is under attack not from the other, but from the United States federal government. Such a calculation causes slippage among the Minutemen as they struggle with how to oppose the institutional representation of the United States. The intricacies of the struggle reveal a dynamic ideological moment and point toward an uncertain future as the Minutemen and groups like the Minutemen rearticulate both who they are and whom they are fighting.

Notes

Names such as "CTHELIGHT," the source for this chapter's epigraph, are the user names for the participants in the public forum maintained by the Minuteman Civil Defense Corps. The quotations utilized throughout this chapter were taken directly from the forum, including misspellings. The Minuteman Civil Defense Corps Forum is no longer active. Portions of the forum are available through the "Internet Way-Back Machine," but it is no longer an active site of exchange.

1. Specifically, I am exploring themes in articulation and antagonism such as those proposed by Angus and later implemented by Brouwer and Hess in their thematized exploration of how military bloggers responded to the military protests of the Westboro Baptist Church.

2. The strained relationship with President Bush was partially the result of Bush's 2005 reference to the Minutemen as "vigilantes" (Elder).

3. President Bush did end up pardoning both agents in his final days in office. This is especially significant given that he granted very few pardons (Gerstein).

4. "Anchor" is a reference to the pejorative term "anchor babies," which references foreign nationals seeking permanent status based on children born in the United States and a general "weighing down" of the nation.

5. Agamben argues that legal code is written with purposeful gaps that allow government officials to reinterpret the law at their own discretion. While there is no mention of Agamben by the forum participants, the similarity to Agamben's argument is striking (*State of Exception*).

6. It is worth noting that this antagonism moves the discussion away from discourses of race and toward an articulation of nation.

IV
Performative Affects

8

Looking "Illegal"

Affect, Rhetoric, and Performativity in Arizona's Senate Bill 1070

Josue David Cisneros

What does it mean to *look like* a noncitizen? How can someone's legal citizenship status be determined by their physical characteristics, actions, or demeanor? These questions point to the embodied and performative levels at which border rhetorics operate in contemporary American society. As essays in this volume by Julia Johnson, Bernadette Calafell, and Dustin Goltz and Kimberlee Pérez demonstrate, discursive and political bordering is situated within a larger body of affects and performances that structure what it means to be a US American. Citizenship and civic belonging are continually (re)enacted, (re)iterated, and read (lacking) on certain bodies through their individual and social performances (Cisneros, "(Re)Bordering"; Hariman and Lucaites).[1] In other words, to enact citizenship is to perform a certain way of being rooted in specific *affects* and emotions (feelings of safety, sameness, belonging, community, and so on).[2] Performing particular types of difference, even if unintentional, can compel feelings of "alien-ness" and be construed as evidence of non-belonging (Ono, this volume).

In the twenty-first century, the illegal, brown, immigrant body demarcates this border between difference and sameness; that is, the figure of the racialized immigrant poses both the principal threat to and the condition of possibility for US citizenship (Calafell, "Disrupting the Dichotomy"; Inda, "Performativity"). From national debates about immigration policy to concerns about the color and legal status of the (nonwhite) US president, recent efforts to "protect" the nation and "preserve" US identity have been enacted in opposition to the threat posed by "foreign," brown bodies (DeChaine, "Bordering the Civic Imaginary"; Hasian and McHendry, this volume; Silva). In contrast, US citizenship and civic identity are enacted through a "national affect" that connotes American-ness, which includes the English language, public displays of nationalism, and certain markers of socioeconomic class and race (Muñoz, "Feeling Brown" 69).

This connection between affects, performance, and citizenship is nowhere more evident than in anti-immigrant campaigns at the regional level.

From the infamous Proposition 187 of California to the recent attempts by local governments to enforce federal immigration law (so-called 287[g] agreements), increasingly state and local governments have taken on the onus of policing the borders (both physical and metaphorical) and prosecuting undocumented "aliens" (Cisneros, "Latina/os and Party Politics"; Flores, "Constructing National Bodies"; Ono and Sloop). The most publicized and most controversial of these recent regional border rhetorics is the state of Arizona's anti-immigrant legislation, Senate Bill 1070 ("Support Our Law Enforcement and Safe Neighborhoods Act").

Passed in April of 2010, SB 1070 capitalized on a wave of anti-immigrant sentiment and fears over the potential spillover of "drug war" violence. The legislation aimed to secure the border with Mexico and eliminate undocumented immigrants using an approach to immigration policy known as "attrition through enforcement." This predominant, aggressive, and nativist approach to immigration policy—which intends to decrease the immigrant population and deter future migration by increasing the surveillance, persecution, and hardship faced by the undocumented—has received support from anti-immigrant groups and is being emulated in states across the country (Chávez, this volume; Fernández). Arizona's infamous anti-immigrant bill has become the model for a host of state and local initiatives to persecute suspected undocumented immigrants, and thus represents a broader materialization in the affective and performative dimensions of contemporary border rhetoric (Wessler, "Hostile State Battles").

I argue that SB 1070 illuminates affective and material dimensions underlying this broader, contemporary approach to immigration developing across the country. In its efforts to police and persecute "illegal aliens," SB 1070 has faced criticism from immigrants' rights groups as well as the Obama administration, and its reach was limited by federal court injunctions in June 2010. Notwithstanding such criticism, Arizona's legislation represents the escalation of militaristic and aggressive efforts by state and local governments to "secure" the border and prosecute immigrants as criminals, an approach that has achieved renewed purchase in states and localities across the country. I analyze both the legislative text of SB 1070 as well as its surrounding discourse to show that this broader approach to immigration policy (e.g., "attrition through enforcement") represents a moment of articulation in an affective economy about citizenship, the border, and Latina/o immigrants. Specifically, SB 1070 codifies and materializes the racialized Mexican-Latina/o-brown-illegal-immigrant body as fearful and threatening, and it makes illegality a performative *affect* emanating from the bodies of suspected immigrants. In other words, the legislation prescribes a series of racial markers and behaviors as the basis of citizenship—all undergirded by a certain visceral evaluation of a person's "belonging-ness"—thereby imputing that nonwhite, immigrant "others" who perform or embody difference are "foreign" or "illegal." Moreover, SB 1070 (and the approach to immigration policy it represents) collapses the distinction between border enforcement and civic engagement, normalizing border vigilantism as a mode of citizenship. In contemporary border rhetorics, border vigilantism becomes a performance of citizenship and (thus) an indicator of belonging. In sum, the heightened border rhetoric evident in SB 1070 points to the anxiety surrounding purported threats of (racialized) immigrants to US (racial) identity and the sanctity of US citizenship.

This argument develops over several sections. First, I discuss the background of SB 1070, and second, I review notions of affect and "affective economies" and their connection to border rhetoric, performativity, and US citizenship. Third, I analyze the discourse of SB 1070 to demonstrate its codification of the connection between immigration, race, and performances of citizenship. Both SB 1070 and the approach to border/immigration policy it represents crystallize a strain of exclusionary border rhetoric that grounds citizenship in performative affect and empowers vigilante citizens to police the (racial) borders of US identity.

The Ever-Encroaching Border

The debate over Arizona's most recent anti-immigrant bill, SB 1070, takes place in a heightened moment of border anxiety. Of course, immigration, the US-Mexico borderlands, and borders more generally have long been sources of historical contestation and concern (Beasley; Chavez, *Covering Immigration;* Demo; Flores and Villarreal, this volume; Holling, this volume). Yet contemporary discourses about the immigration "problem" and border "security" seem to mark a period of the ever-encroaching reach of the border. That is, instead of focusing attention on the US-Mexico frontier as the exclusive site of concern over immigration, contemporary debate expands the definition of the border and border security to include more and more of the interior United States (Demo, this volume; Shahani and Greene 5).

Contestation about immigration and border policy dominated national discussion throughout 2005 and 2006, fueled by federal debate over House Resolution 4437, the nationwide waves of immigrant protests, and the vigilantism of the Minuteman Civil Defense Corps (Chavez, *Latino Threat*). According to the Immigration Policy Center, many state and local government officials contend that the inaction of the federal government has caused them to take on the onus of immigration and border security. Controversies over the presence of immigrants and concerns over the "porous" border now trouble areas and communities far from the US-Mexico frontier such as Prince William County, Virginia, and Davidson County, Tennessee; border anxiety and the rhetoric of border security have spread throughout the United States along with heightened border securitization and policing (Fernández). The federal government itself has enabled this nationwide encroachment through the sharing of responsibility for immigration enforcement with so-called 287(g) agreements authorizing local police to detain and verify the legal status of suspected undocumented individuals (Shahani and Greene).

It is in the context of this heightened concern over immigration, its perceived threats to communities throughout the nation, and the increasing, expanding, and aggressive policing of the border by states and localities, that Arizona's SB 1070 took shape. The law was signed by Arizona governor Jan Brewer on April 23, 2010, yet it was blocked from going into full effect by a federal court ruling in July 2010 that, according to many, sets the scene for a Supreme Court showdown (Beard Rau, Rough, and Hensley). SB 1070 piggybacks on federal immigration law to create several new immigration crimes and also expands police power for immigration enforcement. Its most controversial provisions deal with the work and hiring of undocumented immigrants, expanded police power to verify legal status, the criminalization of harboring/transporting undocumented immigrants, and the power of civil suit to force the enforcement of immigration policy.

The passage of Arizona's SB 1070 incited debate over similar bills in over twenty states throughout the country, successfully spurring copycat legislation in Georgia and Alabama (Wessler, "Welcome"). More importantly, SB 1070 is arguably the most infamous piece in a much larger framework of similar anti-immigrant provisions spanning federal, state, and local levels. This patchwork of initiatives aims to "solve" the "immigration problem" by militaristically persecuting immigrants and suspected immigrants. Thus SB 1070 is arguably the flagship in an entire anti-immigrant enterprise involving unprecedented levels of deportations and detentions by the federal government, over fifty new local laws aimed at preventing immigrants from working or acquiring housing, dozens of English-only ordinances, and, most recently, an organized effort by state and local governments to challenge the birthright citizenship provisions of the Fourteenth Amendment (Wessler, "A Year after SB 1070," "Hostile State Battles").

Therefore, in this chapter SB 1070 serves as a representative anecdote for the discursive and historical moment in which we find ourselves; to me, the legislation represents the articulation of an affective economy surrounding immigration, Latina/o immigrants specifically, and the US-Mexico border. With the term "affective economy" I am drawing on a notion of affects and emotions that locates them not solely in the psychic or discursive realms but "as involving relationships of difference and displacement . . . produced only as an effect of [the] circulation" of signs and bodies (Ahmed, "Affective Economies" 120). In other words, both affects (the embodied and immediate experiences of stimuli) as well as emotions (the combinations of visceral affective impressions and cultural signification) are mobilized in politics and culture through the circulation of images, signs, tropes, and discourses (Massumi 35–36; Lundberg 388). SB 1070 indicates how a relationship of emotional attachments and affective impressions—from fear to disgust to love—has developed around discourses of immigration and particularly around the racialized immigrant body and US citizenship. SB 1070, the most debated in a larger wave of anti-immigrant measures, draws on these affective economies to codify the Mexican-Latina/o-brown-illegal-immigrant body and to situate citizenship in the performative affect of these bodies—that is, in the affects that suspect bodies compel (or are interpellated into) as they are surveilled by law enforcement. To be legal (a citizen) means to display the right feelings, through skin color and demeanor; to be illegal means to spur feelings of suspiciousness, threat, and out-of-place-ness. In the next section I explore relationships between affect, performativity, and citizenship to inform a reading of SB 1070 that illuminates these affective and emotional investments animating the broader anti-immigrant moment.

Affect, Citizenship, and Immigration

The critical focus on affect and emotion demonstrates an attempt to move beyond the role of representation alone by focusing on the place of emotion and, importantly, bodily experiences (affect) in constituting identifications and motivating people to belief or action (DeChaine, "Affect"; Massumi). In sum, the affective dimensions of politics and culture speak to "how bodies are mobilized (called to action) at a material level" for both good and ill (Ott 49). Yet affect does not take shape entirely separate from representation; rather, discourses participate with embodied experience, public culture, and historical memory to articulate affinities and emotional investments. Dominant attitudes about immigration, for example, are articulated, developed, contested, and internalized through affective investments/associations, which are also themselves shaped by both public and personal experience. As Jenny

Edbauer Rice states, "Language affectively articulates a social imaginary within which political discourse is lodged. . . . We are stuck to those beliefs like wooden sticks glued together. We are so strongly invested in (or glued to) certain structures of belief that they seem like part of our own identity. To borrow Kenneth Burke's well-worn term, we are 'identified' with structures of ideology through an affective investment" (205). Concern for affect moves us beyond a focus on ideology as pure representation (thereby denying the place of bodies, feelings, and materiality in influencing our emotional and ideological investments) by illustrating that ideology is articulated through a confluence of signs, bodies, and histories. Though bodies motivate certain affective responses (e.g., fear of "personal violation" or attraction), bodies are also taken up into and influence systems of belief (discourse); bodies, beliefs, and representations get "stuck" together into ideologies (Rice 210).

The notion of "affective economies" explains how affect represents a form of emotional value accumulated in the circulation of bodies, objects, psyches, and discourses. Sara Ahmed writes that "emotions work as a form of capital" (*Cultural Politics* 45). That is, rather than situating affect solely within the realm of either representation or psychology, "affective economies" represent a form of public circulation and accretion of attitudes, investments, and dispositions (affects). As Ahmed explains, "emotions do not positively inhabit any-body as well as any-thing, meaning that 'the subject' is simply one nodal point in the economy, rather than its origin and destination" ("Affective Economies" 120). Just as economic value accumulates through the circulation and relationship of a commodity in/through an economic network, so too affects are articulated publicly through the circulation of systems of signs: "The more signs circulate, the more affective [i.e., affectively invested] they become" (Ahmed, *Cultural Politics* 45). Thus for scholars of rhetoric, not only bodies but also texts and tropes circulate and serve as "nodal points" in the articulation of publics and the (re)articulation of affects (Lundberg).

In terms of anti-immigrant ideologies, immigrant bodies get stuck together with recurring (circulating) representations of immigrants and with material experiences to reiterate dominant beliefs (Ahmed, *Cultural Politics*). The "national affect" of US citizenship contains a number of prior affective investments about what it means to look, talk, and act like a a US American—ultimately, what a US American "feels" like (Muñoz, "Feeling Brown"; Rivera-Servera). Returning to the idea that citizenship/belonging are continually performed for an audience of other citizens, it follows that those performances of citizenship entail the articulation of certain affects that are experienced and judged in the bodies/minds of the citizen-audience who is judging the performance. As Mary Strine writes, "performances become privileged spaces of social reflexivity and occasions of intense critical scrutiny and evaluation" involving "often unconscious investments and desires" (312); performances of citizenship/belonging create pressures of display and assessment. In that sense, then, citizenship and national identity are largely determined through "dimensions of credibility," including affects "that are performed . . . to determine one's potential as a citizen-subject" (McKinnon 218). Of course, the (right) performances and affects of US identity are structured in relation to well-worn affective economies of migrants as strangers—threatening, fearful, dirty, dangerous, or diseased—which justify "alienization" and exclusion of immigrants from the national imaginary (DeChaine, "Bordering the Civic Imaginary").

My contention, then, is that SB 1070 is one such "nodal point" (to use Ahmed's term) in an affective economy surrounding immigration, race, and citizenship. In the next section I analyze the text of SB 1070 and the debate surrounding the legislation for the ways in which they instantiate and rearrange these affective economies. SB 1070 and the contemporary anti-immigrant movement contribute to the "rearticulation of already existing affective and tropological logics" about immigration, Latina/os, and US national identity (Lundberg 408). Specifically, I focus on three ways in which SB 1070 reifies and rearticulates these affective investments. First, I argue that the law codifies (in the sense of organizing and concretizing) the Mexican-Latina/o-brown-illegal-immigrant body as a source of fear, anxiety, and even hatred. Next, I show how 1070 converts illegality from a state-based (juridical) discourse of legal status into a non-state-based, performative affect ascribed onto Latina/o bodies by the audience of (white) citizen-subjects. That is, illegality is performed by and read on Latina/o bodies through their affect rather than determined through legal documents. Finally, I show how, in light of these affective investments, SB 1070 collapses distinctions between border enforcement and civic engagement, normalizing border vigilantism as a performance of citizenship and the US national affect.

Looking Illegal: The Affective Economies of SB 1070

Arizona's SB 1070 enacted a number of anti-immigrant restrictions and represents a broader anti-immigrant strategy that, as I noted above, is often termed "attrition through enforcement" (Fernández). To this end, the Arizona law makes this intent clear in Section 1, the preamble of the legislation. The strategy of "attrition" is motivated by a host of impressions about immigrants as sapping resources, stealing jobs, and disrupting American values. As one Arizona resident clarified, "This law is about respecting the laws of the nation and the economic impact of illegal immigration. . . . [T]hey cost us with spending on schools, hospitals and other services" (qtd. in Archibold, "Two Sides"). Yet SB 1070 was also framed as an initiative to protect Arizona from the crime, drugs, and violence purportedly brought on by undocumented immigration. As Governor Jan Brewer said during the signing ceremony, "There is no higher priority than protecting the citizens of Arizona. We cannot sacrifice our safety to the murderous greed of drug cartels. We cannot stand idly by as drop houses, kidnappings and violence compromise our quality of life. We cannot delay while the destruction happening south of our international border creeps its way north." Brewer's language of crisis and imminent danger—of drug cartels, kidnappings, and even (as she said on previous occasions) beheadings (Davenport and Myers)—goes beyond a systemic threat of job loss or social services spending and grounds SB 1070 in a visceral threat not only to the nation but to the very bodies of citizens (Ahmed, *Cultural Politics* 64). Faced with the threat of crime, violence, and even bodily dismemberment, "attrition" seems an appropriate response. Arizona must choke out the threats from within before their gruesome violence is manifest. The undocumented immigrants' very existence constitutes a threat and hence justifies violence.

The Mexican-Latina/o-Brown-Illegal-Immigrant Body

Scholarship on cultural and political discourses of immigration points to a continual framing of immigrants as "others," as strangers, dangers, or threats. The migrant/stranger must be regulated, surveilled, and potentially even excluded from the body politic for the threat it presents (Cisneros, "Contaminated Communities"). "The ease with which these constructions appear," writes Lisa Flores, "suggests that they have become deeply embedded within the cultural commonsense" ("Constructing Rhetorical Borders" 381). Immigrants' brown bodies threaten the integrity of the nation by association with crime, disease, and danger (Lugo-Lugo and Bloodsworth-Lugo). Because of the prevalence of Mexican immigration in the United States, there is a continual double conflation in this discourse: a conflation of the Mexican and Latina/o body, so that all Latina/o-looking (i.e., brown) people are considered Mexican, and a conflation between the Latina/o-Mexican and the figure of the illegal immigrant, so that all Latina/os are presumed to be illegal until evidence proves otherwise (Hasian and Delgado 257). Yet even in celebrations of Latina/o popular culture icons, Latina/os are presumed to have an "affective excess"—as ethnic, spicy, brown, and so on—that paradoxically leads to their attraction as cultural commodities but also situates Latina/os as *other than* or *outside of* the affect of "normal" US citizens (Calafell, *Latina/o Communication Studies* 27). In sum, Latina/os are presumed to have a suspicious legal status regardless of their true standing, and something is "off" about Latina/os' affect (their race, language, cultural associations, etc.) even when they do "belong" in a strictly legal or limited sense.

The multiple tropes of Mexican-Latina/o-brown-illegal-immigrant difference demonstrate what Rice, borrowing from Ahmed, calls "metonymic slide." That is, a series of affective states or impressions are linked together tropologically and extended out metonymically from bodies to discourses to constitute "an orienting device" (206). These figures are situated within and contribute to an affective economy of immigrant threat and danger that results in alienization and exclusion; Latina/o immigrants are "irredeemable others whose putative exclusion from the national body is virtually absolute" (DeChaine, "Bordering the Civic Imaginary" 45).

Yet SB 1070 is significant, first, because of the way it condenses, legally and ideologically, this Mexican-Latina/o-brown-illegal-immigrant trope/body as threatening and problematic. In other words, through this affective economy the "irredeemable" Mexican-Latina/o-brown-illegal-immigrant body becomes a trope that is materialized and naturalized. One clear example of this process is found in the sections of SB 1070 that focus on work, hiring, and travel. For instance, SB 1070 creates a crime of impeding traffic for the purpose of soliciting work or hiring workers. Though federal law already makes blocking traffic a crime, SB 1070 ties that crime to the cultural stereotype that "Mexican" day laborers are "illegals" who "crowd" street corners and parking lots to "steal" jobs and "disrupt" day-to-day life. SB 1070 also criminalizes the "unlawful transporting, moving, concealing, harboring, or shielding of unlawful aliens" (Support Our Law Enforcement and Safe Neighborhoods Act § 13–2929). While the provision seems to be targeted at criminal smuggling of undocumented people, some legal analysts contend that "even family members or friends who lie to the police" or conceal undocumented loved ones may be liable (Chin et al. 61). Regardless of its intended reach, however, this provision and the section targeting work/hiring seem to operate under an affect of the immigrant body as dirty, dangerous, or disruptive. Notice that the method chosen to combat human trafficking is to target the immigrant body (rather than the crime of trafficking) as a dangerous substance that is transported, moved, concealed, or harbored. Immigrant bodies are best kept off street corners and parking lots, where they can dirty, stain, or just muck up public space and the free movement of citizens. Immigrant bodies are smuggled, hidden, and transported under cover, like dangerous substances.

The conflation of Mexicans-Latina/os with brown and illegal immigrant bodies becomes what Ahmed calls a set of "sticky" symbols. She writes, "The slide between figures constructs a relation of resemblance. . . . What makes them 'alike' may be their 'unlikeness' from 'us.' . . . These figures come to embody the threat of loss: lost jobs, lost money, lost land. They signify the danger of impurity, or the mixing or taking of blood. They threaten to violate the pure bodies" (*Cultural Politics* 44). We see this stickiness in Brewer's own comments about "murderous greed" and violence "creeping" north as well as in the surrounding popular discourse, which works along with SB 1070 to codify this trope. Commented one SB 1070 supporter, "What I'm seeing today is immigrants coming here, wanting us to become like Mexico, instead of wanting to become American" (qtd. in Riccardi). The presence of Mexican-Latina/o-brown-illegal-immigrant bodies threatens and provokes policing to remove those threats.

The most controversial sections of SB 1070, which expand state and local police power to inquire about a person's legal status, also clearly condense this affective association. In final form, the legislation states that "for any lawful stop, detention or arrest . . . where reasonable suspicion exists that the person is an alien and is unlawfully present in the United States, a reasonable attempt shall be made, when practicable, to determine the immigration status of the person, except if the determination may hinder or obstruct an investigation." Yet SB 1070 clarifies that police "may not consider race, color or national origin in implementing the requirements of this subsection except to the extent permitted by the United States or Arizona Constitution" (House Bill 2162 § 3[B], Support Our Law Enforcement and Safe Neighborhoods Act § 11–1051).

The development of this provision of SB 1070 further illuminates the affective economies in which the legislation invests and is invested. The original law, before it was modified, expanded this power to "any lawful contact" between law enforcement and civilians. Under scrutiny and criticism, however, SB 1070 was amended to limit police surveillance over immigration status to "any lawful stop, detention or arrest" rather than any "lawful contact."[3] Furthermore, the original law before amended read that law enforcement officials could "not solely consider race, color or national origin" in determining someone's legal status, which again was amended after public criticism when "solely" was dropped to prohibit racial profiling. The expanded power of surveillance and racial profiling in the original law coupled with Brewer's own public justifications for the law create slippage between these figures and demonstrate that SB 1070 was aimed at targeting and removing the Mexican-Latina/o-brown-illegal-immigrant body. Illegal immigration brings "everything from the crime and to the drugs [*sic*] and the kidnappings and the extortion and the beheadings and the fact that people can't feel safe in their community," noted Brewer in an interview with Fox News (qtd. in Davenport and Myers). During a televised gubernatorial debate she claimed that "the majority of [illegal immigrants] in my opinion and I think in the opinion of law enforcement . . . are not coming here to work. They are coming here and they're bringing drugs. And they're doing drop houses and they're extorting people and they're terrorizing the families" (qtd. in Montini). Affects of fear and anxiety underlying the legislation justified expanded police power to persecute "suspicious" and dangerous racialized bodies during any lawful contact.

Despite the changes, public controversy persisted over this section of the law, which many critics argued would sanction racial profiling of Latina/os. At the signing ceremony, Governor Brewer directed the Arizona Peace Officer Standards and Training Board (AZPOST) to clarify the enforcement of this provision, standards to which I will return below. Nevertheless, the statute itself as signed indicates the codifying of the Mexican-Latina/o-brown-illegal-immigrant body despite assurances to the contrary. Legal scholar Kevin Johnson argues that "border enforcement officers have long employed crude racial profiles—which almost invariably include undefined 'Mexican appearance'" ("How Racial Profiling" 1006). SB 1070 does not break with this accepted practice; rather, it prohibits the consideration of race as a determinant of reasonable suspicion except to the extent permitted by law. Thus, given the racialized affective economy in which SB 1070 circulates, the prohibition on racial profiling is a hollow hope when the conditions for its circumvention are written into the law.

The prohibition of "race, color, or national origin" as factors in determining legal status lies in stark contrast to the implicit and explicit provisions throughout the legislation that stick together Mexican-Latina/o identity and illegality, including those already discussed regarding work, hiring, transportation, and travel. As I noted above, US Latina/os are continuously positioned as potential "others" in public discourse, whether they are celebrated or sanctioned. Therefore, suspicion about illegality "slide[s] across signs, and between bodies" and "becomes stuck . . . in the very attachment of a sign to a body" (Ahmed, "Affective Economies" 127). We see this process in SB 1070 in an affective economy of immigration, race, and citizenship that codifies the trope of the Mexican-Latina/o-brown-illegal-immigrant body. As I have explained, the restrictions placed on space and movement, the heightened "suspicion" about the qualities of a citizen, and the affects that motivate SB 1070 as a policy of "attrition," make clear the identities of "citizen" and "alien" constituted by the law.

Citizenship and the National Affect

SB 1070 not only codifies the Mexican-Latina/o-brown-illegal-immigrant body through this affective and discursive "slide," but the law also presents a view of citizenship and legality as a performative *affect,* as the performance of the right markers of belonging. If, as Muñoz argues, there is a "national affect" ("Feeling Brown" 69) that draws the contours of what it means to look, sound, and act like a US American, SB 1070 materializes this process, making the affect of others' performances the determinant of whether or not, as the law reads, "reasonable suspicion exists that the person is an alien and is unlawfully present in the US." In SB 1070, state and local police (and, as I will show below, ultimately citizens) become the judges of immigrants' performances, with the power to determine whether or not they look, sound, act, ultimately "feel," American enough. As McKinnon describes, this process of reading the immigrant's performances of citizenship often takes shape informally in US immigration courts and during immigration hearings. Yet in SB 1070, and the discourse surrounding it, there is an explicit connection between the performance of "illegality" and the policing of certain populations.

The enforcement standards promulgated by AZPOST, which serve as training materials and guidelines for state and local police, demonstrate the connection between citizenship and performative affect (i.e., the affect derived from those immigrants' performances of citizenship). Building on previous immigration court decisions dealing with "reasonable cause" (Chin et al.), AZPOST wrote that "the totality of the circumstances" should determine whether "reasonable suspicion" existed that a person was unlawfully present (Arizona Peace Officers Standards and Training Board 3). The training materials list a number of "factors which may be considered, among others, in developing reasonable suspicion of unlawful presence." These factors include: lack of identification, "possession of foreign identification" or foreign "vehicle registration," "flight" or "evasive maneuvers," the "attempt to hide or avoid detection," and the circumstances of the stop if it occurs in "a place where unlawfully present aliens are known to congregate" or "in [the] company of other unlawfully present aliens." Other broader factors include "traveling in tandem" or in a vehicle that is "overcrowded or rides heavily," or the presentation of "inconsistent or illogical information" to police. Reasonable suspicion that individuals are unlawfully present in the United States can also derive from their "dress, demeanor . . . [or] significant difficulty communicating in English" (3–4). When taken together in the "totality of the circumstances," these factors can apparently constitute reasonable suspicion that a person is an "illegal alien."

These criteria are significant, on the one hand, because of their breadth and the way in which a variety of factors, from identificatory documents to language use and behavior, can indicate foreignness. On the other hand, the majority of these characteristics demonstrate not concrete evidence, like the possession of legal documents, but focus on the performative affects of the individuals under police surveillance. That is, a variety of possible behaviors—from language use to foreign dress or suspicious demeanor—are "stuck" together (to use Ahmed's words) and also stuck to an overall affect of otherness, alienness, or foreignness. Speaking Spanish, "un-American" or "Mexican" demeanor or dress, flight or other purported markers of nefarious intent, or merely one's presence in an area known as an "illegal" hangout or in the company of other "illegals" marks one as a suspicious, even unlawful and contaminated, body precisely because these markers reinforce an (already present) affective investment in that body's suspiciousness. Not only are these very different characteristics placed in an equivalence, but their sticking together demonstrates the need to identify and categorize the alienized other as such. Thus, the notion that an officer can determine the legality of a person by observing these factors in the "totality of the circumstances" demonstrates that what the officer is judging is the performance of the other, whether or not he or she can come off (or pass) as an American citizen, and, ultimately, whether or not it feels as if they "belong."

Importantly, this affect of US identity is not affirmatively defined in SB 1070 (or in the AZPOST standards) but rather is positioned in relation to its negative or difference. Only the performative affect of foreignness is specified. The white, middle-class, male citizen-subject remains the invisible center in opposition to which the "not" is defined. The conflation of these very different characteristics creates a sort of affect of the other, broadly defined, in which "brownness" becomes a "broader *metaphorical* identity" that is used to stick together a number of different affects into and onto "coloured [*sic*], deviant bodies" (Silva 175). Foreign languages and foreign "demeanor," suspicious behavior, collectively become an affect of "immigrant," "brown," "foreign," and/or "deviant." SB 1070 demonstrates the degree to which illegality and alien-ness become performative *affects* of a brown body about which something (or many things) is foreign and/or "not quite right." Even in its amended form, SB 1070 and the broader strategy of border rhetoric it represents are targeted at a particular affect of foreignness.[4] The result of such affective economies—of citizenship as a performative affect defined only by difference—is the legitimization of a system of racial persecution and terror summarized in the phrase "attrition through enforcement." This affective ascription serves to deflect the determination of citizenship away from the state and onto the alienized subject, thus providing the state with an alibi against charges of racism, and in effect making the alienized subject responsible for her own alienization. Apart from increased racial profiling and unwarranted stops, the legislation also prohibits a number of social services to undocumented immigrants, further contributing to the self-professed strategy of forcing out suspected undocumented immigrants by making life miserable for them.

Border Vigilantism as Civic Engagement

SB 1070 has unexpectedly drawn criticism from some law enforcement officials because it provides for any "legal resident" of Arizona to bring civil suit against any state or local government agent who "limits or restricts the enforcement of federal immigration laws to less than the full extent permitted by federal law" (Support Our Law Enforcement and Safe Neighborhoods Act § 2[G]). In other words, legal residents may sue the state if it fails to enforce the provisions of SB 1070 (and other immigration laws) to their most severe degree. Community members effectively become a second level of border enforcement. If law enforcement officials do not sufficiently police and persecute undocumented immigrants, then the people can hold the state accountable. More than that, citizens themselves are compelled to take on the mantle of policing the borders of citizenship and civic identity, ferreting out those who do not belong. In light of affects of fear and danger, the very presence of the immigrant-other provides the conditions for the constitution of the community of citizens; the members of the national community are called to stand in solidarity against these threats and to participate in making the community safe.

In fact, this affective economy goes further, converting border vigilantism into a performance of public belonging and a form of civic engagement. James Duff Lyall argues that border vigilantism is not a force opposed to or against the state and its control over citizens, but, on the contrary, vigilantism operates "in tandem" with state policies, "mutually ratcheting up rhetoric and policies, each providing cover for the vigilante-style violence of the other" (261). In this sense, SB 1070's civil suit provision connects the practice of surveilling and persecuting suspected undocumented immigrants with the larger value of government of, by, and for the people;

the civil suit provisions are placed in the same "reasonable suspicion" sections that apply to police. Therefore, not only can citizens hold their government accountable for fully enforcing the law, but citizens themselves are encouraged to perform their civic identity by policing their own community. How else can citizens determine, for example, that a police officer has failed to verify the legal status of a suspected immigrant if citizens themselves are not also watching and judging others, deciding whether "reasonable suspicion" exists that those others don't belong?

The actions of "concerned citizens" tap into the affective investments discussed above—of immigrants as dangerous and threatening others and the trope of the Mexican-Latina/o-brown-illegal-immigrant body. More to the point, their actions demonstrate the conflation of concerned civic engagement and vigilante border policing.[5] Citizens are called to take the safety of their communties in their own hands by working to locate and persecute "illegals." When the government fails to do its job, citizens can step in to secure the borders and protect the sanctity of the nation from these foreign threats. In fact, this discourse of citizen border security converts vigilantism into an expression of patriotism and love of country. As Ahmed writes, "The role of citizens as police is translated as an imperative to love, in which love becomes the foundation of community, as well as the guarantor of our future" ("Affective Economies" 133). Fear/hate of the other and the feelings of insecurity produced by his/her presence form the necessary conditions for the constitution of community. More important in light of previous discussions of affect, these provisions stick together border vigilantism and racial profiling with performances of citizenship, creating an affective economy in which to perform love for one's country is to fear/police/hate the other.

Conclusion

This analysis has distinguished three ways in which SB 1070 and contemporary border discourse at the national and (particularly) at the regional level rearticulates an affective economy of immigration and nation. First, the Mexican-Latina/o-brown-illegal-immigrant body is cemented as a source of foreignness and fear, and second, citizenship and legal status become located in the performative affect of bodies (rather than as a product of state-based, juridical discourse) and are felt and judged by government officials who determine those bodies that give off the "wrong" feeling. Third, contemporary border rhetorics call citizens to perform their belonging by participating in the policing and persecuting of immigrant-others, as border vigilantism is converted into a form of civic duty and a performance of national affect.

SB 1070 represents a moment of articulation in an affective economy surrounding immigration and citizenship that materially and discursively constrains the lives of migrants in the United States. The legislation represents a more aggressive and militant shift in anti-immigrant policy (represented in the term "attrition through enforcement"). Yet SB 1070 is also a "nodal point" in the contemporary evolution of border rhetorics. Using theories of affect, performativity, and materiality, I have analyzed SB 1070 and the border discourse surrounding it to illuminate the ways that affective investments and rhetorical linkages become cemented into systems of thought and feeling.

Of course, as previous chapters in this volume have argued, border rhetorics have been fundamental to the articulation of US identity and citizenship throughout history. Yet recent evolutions in the debate demonstrate the diffusion of border rhetoric from the national arena to the state and local level and the intensity of these affective economies. Arizona's Senate Bill 1070 represents a contemporary moment of articulation in this decades-long evolution in border rhetorics. In fact, one conclusion derived from SB 1070 is that the local level may have become the central battleground over US identity and border security. While comprehensive immigration reform on the national level remains gridlocked, state and local governments enact initiatives that impact Latina/o immigrants in areas of education, health, employment, residency, and security. As Seth Wessler ("A Year after SB 1070") recently reported, SB 1070 spurred debate over similar anti-immigrant legislation in more than twenty states, from California to North Carolina, several of which succeeded and many more that could still pass similar measures; supporters argue that even if the measures fail the threat of their passage is enough to strike terror into the states' immigrant population, achieving the intended effects. The ever-encroaching border behooves rhetorical scholars to turn attention to state and local public controversies, which seem to be the forging ground of public attitudes and public policy about Latina/o immigrants.

More importantly, the focus in this chapter on the affective and performative dimensions of border rhetorics signals the need for a broadening approach from the representational realm to the connections between the material, emotional, and discursive (Rice 206). Anti-immigrant and bordering rhetorics stem from an affective economy that (re)constitutes particular expressions of Latina/os, immigrants, and Latina/o immigrants' exclusion and through which moments like SB 1070 are articulated. The fact that SB 1070 is only a small piece in a broader system of similarly styled anti-immigrant measures governed by the aim of choking out the immigrant "threat" further indicates that what we are seeing is rooted in powerful affective investments. These accretions of affect and meaning influence public understandings, political decisions, and societal interactions regarding immigration and citizenship, including interactions between citizens, law enforcement, and Latina/os, immigrants, and Latina/o immigrants. As SB 1070 once again demonstrates, affective economies fuel contemporary efforts to police, persecute, and harass "illegal aliens," especially racialized bodies.

Importantly, connections between performativity and affect also entail the possibility of disidentifying or "unsticking" the tropes and affects that have come to dominate contemporary border rhetorics (Muñoz, *Disidentifications* 18; Rice 210). Fortunately, a number of anti–SB 1070 movements evince strategies of rearticulation that challenge these affective economies. Although space prohibits discussion of these events here, a number of protests, boycott efforts, and organizations have fought against SB 1070 since its passage. The second largest demonstration in Arizona history, for instance, which took place on May 29, 2010, was organized as a direct response to the passage of SB 1070 (Archibold, "Two Sides"; Riccardi).

While grassroots demonstrations or boycotts can neither entirely combat the political power of anti-immigrant state governments nor resist the affective economies of contemporary border rhetorics, at the very least they point to the contestation of these affects and the possibilities for resisting and performatively remaking the US civic imaginary (Cisneros, "[Re]Bordering the Civic Imaginary"). If developments like SB 1070 serve to rearticulate and re-stick affective and discursive associations together, then the activism of pro-immigrant groups also represents a nodal point that, across time, can craft new associations and affective economies. So, too, the efforts of cultural critics can and should play a role in "unsticking" the affective and discursive associations that underlie contemporary border rhetorics, opening up horizons for new ways to think and talk about citizenship and belonging.

Notes

1. By "performances" I mean situated and stylized discursive enactments that are citational, that is, that draw from and repurpose discursive/cultural conventions and are (re)presented to particular audiences (Strine). "Performativity" is a performative paradigm of identity that foregrounds "nonessentialized constructions of identity" continually (re)iterated through large- and small-scale

social and cultural performances (Madison and Hamera xix). My notions of "performativity" and "performance" draw heavily on the work of Judith Butler and performance studies scholars to position identity as the continual social enactment or reappropriation of identity categories. Since performances of identity draw on dominant traditions, are always on display, and are rooted in particular bodies and affects (as is the case with gender or racial identity), performances are "socially determined" and heavily disciplined "by cultural norms of demarcation," often with restrictive and dehumanizing results (Madison and Hamera xviii). However, Butler contends that performativity also entails avenues for resistance and spaces of agency for marginalized groups struggling for identity/belonging because performance allows a level of adaptation and appropriation of these dominant conventions.

2. I understand affect as a mode of perception that is prior to cognition and that is dispersed throughout the body in a visceral state. Thus, affect represents an experience intricately tied to and involved in the act of signification or meaning-making that we know as emotion (i.e., feelings + meanings) but that is also material, distinctly felt, and embodied (Massumi 25–28). As Brian Ott explains, affects are "incipient attitudes, as energies, intensities, and sensations that function as the first step towards an evolving attitude"—that is, emotion (50). I will elaborate on my particular perspective for analyzing affect in the subsequent discussion.

3. In this paragraph I am comparing Section 2(B) of Arizona Senate Bill 1070 and its final form as amended in Section 3(B) of Arizona House Bill 2162.

4. To further this point, it is difficult to imagine a white Irish or German immigrant motivating this "reasonable suspicion" (Cohn).

5. For a contemporary example, see the actions of the "Concerned Citizens of the United States," an anti-immigrant group in Utah (Treviño).

9
Love, Loss, and Immigration

Performative Reverberations between a
Great-Grandmother and Great-Granddaughter

Bernadette Marie Calafell

February 2010

I haven't been "home" in a while. I put "home" in quotation marks because it doesn't feel like home anymore. It's been ten years since I moved. Ten years since I missed the desert and Aztlán, the US Southwest, the Chicana/o homeland. Ten years later a great deal has changed as I have moved from Phoenix to Chapel Hill, to Syracuse, and now Denver. Experiences of a US/Mexico border, then a US/Canadian border, and now back to the Southwest; not quite the border, but its presence remains. Ten years ago, I was solidly Chicana, and now I don't know where I'm really at anymore. The figurative borders shift beneath my feet and my identities seem to follow suit. Though my identities are always in flux, I remain committed to a coalitional queer politics that doesn't erase the bodies and experiences of queer women of color. Ten years later what I consider to be home is a place without any blood relatives and only a family of choice made up of Others who have left their homes because of a lack of connection or support.

Ten years ago, I left to go to Chapel Hill as a doctoral student. Now I return as tenured faculty member and administrator. I come as a representative of my university to interview prospective undergraduates. Ironic that only this "official capacity" could get me to come back "home" again.

My work is done for the day and I meet up with an old friend from college. I haven't seen Jackie in a few years, though we have maintained contact over time. Simply stated, I love her. She is the first woman I ever loved. Years ago, we were drawn to each other for various reasons. She moved to the United States when she was five years old and is originally from Jalisco in Mexico. When we met in college I was in the midst of rethinking my Mexican American identity through a Chicana feminist framework. As I wrapped my head around all the questions of identity, she pushed me to problematize the ways I thought about my sexuality. In some ways, I problematically fetishized her as "authentic" as I sought to find myself. She was drawn to me because I was the only other Latina in our class and I was white. Much like my grandmother who proudly called me *guera*[1] and embraced my whiteness, Jackie also desired my whiteness.

After all this time we remain friends, and she comes to see me while I'm in Phoenix. We find a local bar by the hotel for a drink. As we sit sharing memories and thinking about the future we see a large group of men gathered on the patio dressed in matching jackets that announce the name of an organization. These men are bikers; however, we do not know what brings so many of them together. We venture to the patio to see if we can figure out this mystery. The group of men is mostly white, and in their forties or older; however, suddenly another group arrives. These men are slightly younger and Latino. Jackie begins a conversation with one, perhaps the youngest there, asking him what their organization is about. He explains that all of the men are border patrol agents and they have formed this bike club. The majority of them are from Tucson. Seeing us engaged in conversation with their friends, some of the other Latino agents come over and start asking us questions as well. We give some background information and exchange pleasantries. Jackie and the men speak in Spanish and I sit trying to make sense of their conversations. Jackie marks my identity for me and lets them know I am Latina. Suddenly their demeanor toward me changes and things become a lot friendlier.

As the night wears on we are invited back to the resort where they are staying for an after-party. Though the days of after-parties are long behind me, perhaps it is being with Jackie that makes me feel youthful. Memories of her and me taking youthful risks, and seeing the desire in her eyes for one more adventure, I agree. Once we arrive at the resort we sit together on the couch and start talking with some of the Latino officers with whom we had exchanged pleasantries earlier. At this point, my emotions are mixed. I do not want to know the border patrol agents. I do not want to put a face to them. I do not want to imagine that they are Mexicanos, too. I feel like I'm being a traitor sitting with them. I don't even know what to talk about so I remain silent.

This is not a problem for Jackie. As we continue sitting with the Latino agents we met earlier, another agent, an older white man who is clearly intoxicated, joins us. He is introduced to us and as he hears Jackie speak he catches her slight accent and the interrogation begins. "Are you in this country legally? Do you know we could take you in?" The young Latino officer next to Jackie with whom we first started the conversation gets embarrassed and starts laughing nervously. Jackie likes to play games and knows he's drunk, so she refuses to give a straight answer about her status. His interrogation continues as he states, "You know, I could have you arrested and deported before you even had a chance to call a lawyer." Jackie laughs and continues to evade him, while another Latino agent tells him to stop that: "Now is not the time for work." The agent who interrogates Jackie says, "Hey, even if you were illegal, I wouldn't turn you in because we're partying." His statement brings me little comfort.

Though Jackie is a US citizen, I am nervous. This is not the first time I have witnessed these kinds of tactics, as I am taken back to another life in Syracuse, New York, when my then-partner, Mohamed, and I went through the process of permanent residency and then the application for citizenship. "Rights" and "protections" haven't felt like rights and protections for years since we started that process shortly after 9/11. I'm always on guard and always suspicious. The Latino agents seem nervous and embarrassed by this whole scene and even begin saying, "Dude, she's legal. She came when she was like five years old."

In the background one of the other men falls in a drunken stupor and the conversation stops, as Jackie had begun to turn the tables and start interrogating the officer about the politics of the Canadian border versus the Mexican border. Just as he had started to tell us that it was just all about "terrorists," the conversation halts as he runs outside to make sure an agent they call "Froggy" is okay. I give Jackie our prior agreed-upon signal for leaving, and we say that we need to get back to the hotel because it's late. We leave a little shaken and just wanting to be away from the surrealness of the whole scene. Jackie and I deconstruct it all as we try to make sense of the interactions and the Latino agents.

Later, as I reflect on the events of that night, I wonder if the people I love will always be subject to surveillance and suspicion. The first suspect of this suspicion was my former partner, Mohamed, an Egyptian-born man, and now Jackie, a Mexican-born US citizen with whom my relationship continues to be complicated. After 9/11 they are interpellated by a shared Otherness or affect of brownness that links their differently storied and historied bodies. Ten years ago, south Phoenix hadn't yet been gentrified, and Sheriff Joe Arpaio had just started his crusade of hate. Ten years ago, I hadn't yet considered the possibility of a shared affect of brownness that moved beyond a Latina/o body, but my experiences in the last ten years have forced me to consider it. This shared affect also causes me to return to the story of my great-grandmother, Teresa Carbajal Benavides.

And so it begins . . .

This is a story that has been waiting to be told, but I don't know if I was always ready to tell it, or for that matter hear it. It's not like I even know the entire story. I remember her. But my memories are not always complete or in necessary order. Instead they are fragments. They are sounds. They are moments of intimacy that defy the confines of language.

I performatively write to explore the story of my maternal great-grandmother or, as I used to call her, Little Grandma— Teresa Carbajal Benavides, who lived with me in my grandparents' house in which I grew up. We spent a great deal of time together; however, I never completely knew or understood the significance of her story until now. It was during the past eight years that I began to feel the reverberations of her story in a way I never had before. My affective connection with a discourse of Otherness post-9/11, based on incidents such as the previously described one, made my body remember.

I become obsessed with her story, wondering if perhaps it might shed some light on my own. Is this where my feminist consciousness began? *But I move too quickly.*

In the past I have written about my own troubled relationship with immigration post-9/11 (Calafell, "Performing the Responsible Sponsor"), or perhaps it would be more accurate to say, Mohamed's troubled relationship with immigration and my performance in helping him secure citizenship. It was a story based in love, fear, and performance. It was a story that finally had an ending that was somewhat satisfactory, but far from anyone's American Dream. In the end, I was a responsible sponsor and he performed patriotism and a desire for citizenship in ways that were acceptable and lauded.

On May 8, 2002, in the blink of an eye my life changed forever with the words "I do." The changing of one's life after marriage is certainly not a remarkable or unique situation; however, the specifics of my marriage created a series of events I could not even imagine. You see, I was a twenty-seven-year-old Chicana doctoral student far from home, newly married to an Egyptian citizen after 9/11. Though I knew we would have to begin the process of applying for residency and eventually citizenship, I had no idea just how much this process would forever change me or us. Narratives of immigration and border crossing were not outside of my frame of reference, both because of my background as a scholar doing work in Chicana/o studies and because of my family's narratives of crossing the border from Mexico. This encounter with immigration was the starting point for thinking about her: Teresa Carbajal Benavides and my desire to know her and understand her so that in some ways I might know myself.

In this exploration I engage in a performative writing methodology or framework because of its ability to tap into the affective or emotive. This is both a scholarly and personal story that continues to have reverberations in my day-to-day experiences. This is a story I juxtapose in many ways with my own. I consider it alongside my recent experience with immigration with my then-partner and in the everyday incidents I experience after 9/11, such as my encounter with the border patrol agents. I juxtapose it with my experiences as a Chicana in this anti-Latina/o nativist time and place (is there ever a time that isn't?). I think about the politics of love that tie the stories together. In engaging in this methodology, I turn to Ron Pelias and Della Pollock to frame my understanding of the politics and form of performative writing, but I also turn to others such as Sandra Faulkner and Diane Grimes (Faulkner, Calafell, and Grimes) to engage in poetry as research method. Scholars such as Pelias and Pollock ask that performative writers create experiences on the page that affectively connect with readers. Pelias writes, "Performative writing features lived experience, telling, iconic moments that call forth the complexities of human life. With lived experience, there is no separation between mind and body, objective and subjective, cognitive and affective" (418). Furthermore, this work stakes a claim in an experience, or position, persuading through narrative identification or empathy (Pelias). Similarly, Faulkner, Calafell, and Grimes wonder how we might use poetry as a method to explore and nuance experiences, particularly as they relate to those in marginalized positions.

Like other feminist scholars who set the standard for the politics that should drive a performative writer, I understand the importance of theorizing and unpacking experience as a way of knowing (Hill Collins; Moraga and Anzaldúa). As Anzaldúa has long argued in her framing of theories of the flesh, experience is fundamentally important to the ways that women of color have long theorized. Barbara Christian and Patricia Hill Collins explicitly connect theorizing through experience and the body to a history of oppression (for example, slavery, and not having access to education) that has often forced women of color to theorize through everyday actions and ways of making do. Furthermore, examining experience can point to the ways that the personal is located within what Hill Collins terms a larger matrix of domination that speaks to the intersecting nature of race, class, gender, and sexuality and how power shapes them. The critical examination of experience, particularly of historically marginalized groups, is also of central importance in performance studies as scholars have examined personal narrative (Corey, "The Personal"; Langellier, "Personal Narrative") or what others term a performative autoethnography (Alexander, "Performing Culture"; Holman Jones; Spry). From a performance ethnography paradigm undergirded by Conquergood's dialogic performance ("Performing as a Moral Act"), the personal acts in dialogue with the larger frames of the social, political, and cultural in order to theorize beyond the self. Enrique Murillo Jr. describes his positionality as scholar and Chicano as traveling in blurred boundaries, when "Other becomes researcher, narrated becomes narrator, translated becomes translator, native becomes anthropologist, and one intermittent identity continuously informs the other" (166). Like Murillo, I draw upon my experiences or theories of the flesh to performatively understand the experiences of Otherness as they relate to the here and now, as well as those that occurred within my great-grandmother's story.

Looking for Teresa Carbajal Benavides

In first looking for her story I turned to my own body. Looking in the mirror, I longed to see something of her in my face, yet I did not see it. Somewhat disappointed, I turned to my grandmother, Consuelo Muñoz, and started asking questions. I asked about love. I asked about citizenship. I asked about family history. I wanted to know everything.

I feel like being the good scholar and I'm documenting family history. Maybe I'm a little too self-congratulatory. I'm going back to Phoenix to do an interview with my grandmother, Consuelo Muñoz. Bryant Alexander, like other scholars of color before him, writes poignantly of going home and negotiating the self as PhD/professor versus son/sibling/etc. In this moment I know that feeling all too well. My grandmother and I sit together in the living room across from one another, near the front window. Ironically, this is the space where my great-grandmother used to sit stationary. It is as if she is ghosting us. I test my recorder and our conversation begins. We start out with the basics: place of birth, any family history, and such. I've got my list of prepared questions, but I'm thinking things will probably deviate. At least I'm hoping so.

I want to flesh out the story of a woman whom I knew, but never *really* knew. As a woman, then thirty-three years old at the time of this conversation, I want to know about her desires and challenges. I want to know about things like love and loss. I push because I need to know so that I might also know myself in the process. This desire is in my blood as I'm always looking for the stories of my mothers before me (Calafell, *Latina/o Communication*

Studies). Through the fleshing or reclaiming, I hope to enable some kinds of potentiality. Potentiality for me to find a space of identification across time and beyond bloodlines. Writing on possibility within the framework of performance ethnography, Corey argues that it "is one way of releasing suspended voices, building connections between the expression of a people and those people themselves, with power, possibility, and integrity" ("On Possibility" 332). I look for potentiality or possibility that might give me some kinds of mechanisms, theories of the flesh, or ways of knowing that defy dominant logics, particularly those that emerge around constructions of Otherness. Are there things she can teach me about love and loss? These are the potentialities I hope for.

I like to imagine my great-grandmother as a Chicana feminist blazing new trails and performing the theory of the flesh that I now like to write about.

> Single mother
> moving her family
> across borders;
>   from Chihuahua,
>   to Jerome,
>   and finally to Phoenix.
> Shifting borders,
> shifting desires,
> shifting priorities.

Perhaps my desire to see her as this everyday feminist is driven by a narcissistic desire to imagine myself in the same way. Where do my scholarly interests end and my personal desires begin? Are they even separate? Is this a question even worth asking?

I continue looking for answers. We get to the questions about her crossing the border:

"So, she was here in the United States the whole time without papers?" I ask the question to understand contexts. I ask the question though I feel the irony of getting your "papers" in Aztlán of all places.

"No, she became a citizen."

Taken aback, I pause for a moment and consider my quick jump to illegality. Does this come from the fact that as Chicana/os or Mexicana/os we are always depicted as forever foreign or outsiders (Calafell, "Mocking Mexicans")? As the good academic, the Latina/o Studies scholar, wouldn't I know better than just to assume illegality? Have I been so warped by discourses of crossovers and invasions that my sense of self is so distorted? Have I forgotten about all my talk of Aztlán? Or is this assumed illegality a symptom of my living in suspicion for years and years as my former partner and I strived to "prove" the legitimacy of our union (Calafell, "Performing the Responsible Sponsor")? The scholar turns the mirror to herself to see the way *I perform and embody hegemony* . . .

"I didn't know that . . . when did this happen? Do you have her citizenship papers?"

"She was seventy-three years old when she became a citizen."

I sit quietly for a moment wondering what possessed a seventy-three-year-old woman who had lived in the United States for many years, never speaking English (even until the day she died at age ninety-six), to become a US citizen at such an advanced age. Is this about patriotism? Is this about claiming one's space in the face of denial of everyday rights in the racial tensions of the 1960s, the era in which she became a citizen? I desire to know; however, I am fully aware that I will never know and can only think of possibilities. I draw on my theories of the flesh, my lived experience as a woman in this country, to consider the various possibilities. I draw on my experiences of having been partnered with someone going through the process of immigration and citizenship to consider the desire that motivated her choices. My grandmother interrupts my thoughts as she continues . . .

"I have her citizenship certificate if you want to see it."

My mind is flooded with all kinds of thoughts. It's as if I have found the holy grail. It's been here the whole time, and yet I never knew any of this. I imagined a family history of migration that was much different. My former partner Mohamed received such a certificate just a few years ago and I wonder how time has changed these documents. What would these certificates look like side by side? We move to the bedroom and from a small metal box my grandmother produces the immigration certificate along with a US flag that was given to my great-grandmother on the day that she received her citizenship. I move in closely to inspect it all.

I survey the certificate, looking over the date it was issued, the date of my grandmother's birth, and such. However, one thing stands out. This document lists her "complexion" . . . is this a way of getting at race? Is this how her difference would be forever marked? According to the United States of America, she is "dark." How does this fit within larger discourses of blackness and whiteness? All of these thoughts race through my head. I consider how this marking of difference feels like a colonial racial hierarchy similar to the ways that *mestiza/os* have always been marked and assimilated based upon the idea that "whiter is better." I think of my grandmother, who is darker skinned, always alluding to her fear of us being ashamed or embarrassed by her because she was dark. I remember her attachment to *Imitation of Life*, a story in which a young African American woman who can pass as white continually tries to distance herself from her mother who cannot make the same pass. My grandmother who loves me unconditionally, but also loves the whiteness of my skin. This is another moment of our difference being marked in an official way that would again have everyday reverberations. I think of the politics of my Egyptian former partner being racially classified as white, though he was certainly never privy to the benefits and privileges of whiteness, particularly after 9/11. I consider the interrogation of Jackie by the border patrol agents. Her accent and appearance immediately marked her as Other in their minds, while I remained inconspicuous. How have discourses of whiteness and difference shifted over time? Have they? How are these shifts tied to the shifting or tightening of borders?

I look closer at the photo on the certificate, once again looking for some kind of resemblance. This time, instead of seeing any trace of myself, I see my grandmother's face. It's a somber face I can't read, one that stands in contrast to Mohamed's wide smiling face in the photograph that graces his certificate. His picture says, he's made it. But hers has something else behind it. Perhaps the circumstances of being a woman, and a Chicana at that, inform the somber yet straight-ahead expression she gives. So many questions remain unanswered, and so I began to dream . . .

The Politics of Love

"I don't want to do this anymore," and with those words he broke
my heart.
　　Sitting here alone I wonder if those words were all too familiar to
you as well.
A Mexican woman in a foreign land
Persevering
Journeying
Crossing borders in ways that are not
Glamorous
Or trendy
Eventually granted citizenship
But never the full rights it promised.

Alone
But with children
Yes, that's a plural
Seven to be exact
So you're never really alone.
Making do
Was love a luxury you had time for?
Or did it just get in the way?

I like to imagine you briefly brokenhearted
But the tug of a child at your sleeve
Makes the pain seem not so important
Or at least a privilege
Maybe the pain is gone for the moment
But the affect of it remains
And you wear it in the lines of your skin
Thinking of lovers past
Wondering if you might ever feel that way again

Decades later I sit brokenhearted
Yet again
Wallowing in my pain and self-loathing
which in many ways seem so miniscule to all you shouldered
For all of us
But remember I'm not about comparing or ranking oppression
So why am I asking these questions?

Aretha told me that "a rose is still a rose."[2]
While my Lady says she'll never talk again
And she'll never love again[3]
Kind of dramatic, but that's exactly what I need right now
I listen to those words like they're some kinda feminist melody
Thinking if I listen hard enough just maybe my mood will change

American great-granddaughter
Always hyphenated
Always feeling like second class.
Both in work
And in love
Unlike you the love I desire is queer
Despite the promise of citizenship that you ensured

For me in this place and time love does not feel like a luxury
It feels like a necessity that I'm always in search of
So much so that I've become the professor who's always writing
about love
But it's hidden behind different kinds of veils.
The sacrifices you made give me time to dream of possibilities

And so I sit alone
Thinking of you
Thinking of love
Thinking of borders
and spaces I still can't cross
and spaces you have overcome
Looking to you for some answers across the years
A maternal connection of love
that binds beyond time
and leaves me asking like Cherríe
"What kind of lover have you made me mother
So in love with what is unrequited?"[4]

Final Thoughts

The narrative I have crafted is incomplete. The story continues to unfold as the borders shift and tighten around us. As I stated at the beginning of this chapter, I construct this story only out of fragments and perform possibilities out of a desire for connection. The border shifts all around, inside of us, and beneath our feet. Ideologies of race and Otherness are re-crafted as old scapegoats become new again and new scapegoats get marked in old ways.

In this performative piece I have tried to bring together fragmented narratives of Otherness to understand or feel affects of difference that permeate across space and time. In doing so, I have ended with a poem that attempts to bring together the past and the recent present through love, both romantic and familial, immigration, and borders. The borders crossed in each narrative are different, both as physical spaces and experiential. It is my hope that this performance piece might get us to *feel* the shifting borders around us, both figuratively and literally, as a way to connect with and understand affects of Otherness. Through these narratives I have pointed to shifts in borders and the feelings that span them. In these scenarios, the contexts, their specificities, and nuances might vary, but in ending with the poem "The Politics of Love," I try to perform the theory of the flesh handed down generationally through a Chicana feminist ethic of love. This ethic of love guides a previously written-about narrative with homeland security, the contemporary narrative of interactions with border agents, and that of a Mexicana who at an advanced age sought "legalization" through citizenship so decades later, a great-granddaughter who continuously feels the pressure of the border might garner some everyday knowledges of resistance. In offering these narratives, I do not try to answer specific questions; rather I invite you to feel so that we can begin the conversation and start to name or consider the layers of shifting borders (political, social, historical).

Notes

1. *Guera* is often used to refer to light-skinned Latina/os.
2. Aretha Franklin, "A Rose Is Still a Rose."
3. Lady Gaga, "Speechless."
4. This quote is from Cherríe Moraga's *Loving in the War Years*.

10
Borders without Bodies
Affect, Proximity, and Utopian Imaginaries through "Lines in the Sand"

Dustin Bradley Goltz and Kimberlee Pérez

Mainstream discourses circulate to construct images of the Mexican–American border and Mexican Americans: as perpetual immigrants (Flores, "Constructing Rhetorical Borders" 363) outside of belonging to the nation (Carrillo Rowe, "Whose 'America'?" 122), economic and criminal threats to the nation (Ono and Sloop 28), and a complex and changing group (Calafell and Delgado 2). In this volume, Ono theorizes the relation between borders and bodies, demonstrating the ways immigrants (and people whose phenotypes signify Latino/a and are therefore rhetorically conflated with immigrants) move with borders. Following Anzaldúa's theorizing of border as psychic and embodied, Ono explains how immigrants who cross the geographically legislated border between the US and Mexico continue to "carry" it with them. Therefore, as a discursive construction, the border is constantly redone through and around the bodies of immigrants; the border is as much in the Southwest as in the Midwest and North. As we demonstrate in this chapter, the performativity of the border mediates relational and spatial meanings and interactions.

Although we certainly confront the pervasiveness of border rhetorics (alongside critical resistance to them), quite simply, *we* need not confront *them*. Spatially and discursively distanced from our daily lives, we can and do occupy a privileged removal from the border, as intersecting discourses of nation and whiteness certainly produce our bodies as non-immigrants (citizen, white, Mexican American) and apart from immigrants (Flores and Villarreal, this volume). It is only when we deliberately confront and reflect upon the intentional and circumstantial, the mundane and spectacular moments of our daily lives that place us in direct bodily contact with immigrants, that we get at the meaning of living that discursive production on individual and relational levels. How does the story of *my* understanding of immigrants and border rhetoric change in relation to *us*? How does it change the meaning of a relation, of difference, of distance? Does it bring us closer together in identification or pull us apart? Do the contours of us take on a different shape, texture, tone, and feeling? The spatial and discursive issues surrounding US/Mexican immigration complicate, rupture, and pry apart our relations, emphasizing our differences along the lines of identity politics.

The tension of distance and daily interanimation of the border in our lives lies at the heart of this chapter. What does it mean to confront these constructed illusions of distance, the deliberate binary production of border rhetorics that separate *us* from *them*? What can/might/ought this look like? Through a performative methodology,[1] we enact a self-reflective process in order (or in an attempt) to understand our complicity with, and the challenge of, border rhetorics. Discourses of the border produce relations between and among difference: Mexican, Mexican American, and other non-white bodies are lumped into a homogeneous body of Others who negotiate tense dynamics with whiteness.[2] The effect is a circulating border that has an effect on, but is discursively without, bodies and their lived experiences. Our efforts here are to follow critical race scholars who theorize white privilege alongside its damaging consequences (Segrest; Nakayama and Krizek). We consider how border rhetorics produce non-immigrant and white signifying bodies through reflecting on how border rhetorics produce *bodies,* namely ours.

Border discourses work to produce and sustain many parts of us—as scholars, as white signifying bodies, as teachers, as citizens, as hypocrites. What we write on the page, discuss in classrooms, or present at conferences is not divorced from the bars we drink at, the stores we shop in, the daily movement of our bodies through the world. In each of these moments, we are doing border work. We are working the border.

Grounded in the awareness that our point of entry as a self-reflexive examination of this choice is riddled with complications and potentials—the risk/charge of recentering whiteness through calling attention to it without nuanced criticism of it (Projansky and Ono 156)—we mindfully intertwine our embodied knowing with cultural critique (Conquergood, "Rethinking Ethnography"). Working from tradition of performative engagement, both outlined and enacted by Calafell in the previous chapter, we call upon the affective connections forged through our embodied experience. We offer this process as a complement to, rather than a replacement of, other activist and scholarly work featured in this volume and elsewhere that directly relates to the lives of immigrants and the material effects of border discourses. By challenging these notions of perceived spatial distance of the border from our lives, we open the possibility for us to both reflect on and engage the border differently—to do the border differently. We problematize illusions of distance. We practice critical, cultural, and feminist calls to politicize the personal and to do *our* work. We do so through narrating our individual and relational experiences in our daily lives and through performance.

In spring 2006, our then-home state of Arizona was one of the many sites to garner national attention in the ongoing struggle between the violences of xenophobic speech and action (Sheriff Joe Arpaio, the Minutemen, legislation targeting immigrants and undocumented workers) and resistance movements for social justice (for example, No Mas Muertes, Immigrant Solidarity Network). In the wake of domestic immigration marches garnering international attention, the mediated representation of these public displays consumed our attention. Particularly interested in how Mexican immigrants, the US-Mexican border, and US citizenry were being constructed through local and national news, we began a collaborative performance process, which resulted in the performance "Lines in the Sand: Fear, Loss, and Whiteness in Contemporary US Representations of Mexican Immigration." The piece offers the relational interrogation of privilege, citizenship, race, class, and queerness through dialogue between a queer white Jewish male and a queer Chicana. As friends, colleagues, academics, citizens, teachers, and collaborators, our authoring of this piece works to enflesh and embody the affective, mundane, and temporal dimensions of border work through our daily lives and interactions.

The "she," "he," and "us" who authored the performance and this chapter move in and out at points where our voices speak collectively, as well as individually. The movement between "she," "he," and "us" designates the tensions, differing histories, and divergent perspectives, preventing the easy and seamless collapsing of a "we" inherent in collaboration. The personal experiences of "she" and "he" also trace the process of moving toward a "we" in *coalition,* designating difference and important breaks present in our claiming of a "we."

This chapter will first address how a move to performance highlights embodied, personal/relational, and affective dimensions of the border, complementing broader discursive investigations. Next, the chapter examines how performative methodologies draw attention to the simultaneous and multiple border discourses that shape, define, and complicate fixed, finite, or singular border frameworks. Finally, the chapter looks to how our performance seeks to stage and embody a utopian imaginary that interrogates and works to disrupt geographical, historical, and temporal borders.

Borders without Bodies: The Move to Performance

The collusion of whiteness and our critical academic positionings was never so pronounced as in our preliminary discussions about the border in the early stages of our collaborative process. We sat across from one another and talked about immigration, the local marches, the media coverage, our community college and university students' families, and the discourse surrounding our state and the Mexican border. Theories of race, privilege, class, and nation danced off our tongues with suspect confidence and clarity, the ease of instruments as shaped, molded, and disciplined as a ballerina's body. We could talk privilege. We could talk entitlement. We could even talk fears. Yet the cool liberal glide of our analysis was sidestepping something more hideous, uncomfortable, and off-balanced. What escaped our discussion were the depths of its infestation, the ways our conflicted dances sustain its affective integrity while they claim to dismantle its logics. The border became a place, a marker, a metaphor, and a system in our talk. We place the border elsewhere, critique it from afar, study its contours, yet it is through our fears, angers, embodied experiences, avoidances, unspoken assumptions, and the dancerly calm of our discussion that we believe we are complicit in its elusiveness. Turn the scholarly microphones off, and we return to our worlds, our bodies, and our existence beyond abstractions.

I, Dusty, live in a primarily Latino/a neighborhood, and literally play white noise in my home to construct an audio wall to cancel out the Mexican music from the apartment complex parking lot next door. I drive across town to certain grocery stores because "I just enjoy shopping there" more. I avidly support the immigration marches in Arizona, and allow my students to miss class in order to attend them; yet I do not attend myself due to feelings of displacement that I rationalize as respect. I am quick to grow angry when I am inconvenienced by someone not playing good neighbor, good student, or good citizen by my standards, which secretly reifies my own goodness, rightness, correctness, entitlement to my self. In those moments I use a different vocabulary from my academic-ese. Surely, I correct and shame myself, rescript impulsive flinches with critical concepts to challenge the dehumanizing entitlement passed down to me. These parts of myself fight to navigate my movement through this world. I do not believe in master narratives of nationalist neo-liberal privilege and entitlement, yet I feel them; and these are but the ones I can see and locate. What hides beneath my shame, rationality, and obliviousness?

I, Kimberlee, a second-generation Mexican immigrant on my father's side, sit alongside my friend who is a first-generation Mexican immigrant. He came to Arizona as a baby. In the relative safety of a south Phoenix Starbucks, we debate the complexity of revolutions (acts of resistance paradoxically riddled with sexism and homophobia) when he reminds me of the immigration rally happening at the capitol building. The irony and privilege of our distances, the small distance of space from the rally yet vast distances of citizenship, history, and economic status, are not lost on us. We race downtown, transported from the cool spaciousness of our conversation to the crowded heat of mid-morning April. We pause at the Starbucks cups in our hands and leave them in the car, then make our way toward the crowd of predominantly brown bodies holding signs, chanting, and speaking. My belonging feels conflicted. My identity as queer Chicana rubs against skin that signifies and benefits from whiteness. My *grandparents* were immigrants and while they leave me their names I don't hold their stories or experiences.[3] I am visible in name—in speech—a rehearsed and careful narration I can *choose* to mark or not mark. As I make my way to the margins of the crowd, I feel inauthentic and outside as I follow the cues to clap and chant, unable to attach meaning to much of the Spanish. It's a familiar dance. Feeling fraud, feeling longing, offbeat and out of touch. There and not there, seen and not seen, I wonder at my choices, my inheritance, my location. How do I stand in alliance to that which I do not know but to which I am tied, to identify difference alongside what we share—to motivate and generate collective action?

We use performance to engage our questions. Although discourses of whiteness and our white bodies enable our distance from immigrants, our focus on the sites of our bodies and experiences and relations expose the interdependence. While whiteness renders us "invisible," the reality is that *our* invisibility depends on the hypervisibility and calling attention to immigrants through rhetoric. Following Ono's "border effects" (this volume), through lived experience we challenge and unpack the notion of the border as a thing that is far and away from our lives. Invested in the affective dimensions at work in our own performance of border, of doing border, we mined our experiences for stories, discomforts, shames, complicities, affinities, and ruptures to begin mapping the emotional, historical, and contextualized complexity we evaded in our scholarly banter. We interrogate our performances within the classroom, the immigration rally, the grocery store, the academic seminar, the gay bar, and the south Phoenix Starbucks to understand obscured relations of our bodies to the reproduction and potential rearticulation of borders and bordering discourse. The performativity of the border grew complicated through the simultaneity and multiplicity of many borders at work, being worked, and working upon us.

Performing Borders: "We Are Never One Thing"

The frames applied to "us," "he," and "she" in this process fuel suspicions, distances, and borders from the inception. She is half-Mexican and half-white. He is white. He is Jewish; she was raised Lutheran. He is gay, she is lesbian, and they are queer. They are academics. The borders, suspicions, and identity categories that drive and dictate these designations and divides raise eyebrows and concerns. "Why are *they* talking about border rhetorics?" Divide by divide, the categories break and bind "us," manufacturing our distances from the border. Rigid enforcement and/or uncomplicated commitment to identity politics sustain these boundaries and rub against our political commitment to reconfigure these relations, our relations, both to ourselves, each other, our immediate world, and the border seemingly far, far away.

We all are working the border, aren't we? I, Dusty, locate borders at work when an uninsured immigrant motorist crashes into a car in an intersection, and my lawfully stopped truck—waiting patiently for a green light—is hit head on. "Innocent," law-abiding, and cool-tempered, I listen to the police officers explain the "immigrant" situation to me while shaking their heads in frustrated helplessness. Both drivers involved in the initial accident appear Latino, as far as I can tell. I am positioned on one side of the intersection and they on the other. I do not recall how they ended up on the northwest corner, and I the southeast. A police officer moves between us, apologizing to me continually, thanking me for my patience, and expressing appreciation that I "understand the situation." "Nowadays, we all have to have insurance," he comments. I nod, agreeably, following his cues. Police officers scare me to death, and I usually get very masculine in their presence, adopting a likeable "guy's guy" Vince Vaughn–like performance. I wonder if the "we" who need insurance "nowadays" are all motorists, or a different "we" is being marked between the white male officer and me. Is he as chummy with the folks over on the northwest corner of the intersection? Am I performing, as Cisneros discusses earlier in this volume, my own national belonging through "guy's-guy" complicit smiles that can be seen to endorse the policing and othering of nonwhite bodies?

That border, 180 miles south, lives here. We feel it, we talk it, we interrogate/sustain it. Do we humanize it—its blood, its flesh, its anxiety, and its material violence? I wonder how the guilty ease I brush off when casually chatting it up with local law enforcement is tied to the physical pain of bodies far away, collapsing the distance between Nineteenth Avenue and Camelback and the border 180 miles south of Phoenix. We ask each other what it might look like to posit a relationship—place our bodies in relation to others' bodies, stand in coalition, forge identifications across that border 180 miles south on I-10 to I-19 and the borders severing us.

I, Dusty, play a VHS recording of the previous night's news about upcoming immigration rallies. As a class, we observe the emphasis placed on the number of police who will be present, suggesting a building threat, a danger to be contained. More than half of this class identify as Latino/a and about one-third mark themselves or their parents as Mexican immigrants. That physical border, 180 miles south, is a familiar place for many of them, separating family, friends, and, for some, what is "really home." Voices grow loud, confident, and angry at the newscast, critiquing what is forefronted and constructed through absences and omissions. In facilitating and fostering this interrogation, I become an ally to some, performing the well-intentioned white liberal professor. A small collection of white students, however, grow increasingly frustrated. I offer a space for voicing their affective experiences, though none speak up until after class—in private— lingering around the room until only white signifying students are present. In this newly constructed all-white space, I am challenged for favoring "one side" of the discussion. I reply that there are more than two sides to this discussion, and a student clarifies "their" side. Framings of "them," "those people," and "the Mexicans" are tossed out, along with a designation of "us"—into which I was interpellated. I refer them to the "respect" clause in my syllabus that explicitly states that the denigration of human integrity of any group or identity (racial, religious, sexual, gendered, economic, age) is not acceptable. I patiently explain that while they may feel their own viewpoints are not always endorsed in class, their humanity is never compromised. I try to show how their viewpoints, however, diminish the humanity of others inside and outside the class. I listen. I am listened to, and being a white male in these moments carries privileges when engaging these students. "We" talk it through. I work to negotiate the problems and potentials of how I speak, talk, move, and am read within that space.

Following an immigration march in Phoenix, I show additional news coverage in class. The segment focuses on how "Mexicans" are being courted by Republican "family values" campaigns—specifically anti-gay rights. I am disheartened to hear several of the outspoken Mexican students, with whom I was an ally a week prior, confidently speak to the evils, sin, and moral deficiency of "those gays." Other members of class, more attuned to my (subtle?) cues, are awkwardly silent, conscious that their classmates are oblivious to my own sexuality—operating under the common assumption that the classroom, as all-public space, is an entirely straight space.

I realize, in this moment, that I do not fall under the category of "human" according to these students. My syllabus, for them, does not include my families and myself. I am not one of "us," but one of "them." Another border, a different border emerges, with these degenerate gays somewhere far away, miles away, on the other side. I retreat into my white masculinity.[4]

I am abstract, logical, critical, and hypothetical, denying the anger, sadness, and affective overload of my body in that space. Students who read my queerness commend me after class for being "fair and objective." I am thanked for my lack of affect and calmed reason—my performance of whiteness (Muñoz, "Feeling Brown"). One of the more outspoken anti-gay students later apologizes, "not knowing" I was gay. She does not retract what she said, only that she said it in my class. I calmly steer the discussion to borders and broader discussions of difference—immigrant families, queer families, their identity, my identity. "It's different," they reply. The litany of scripts, of "choice" and "God" is the justification for this difference, collapsing "family values" rhetoric and Mexican immigration, seemingly producing all immigrants as only possibly straight Catholics. As ally, I am produced as white straight ally when I stand with my Mexican students. The queer ally is cast outside of possibility for coalition, as one movement is "just" and one is so easily cast as morally deficient. I listen, though it's difficult. I perform calm. I am a teacher, and I respect and believe in process. Maybe I just want to believe that. Maybe it's a cop-out. Maybe I'm all too familiar with these logics, shamefully empathetic to them, or afraid to speak. My white masculinity does not feel so powerful this week. I want to scream, cry, argue, or protect myself with emotions I am not allowed to express in this space, this body, or this role. I listen, stilled, "neutral," fighting to convey the poised "objectivity" my students so admire. I close the discussion with a few questions to reflect upon and run out the door to a meeting that I make up on the fly. After all, next week is a new topic, a new frame, and a whole new set of potential borders, alliances, and "thems."

The subsequent months following the immigration debates in Arizona provide endless opportunities to place my, Kimberlee's, body alongside my politics, to directly engage rhetorics of the border in action. I opt for the coolness of the classroom: the careful yet distanced alliance of provoking dialogue in academic spaces that are sheltered but not protected, yet distanced from the streets. I excuse my students' absences, encourage them to participate publicly in the protests, subversively and directly advocate the action of those who choose it. I want to be there but feel bound by the powers and authority of the administration. E-mails circulate in anticipation of the rallies, reminding us of the terms of our contract to not cancel classes, to uphold our agreements to "teach." What am I teaching? The untenable position of academic surveillance is uncomfortable but not impossible. I follow the lead of my experience as an undergraduate during the 2003 war on Iraq: some professors and students had formed a Peace and Justice coalition against the war and planned to hold a walkout on the day bombs dropped. United together, we simultaneously held different relations to the institution. While students missed out on attendance or scheduled work, for professors a walkout violated their contracts and threatened their positions. Many, then, while supporting the walkout, held classes. Here I am the teacher. Do I place my body alongside my allies in the street? Risk visibility? Perform resistant vulnerability? My activist allies voice suspicion about what's possible inside the classroom. I face division once again. Defeat and uncertainty creep in. Am I complicit in the production of neoliberal subjectivities? Do I maintain the nation-state through a liberal education? Is there potential for resistance? I redirect my lesson plan to tilt us toward the issues. Fear of falling, fear of failing, we consume and produce our narratives that keep us inside and keep us distant.

As these narratives demonstrate, we are never one thing; never singularly gay or lesbian, teacher or student, racialized white or of color. While we might identify ourselves as one thing in any one encounter, these categories swiftly dissolve, overlap, and intersect.

The US/Mexican border, seemingly so far from our reality, was a struggle to get to—to touch, feel, comprehend. Our process drove us to the borders we could feel, the borders we learned and do. Dusty grew up in a very white suburb that instilled logics of inside and outside, safe parts of town and unsafe parts of town, "our" people and others. These borders attempt to legislate who can be tied to whom, which relations matter and which do not. Cultural borders mark "friends" and "real families," designating these "labels" with meanings that fail to account for "us"—Dusty and Kimberlee's queer intimacy. Historical borders dictate ancestry, as Kimberlee fights to claim a history that whiteness works to erase—sanitizing its threat. Religious borders are drawn on earth and in heaven, and racial borders are scripted through significations of body, voice, accent, name, and affinity. Gendered and heterosexed borders police the ways our bodies are read in relation and apart. Academic borders hold us together, yet sever us apart from so many others in a hierarchy we rarely speak of. Economic borders work to naturalize our interactions with other borders through the workings of consumption, consumer, and authority. National borders are deployed daily on our TV sets, positioning us in a chair of citizenship, judgment, and entitlement. So many lines at work, being worked, in our lives that inform, shape, and uphold borders seemingly so far away. We worked to visualize this web, and to learn the ways it choreographs our relations, movements, and bodily doings so that we might make this choreography visible and place pressure at its demands, push back, dance outside, and across its lines. Moving to staged performance, our integration of performance methodologies allows us to intersect narrative with embodied movement, images with text, to communicate the simultaneous intertextual layers that are difficult to present on the page.

Bodies without Borders: Utopian Imaginaries

Border rhetorics viscerally calibrate Othering, facilitate hostility, provoke suspicion, and tend to incapacitate dialogue. We find through our experiences above, as well as in other academic settings, that identity categories are often deployed when dialoging about border rhetorics. While Spivak instructs us as to the political efficacy of strategic essentialism, or strategic identity rhetoric, in moments such as those detailed above border rhetorics work to distance us from one another rather than bring us closer. The risk, we find, is the conflation of identity with experience as a move to either discount or solidify a particular position. For example, in our collaboration, during tense moments of considering volatile topics and experiences Kimberlee sometimes relies on her Mexican ancestry to collapse her distance from the border to enforce a particular position. In this moment her Chicana identity is conflated with an alliance with immigrants, an experience she knows little of. Rather than effect an alliance, in reflection it is a move that is enabled through the distance procured by the privileges afforded her through whiteness. Likewise, Dusty's move into a Latino neighborhood while simultaneously blocking out his neighbors is a choice, a claimed distance, entitlement, and mobilization calibrated through whiteness. Rather than position us collectively in reflection of our similarities and differences, we retreat from one another through identity politics. These uncomplicated claims that position us closer to or farther away from the border simultaneously reify and substantiate OUR distance from the border. It positions us on either side of a line. It's a tension we interrogate through performance.

Projected images flicker behind us, of immigrant bodies policed, contained, and disciplined geographically, filmed as fuzzy infrared movements violating spatial plans, stepping over, running across, pulled back. On stage, we explore the multiple borders that connect, distance, define, and constrain us. As critical academics, "we" glide across the dance floor with suspicious ease. As dear friends, our "I"s and "you"s are patient, flawed, but contextualized, narrating stories of discomfort, dissonance, anxiety, ambivalence, hurt, and resentment. We are academics. We are US citizens. We live our lives with an authority and mobility granted by vocabularies, degrees, and an affective performance of American citizen (see Cisneros, this volume) that produces belonging (and entitlement). We audience and engage each other's stories with suspicion, questions, complications, and discovery. The "us" is always tied to a delicate temporality, a commitment to stay in the room when comfort, patience, connection, identity, and/or identification break down. Yet always, in the shifting dimensions of our interrogations, there remains an unnameable "them" beyond our own borders, which always ties us together, pulls us close, and separates us out.

By inviting the audience into these multiple borders that connect and sustain us, we sought to rupture illusions of distance. It is a project of self-reflexive investigation, due to an understanding that for us to speak to (and thus "at") the border was dangerous. Rather, we chose to examine how we—both as an "us" and two individual "I"s with unique experiences—produce, benefit, and sustain border discourses through our affective and embodied interactions. From "disrespected" neighbor and childhood cruelty on the playground, to neighborhood watches and a Mexican father's insistence that "my babies are white," our stories narrate the ways we embody, perform, and reify borders. We invite the audience into a complicated and uncomfortable dialogue with hopes of continuing a self-reflexive discussion, a discussion in which we don't get to say the right thing and walk away, a discussion in which neither one of us is an innocent bystander, a victim, or a well-intentioned worker of good. These trappings support the distancing of borders and erase our daily bordering performances.

On stage, we explore what it might look and feel like to move through and beyond the identity and national boundaries we often cling to—the surrendering of entitlement, privilege, boundary, and definition between self and relation. It's a temporal and future-driven utopian imaginary, one that cannot be fully sustained or withheld, yet we aim to potentialize a different way of thinking of self in relation to other in the effort of coalitional work, a political commitment to work across difference without collapsing that difference. It is a project committed to working past the trapping of this bordered and limited present (Muñoz, *Cruising Utopia*), reimagining logics of citizenship and home to connect bodies across spatial and discursive borders that work to sever and designate what is and is not "our" problem—who are and are not "our" people (Sandoval). That concept of coalitional work sat at the heart of our project, not as an ideal but a process. We move together and apart, aligned and disconnected, in a frustrated act of love and commitment. The fears, angers, resentments, and dissonance we faced, conjured up in one another, and put on the table were always about coming together, standing together, yet the movement to that togetherness was not linear or unidirectional. Standing together is a temporal gesture, not frozen in time, but ever-present with tensions, ruptures, hesitation, and risk. Yet, to stand and commit: this was our performative utopian imaginary, gesturing and potentializing a future nation and identity reconfigured through queer intimacy, love, and kinship. At the end of our performance, having removed differing artifacts of gendered, raced, and national identity, we stand across from one another in silence. With curiosity and care we explore each other's body. A recorded, shared narration plays in the background, cataloging the difficulty, the paradox of longing for a queered future as it intersects with present discourses. We end with silence, in darkness, and in an embrace. We map a hesitant utopian gesture, a hope, and a moment of suspension gesturing elsewhere, through this self-reflexive and dialogic investigation. Yet the staging of this process was not in spectacle or sheer imaginary, but pedagogical and process driven. The space of silence, of performance, holds our utopian imaginary—a gesture to a future not yet possible, but one that our performance seeks to potentialize (Muñoz, *Cruising Utopia*).

While we as performers/academics occupy our citizenship with privilege and leverage in our daily lives and are largely without threat, we also poke holes in the illusion of security and of the sanctity of citizenship. Kimberlee narrates the surveillance of her body as a woman as she moves throughout the world and as a queer woman kissing her girlfriend in public. Dusty challenges how mediated discourse interpellates him as US citizen, through enmeshed anti-immigrant and self-hating anti-queer logics, casting him as "full citizen" and "evil threat" at once. There are degrees of citizenship that posit us in alliance with immigrants—not equated to be sure, but in a certain alliance that the performance gestures toward through dismantling the unifying logic of American. Animating utopia through the remapping and reimagining of borders is necessarily a political tool and though it doesn't necessarily place our bodies next to immigrants in physical or intimate relational proximity, it does expand space in ways that challenge discursive formations that aim at solidifying their differences and distances of citizenship, relation, and identity.

Conclusions: Identifications, Identity, and Remapping of Distances

We aimed to unearth affective dimensions of whiteness, our investments in and production through whiteness, and how whiteness works to shape, define, and constrain all of those interpellated into constructions of US citizenry and identity—these lines in the sand. While we invoke discourses of immigration and even posit the complexity and certain impossibility of those relations, we look to performance as a site to rescript ourselves, our audiences, and immigrants in politicized and reimagined relation to one another. By attending to embodied experiences, our performance imaginary pushes at the edges of the border rhetorics and identity politics that shape us. We, in turn, sought out avenues and strategies to challenge and rethink the bordered discourses of the present, in a commitment to hope that potentializes a future not yet imaginable (Muñoz, *Cruising Utopia*).

Our temporal remapping of identity, spatial relations, and border discourses is surely a contested approach, loaded with obstacles, fears, anxieties, and suspicions for our multiple audiences and us. Differing spaces and audiences brought differing reactions, from suspicion and soberness to celebration and laughter. Levels of audience resistance were fueled through strong identifications with *either* "him" or "her," the white guy and the Chicana, weary of our temporal assertion of a politicized "us." These severing identifications across identity systems lubricate a prying apart of us from one another, a stabilizing of individuated rather than relational personas.

The politics of recognition seemingly led to some audience members locating Kimberlee as only a Mexican American woman, one upon whom they can narrate their own stories, engage themes of Mexican American identity (making no mention of Kimberlee's queerness or Dusty at all). Other audience members engage Dusty's body and story solely through frames of white US masculinity, finding identification with and through border anxieties, apprehension in racial discussion, fears and losses through constructions of whiteness, and subtle angers unearthed through the challenging of tacit (and violent) privileges. At the same time, Kimberlee's proximity to whiteness enables a politics of recognition with some anti-racist and/or liberal white men through which other forms of identification occur, framing her as the reasonable, mild-tempered, light-skinned, and palatable woman of color. Both spoken and unspoken in audience interactions, these moments indicate how whiteness haunts the production of the performance and the politics of reception in ways that we can neither anticipate nor control.

Such identifications offer productive avenues to locate affective dimensions of border discourses and self-reflexive opportunities to examine how we all perform borders. However, when the divisions between "he" and "she" are reinscribed, thus resisting the coalitional potentials of "us," there is a glossing over of the queer/relational politics of the piece. Identity politics work against the suturing of distances between multiple "us"s and "them"s. Perhaps such responses are indicative of whiteness, emphasizing and reproducing individualism, and rejecting relationality in the service of preserving discrete identities and particular identity discourses.

After all, discourse resists its own interrogation, reifying concretized divides, by designating who is allowed to enter the discussion, who these bodies are within this discussion, which bodies and relations we are connected to, and which bodies we are not. Questions such as "who are we to engage these discussions?" mark territories that need to be remapped, for as we have sought to demonstrate, we all do the border, just as the border does each of us. Audiences should and must engage "us" with suspicion, yet fully retreating to the discourses of "she" and "he" only reifies and substantiates difference, disconnection, and the individualistic workings of whiteness. The turn to performance is an attempt to suture discursive distance, asking audiences to enter this discussion through their bodies, unearthing and interrogating the layers of fear, guilt, shame, anger, and privilege we struggle to work through. It's an invitation, both to self-reflexive investigation and utopian relational imaginaries.

We are conscious that our audiences, our discussions, and our epistemological productions do not necessarily bring us any closer to the bodies of immigrants. They are invoked discursively through mediated images, through our narrations of distance from them and the discursive productions that posit us in relation to them. Again, this is about choice; we do not have to locate our bodies in relation to immigrants or to discussions of the border. The discourse privileges us through this distance, this removal. We are both confined, yet not fully defined, within systems of whiteness. Rejecting the cool-headed rationality of tail-between-our-legs liberal guilt, we stand together in risk, love, conflict, and commitment as we continue developing vocabularies about the movement, presence, and day-to-day performances that sustain and uphold so many borders—how we do border, how the border does us, and how "we" are connected to, connected by, and pried apart through larger discourse. "Lines in the Sand" aimed to construct a physical space where the anxieties of borders and difference could be renegotiated, reimagined, and rearticulated—rewriting politicized discourses of affinity, kinship, and nation and through a utopian imaginary where and when our alliances and proximities to one another rupture the bordering discourses and the present and cast us elsewhere.

Notes

The authors/performers worked together in the generation and revision of this chapter, and would like to explicitly mark equal contributions, rather than offering a designation of a lead author.

1. At times, critical scholarship tends toward analysis of discourse that can be abstract or distanced from concrete lived experience. At other times, eth-

nographies provide insight and strategies to resist power from lived experience. While we both recognize the value of these methodologies and at times rely on them ourselves, we also find performance methodologies to be a critical and productive point of entry into analyzing discourse and lived experience, including our own. In this chapter, we rely on personal narrative and reflection to accomplish this. Performance studies in communication has a long history of using personal narratives as a strategy both to *do* the work of theorizing, critical reflection, and resistance (Langellier, "Personal Narrative") as well as to place narratives alongside larger discourses (Corey, "Personal"). While these often focus on the individual in relation (Langellier and Peterson), elsewhere we (Pérez and Goltz) have developed the idea of collaborative personal narrative, or the generation of personal narrative between two people in relationship to extend the personal. In placing our stories and experiences next to one another and dialoging and reflecting on them through our relation and in collaboration (here and in performance), we pry apart the personal to ask further questions of identity construction and relationships, and to confront the intersection of border rhetorics and personal experience.

2. In this volume, Lisa A. Flores and Mary Ann Villarreal read the 1948 case of Delgado v. Bastrop Independent School District to theorize the dynamic production of whiteness as a marker of difference. In this desegregation case, the plaintiffs' challenge to segregation of children relied on linguistic strategies that marked their proximity to whiteness. The children were referred to as being of Mexican descent or extraction rather than "Mexican," which was always used in quotations. This strategy, Flores and Villarreal argue, of utilizing the language of extraction or descent discursively distances them from both Mexican and immigrant and moves them closer to whiteness. While the decision to desegregate was ultimately not made on that particular argument, it certainly points us to the ways in which whiteness works as an organizing principle. Even where border rhetorics prevail in producing a white/brown binary of difference, we see the ways in which whiteness shifts to integrate and outcast different people in different moments.

3. Following the arguments laid out by Flores and Villarreal, we see that Kimberlee's family deliberately worked to distance itself from being Mexican and therefore placed in closer proximity to whiteness. While they moved from Texas to Michigan, we might see them moving farther and farther away from their brownness as the Midwest at that time was predominantly organized by a white/black binary. They would not have made "sense" as black, even though they were clearly not white. Kimberlee's own distance from Mexicanness, and her ancestry, doesn't necessarily place her securely in brown or white categories. In the instance of an immigration rally, her identity is mul-

tiply complex: on the one hand, border rhetorics produce her phenotypically white body, placing her closer to whiteness and its privileges and farther away from brownness/immigrants. On the other hand, to a Minuteman or white supremacist on the outskirts of the rally she would be excluded from whiteness and be seen as a traitor. The point here is to remind us that racial and identity markers are always relational and contextual.

4. The increasing rhetorical and physical violence of border rhetorics against immigrants has possibly contributed to the shift of resistance at rallies of signs from "We Are American" to "We Are Human." That people feel compelled to mark their humanity is not only a terrifying state of affairs but a clear signification that they are not seen as human in all contexts. The dehumanization of immigrants follows a similar logic of differentiation and dehumanization of lesbian, gay, bisexual, transgender, and queer (LGBTQ) persons (Butler, *Undoing Gender*). However, as this example shows, rather than working as a catalyst for coalition and solidarity among groups that are similarly cast out of belonging and in some ways citizenship, it serves as a further divide. As a marker of identity, this discrete example also further cements the discursive borders between immigrant and queer.

V
Media Circuits

11

Transborder Politics

The Embodied Call of Conscience in *Traffic*

Brian L. Ott and Diane M. Keeling

In 1969, President Richard Nixon sought to curb the manufacturing, distribution, and use of controlled substances by initiating a "War on Drugs." Following the launch of this initiative, "the US-Mexico border became . . . the frontline in a never-ending war between the US government and the drug-smuggling cartels" (Payan 23). In the ensuing years, the War on Drugs has been central not only to US foreign policy with Mexico, but also to public perceptions of the US-Mexico border itself. For many US Americans, the border is experienced, and thus understood, chiefly through film and other popular media. Consequently, citizens' attitudes toward the border, their border politics, are powerfully shaped by popular images of the border. Given that the US-Mexico border is one of the most "frequently screened landscapes of North America" (dell'Agnese 204), there is no shortage of cinematic representations that contribute to how the border is rhetorically constructed in the public imagination.

One of the most significant is Steven Soderbergh's celebrated 2001 drama, *Traffic*. The importance of this film is evident across two registers: timing and critical acclaim. Though the US-Mexico border has been a site of tension since the 1848 signing of the Treaty of Guadalupe Hidalgo, which demarcated national boundaries, the issue of drug trafficking has been a matter of particular public anxiety and political contention in the late twentieth and early twenty-first centuries. Notably, *Traffic* "was released during a time when the border was experiencing the most militarization since its inception" (Beckham 140). The political import of the film owes not simply to its apposite timing, however, but also to its considerable popularity and commercial success.

Although numerous films have taken up the issue of drug trafficking in recent years (see dell'Agnese 205), few have done so as compellingly as *Traffic*—a film extolled as "a powerful overview of the contemporary drug culture" (McCarthy). Grossing over $124 million domestically, *Traffic* garnered four Academy Awards (Best Director, Best Editing, Best Actor in a Supporting Role, and Best Adapted Screenplay), as well as a nomination for

Best Picture. Michelle Brown attributes the success of the film to "its successful invocation of deeply-held American values and moral systems" (21). Identifying and assessing the precise contours of those values and moral systems is the central aim of this chapter.

Despite its noteworthy critical acclaim and resounding commercial success, *Traffic* has not been without its detractors. Beckham argues, for instance, that the film portrays Mexico as subordinate to the United States and reproduces a number of damaging ethnic stereotypes (131). Other scholars have also lamented the limiting depiction of Mexico and minorities within the film (e.g., Michelle Brown, dell'Agnese, Shaw). But even as *Traffic* perpetuates some stereotypes, it challenges others. Not all Anglo-Americans are celebrated as infallible, nor are all minorities villainized, for instance (Shaw 221). Since several critics have already carefully studied the film's representations of race and ethnicity, the primary focus of our investigation concerns the processes of decision making, moral character, and rhetorics of conscience that emerge in the border politics of the film.

As the title implies, *Traffic* is about movements, passages, and above all border crossings. It is about the unrelenting flow of drugs across all manner of boundaries: national (US-Mexico), cultural (race, class, and gender), and corporeal (individual bodies). Though boundaries are typically seen as impediments to mobility, *Traffic* suggests that, at least in the War on Drugs, borders are so permeable and porous—so indistinct and indiscriminate— that they are utterly ineffectual in regulating and controlling the flow of illicit substances. Soderbergh's film, then, sees little chance of the $19 billion-a-year drug war being won or even improved on policy grounds or through law enforcement (Ebert). Instead, *Traffic* advocates a personal perspective, urging viewers to focus on the individuals and communities afflicted by drugs. To advance this perspective, the film appeals to conscience as embodied in the actions of its lead characters. "Ultimately told from the point of view of individual actors," explains Michelle Brown, "the film's [rhetorical] effectiveness relies a good deal on its ability to build a structural narrative through empathetic, individual characters" (20). Collectively, the actions and decision-making processes of these characters participate in *Traffic*'s rhetoric of conscience, which we contend, while complex in effect, generally fosters and promotes a transborder politics rooted in the protection and nurturing of children.

In support of this argument, our chapter proceeds in three stages. First, we identify the relationship between bodies and borders in the film, attending to the framing techniques that structure the cinematic experience. Second, we move to a discussion of the three main characters in *Traffic*, each of whom must make moral choices concerning their lives and their communities. Finally, we analyze the film's rhetoric of conscience as articulated through the embodied decision-making processes of its primary characters.

Bodies and Borders

Space is necessarily a bodily experience: an emplacement. The location of the body in space is governed by boundaries, by the distinction between inside and outside. In this view, the body is a container with clear borders—borders that hold the materials (infectious pollutants) of its surrounding environment at bay. Though borders have material entailments, the regulatory processes of demarcating between inside and outside are largely symbolic. Borders are social structures, then, that require "a high degree of conscious control" and "a high level of formality" to maintain (Douglas 86). In the iterative practices of maintaining borders between inside and outside (Self and Other), there is simultaneously a desire for and fear of border crossings. This ambivalence fuels the inevitable anxiety surrounding borders.

To the extent that individual bodies are reflective of any bounded system (Douglas 74), the bodies in *Traffic* function synecdochically for (trans) national politics. The film's central theme is a geopolitical account of drug trafficking as depicted through the choreography of multiple characters, each embodying a different element of the drug trade: Javier Rodriguez-Rodriguez (Benicio Del Toro) is a committed law enforcement official; Robert Wakefield (Michael Douglas) is a father and politician; and Helena Ayala (Catherine Zeta-Jones) is a mother and socialite turned drug distributor. *Traffic* is a film about the lives and motives of these three characters, each of whom confronts challenging moral dilemmas.

Traffic covers extended territory, "sprawling from the slums of Mexico to the corridors of power of Washington, DC" (dell'Agnese 214). But as important as "territory" is to the film, the ways that characters occupy and move through space are even more crucial. This is communicated by the film's signature use of three filters: sepia, blue, and transparent. Each photographic filter, we contend, indicates a spatial "orientation"—its entailing logic, rather than the place itself. A number of critics have suggested that the filters' purpose is to stabilize the portrayal of both place and characters (see Beckham 138–39; Brown 19; dell'Agnese 214; Shaw 218), but Washington and Cincinnati are not consistently shot in blue, and several characters are shot through different filters at various points in the film. Thus, we argue that the filters reflect the basic orientation of the characters' embodied emplacements, which is fluid throughout the film. Attending to these orientations reveals the inner workings of the rhetoric of conscience within the text.

Confusion regarding the filters arises, in part, because the homes of the characters living in Mexico and San Diego never change from their correlated colors—sepia and transparent, respectively. All scenes south of the US-Mexico border, for instance, are shot using a sepia lens, also known as a tobacco filter. This creates a dirty, gritty, grainy, and washed-out mise-en-scène, as though the entire landscape has been scorched by the sun. The yellowish hue of the sepia filter, which is equated with the corruption of the drug cartels, evokes a sense of stillness and immobility (Kandinsky 40), suggesting that the drug situation is bleak and unchangeable. The majority of people live modestly, and the bodies shown tend to be light brown, unless they are tourists or US government officials on visits. That the corresponding dialogue in these scenes is in Spanish lends an air of authenticity to the images and invites spectators to see them as unmediated reality—Mexico as it "really" is.

Scholars have been critical of Soderbergh's representation of Mexico and, by extension, his use of the sepia filter since it evokes chiefly negative associations. In framing Mexico as both the *source* of drugs and the *location* of governmental corruption, the film urges the audience to see Mexico as a place of infection and illegality, of infiltration and immorality. Commenting on the sepia filter, Porton explains, Mexico "becomes a mirage-like, evanescent realm where life is cheap and morality is infinitely expendable" (42). Though a few images and scenes within the film challenge this perspective, they are, nonetheless, the exceptions, and it is not hard to understand why academics have been so critical of the film's portrayal of Mexico and Latino/as. Generally, the sepia "orientation" is a signifier that the social order is unjust, unprincipled, and unchanging.

The blue filter is, by contrast, used to frame locations in the United States, namely Cincinnati, Ohio, and Washington, DC, though it is less strongly correlated with place than the sepia filter. Blue is regarded as a cool color, and according to Kandinsky, it draws away from the spectator, fostering a sense of distance and detachment (37–38). In *Traffic*, the blue filter is associated with legal and political institutions; it suggests a rational approach to drug trafficking in which the impulse is to legislate and police the flow of drugs. The blue filter favors a cool rationalism that downplays affective attachments and sympathies in favor of logical, calculated responses to social problems. In doing so, it erases social, cultural, and historical complexities, suggesting naïvely that drug trafficking can be addressed uniformly through policy and police intervention. The film, however, is no less skeptical of the simplistic rationality of US-led initiatives bathed in blue hues than of the unbridled corruption of the Mexican government and the illegal actions of drug cartels coded in yellow.

The third and final filter is transparent, and appears in mostly liminal spaces between the cool (blue) rationality of US governmental institutions and the dirty (yellow) underbelly of the Mexican drug trade. The clarity of the third lens (re)presents the harsh reality in which these two worlds and their corresponding logics collide, where order is infected and disrupted, and the drug trade confronts the law and sanctions. Through this orientation, the "reality" of the War on Drugs is played out on US soil. Because legal institutions are cast as impotent, these scenes occur in homes and on streets rather than in courtrooms, and they privilege family and community over institutions. The transparent lens suggests a hybridized landscape that blends two sides/logics into what Gibbs has called "Amexica" (42) and Anzaldúa has described as "the lifeblood of two worlds [that] form a third country—a border culture . . . [a] vague and undetermined place [that is] in a constant state of transition" (25). Correspondingly, there is greater fluidity, and racial stereotypes are less strongly pronounced. The transparent, or unfiltered, lens is most commonly correlated with San Diego, but also includes moments where typically "blue" characters, such as Robert and his wife, confront the difficulties of competing logics.

Embodied (Border) Politics

Structurally, *Traffic*'s narrative unfolds in relation to three principal characters, whose stories and experiences intersect around various aspects of the US-Mexico drug trade (e.g., policing, parenting, and distribution). As each character confronts and negotiates difficult moral choices, his or her decision-making process fashions a particular rhetoric of conscience. In this section, we identify those rhetorics in relation to the embodied actions of the film's three major characters: Javier Rodriguez-Rodriguez, Robert Wakefield, and Helena Ayala. Our argument is that Soderbergh's film—using the War on Drugs as anecdote—advances a rhetoric of conscience, a model for behaving morally in the face of the "not-yet of the future" (Hyde, *Life-Giving Gift* xiii), and, in the process, promotes a particular border politics. We examine the lead characters in the order in which they appear in the film.

Javier Rodriguez-Rodriguez

Javier is a Mexican police officer who lives alone near Tijuana just south of the US-Mexico border. Although he is never shown with a family of his own, he is close to his partner Manolo Sanchez (Jacob Vargas) and Manolo's wife, Ana (Marisol Padilla Sánchez). When Javier is south of the border he is filmed through the sepia filter, but when he travels north he is filmed through the transparent lens. Amid rampant governmental corruption, Javier is an honest and dedicated officer. But his efforts to curb the drug trade prove largely futile. Despite his relative ineffectualness, especially early in the film, Javier is a concerned, committed, and conscientious law enforcement official.

Traffic's opening scene begins with a wide-angle shot of the desert landscape littered with drought-distressed shrubbery and weeds. An unmarked police car is barely visible in the distance. Though spectators cannot yet see inside the automobile, they hear the voices of its occupants. Speaking in Spanish (accompanied by English subtitles), Javier describes a dream to Manolo. In the dream, Javier's mother is suffocating, but he is unable to save her—a symbolic expression of his inability to liberate Mexico from the suffocating grip of the drug trade. As the two talk, a plane flies overhead and lands in the distance. Shortly thereafter, a white cargo truck approaches. Javier and Manolo stop the truck, revealing the large drug shipment it is hauling for transport across the border. The officers arrest the smugglers and confiscate the cargo truck. The use of handheld cameras throughout the scene fosters a feeling of uneasiness and instability.

While in route to the police station to book the smugglers, General Salazar (Tomas Milian), head of the state police unit and federal drug forces, and his men surround Javier and Manolo in four black SUVs. Salazar commends Javier on his "excellent job," but explains that he will take over the investigation from there. The drug smugglers are transferred to the black Suburbans, and the cargo truck is impounded. The General asks Javier how he knew about the operation, but Javier refuses to disclose his sources.

Although Salazar is head of federal drug forces, he is acting covertly on behalf of the Juarez cartel in Mexico City (against a rival cartel in Tijuana). After learning of this corruption, Javier urges Manolo not to disclose this information to authorities out of fear for their safety. In an earlier scene, US Drug Enforcement Administration (DEA) agents approached Javier and invited him to work as a US informant. He declines to cooperate, however, due to the agents' approach and ambiguous intentions. The agents attempt to entice Javier with money to give up information about the Mexican cartels, but Javier takes offense at their assumption that he can be bribed. Javier responds, "You like baseball? We need lights for the parks, so kids can play at night. So they can play baseball. So they don't become *burros para los malones* [donkeys for the mobs]. Everybody likes baseball. Everybody likes parks."

In this scene, Javier puts the welfare of his local community ahead of himself (and personal monetary gain). He is reluctant to assist the DEA unless it benefits Mexico as well as the United States. In particular, Javier demonstrates concern for Mexican children, whom he does not want to see get caught up in the drug trade. Though Javier, unlike Helena and Robert, is not a parent, his actions are nevertheless guided by a commitment to the safety of children and future generations. This intersubjective stance is the "constitutive dimension" of moral life (Todorov 286), and Javier emerges as the most moral character in the film.

Going against Javier's advice, Manolo schedules a meeting with people whom he believes to be US officials to discuss his newly acquired information. The persons who meet him, however, work for Salazar. They kidnap him and throw him into a car where Javier is already captive. Manolo and Javier are driven deep into the desert and forced at gunpoint to dig their own graves. Manolo is killed, but Javier is spared because he was not caught snitching. As a consequence of Manolo's death, however, Javier decides to become a US informant.

Feeling as though he has no other options, Javier resorts to working with the DEA—an ambivalent choice, causing him to "feel like a traitor." After a detailed on-the-record interview, Javier perceives his actions as betraying his heritage. While Javier's collaboration with the United States potentially reinforces the idea that "the good Mexican cop can only get results if he works for the US agency" (Shaw 219), it is also a moment of border blurring, where the "sides" and their interests no longer seem at odds. Indeed, the film's final scene—a children's baseball game in Mexico—seems to suggest that Javier's actions have made positive contributions across these communities. As one critic explains, Javier "succeeds in bringing prevention and vision to his troubled community in the form of baseball, all in an anonymous, lonely silence" (Michelle Brown 21). But this final scene, filmed in sepia, suggests there is still much work to be done.

Robert Wakefield

Formerly an Ohio Supreme Court judge, Robert has recently been promoted to US Drug Czar by the president. In his new position, he is depicted as idealistic and naïve. Though Robert is the only character seen in all three spatial orientations, he primarily occupies a blue, institutional perspective, especially when enacting his position as the head of national drug control policy. While being trained for his new role, Robert is introduced to his staff and learns how the system works. The primary advice he receives, as communicated by the previous czar, is how to sweep the drug problem under the table. Robert's new job, viewers overhear, has a high turnover rate and is rarely rewarded. Laments the previous czar, "I'm not sure I made the slightest difference. I tried. I really did." Robert is undeterred by the pessimistic view of his predecessor, however, and unsympathetic toward him for having given up hope.

The first time Robert is depicted through a transparent lens, and thus framed as beginning to understand the complexity of the drug problem, he is attending a social gathering in Washington, DC, where he is officially introduced as the new Drug Czar. As he meets and mingles with politicians, lobbyists, and other White House staff, he is offered unsolicited advice and information: the problem cannot be solved on the supply side because there is demand in US cities; it is not a war with traditional winners and losers; 25 percent of high school students use drugs—a number that can be reduced but not erased; the price of coke and heroin is dropping; law enforcement makes it easier for kids to get pure drugs cheaper; reporters do not care about education, rehabilitation, or prevention—they just want to see the gory aspects of the war.

Disheartened, Robert returns to his home in Cincinnati, where he is, again, viewed through the blue filter. Unbeknownst to Robert, his daughter, Caroline (Erika Christensen), is already headed down the path of drug addiction—the use of the blue filter suggesting that governmental and legal institutions are utterly ineffectual in combating drug use, as they cannot even protect the Drug Czar's own daughter. Caroline is exposed to hard drugs by a school friend, Seth (Topher Grace), with whom she begins freebasing cocaine. Significantly, Caroline's early drug use is shot using the transparent lens, stressing the complexity of the US drug problem—one that cannot easily be explained in terms of victims and perpetrators (Michelle Brown 21). Is Caroline an innocent casualty of the drug trade, or is she part of the problem, actively enabling it through her own drug habit?

During this period, Robert is rarely home, focusing instead on his official responsibilities and pursuing public strategies for the War on Drugs both at the border (San Diego and El Paso, which are framed with the transparent lens) and south of the border (Mexico City, which is shot through the sepia filter). His attempts to gather intelligence, however, only complicate "winning" the War on Drugs. When Robert learns that his daughter is using narcotics, he disagrees with his wife, Barbara (Amy Irving), about how to address the issue, creating a tension between supporting responsible experimentation (his wife's position) and enforcing complete abstention (Robert's position). This is one of the few family scenes shot through a transparent lens. Robert passes up the opportunity to understand Caroline's desire to experiment with drugs and, instead, has her cleared of recent drug-related charges and sends her to rehab, which reinitiates the blue filter. But the enforced abstinence fails to help her, as she runs away from the rehab center, sells her body for drugs, and lives off the streets to feed her addiction.

Upon learning that his daughter is missing, Robert returns home and begins searching for her—the blue filter framing these scenes. After a failed effort to locate her, the framing of Robert shifts to a transparent lens, signifying a realization that the US-Mexico border is not the only site in the War on Drugs, but that families and local communities are sites as well. After nearly giving up, Robert discovers that several valuable possessions are missing from his home, renewing his hope that Caroline is still alive. Forcing the assistance of his daughter's friend Seth, he begins searching for her again. Traversing the urban environment, Seth lectures Robert about his simple view of the drug trade and his reductive understanding of the perpetrators. Eventually, Robert locates Caroline in a filthy hotel, where she has been pimped out to a middle-aged white businessman. Her subsequent recovery is filmed with the blue filter, an orientation that remains with Robert and his family for the remainder of the film.

After locating his daughter, Robert returns to DC to give a press conference on recent developments concerning the Mexican drug cartels. The speech he prepares is filled with platitudes, war metaphors, and binaristic thinking, reinforcing the idea that the War on Drugs can be won. As he delivers his speech, however, he becomes increasingly unsettled and unable to continue with his prepared message. Recognizing the shallowness of his own rhetoric, Robert concludes by resigning his post as Drug Czar, returning to his family in Cincinnati, and attending rehabilitation meetings with his wife to support their daughter.

Helena Ayala

Helena is a glamorous socialite who frequents country club luncheons and charity events. She is six months pregnant and lives in an upscale community overlooking San Diego beaches. She appears to be Latina (Zeta-Jones is Welsh), though she does not have a discernible Spanish accent. Helena is shot through a clear lens (except while in Mexico), designating her liminality and extraordinarily complex relation to the drug trade. She is initially oblivious of her husband Carlos's (Steven Bauer) drug business and the source of her family's fortune. So, when he is arrested, she is physically shaken by what she believes to be false charges. Genuinely concerned for her husband, her vulnerability resonates with the audience.

Helena eventually learns from Carlos's business partner that he is a major player in drug trafficking operations from Mexico to the United States. She is shocked and confused upon learning this and initially takes no action.

But after her family's bank accounts are frozen, the bills begin to pile up and she struggles to maintain her extravagant lifestyle. Gradually, she is ostracized by her neighbors and community. Though her economic troubles seem trivial given her standard of living (and how it was achieved), the audience's empathy is maintained by her clear desire to raise her children in a safe community, unlike the one in which she was reared. Despite this desire, Helena's son is kidnapped while playing on the beach, and she is told by his abductors that he will be killed if she does not repay her husband's $3 million debt to the Tijuana drug cartel.

Unable to acquire $3 million by legal means, Helena takes over her husband's drug smuggling business while he is incarcerated. This decision implies that she does not trust the government to protect her family and that preventing her husband from going to jail is more important than obeying the law. Continuing her husband's business plan, she meets with a member of the Tijuana cartel and explains a new way to transport cocaine across the border, ironically titled "The Project for the Children." The "project" disguises cocaine in doll form through a high-impact, pressure-molding process. To guarantee that the dolls are indeed cocaine, a cartel member insists that Helena test it. Citing her pregnancy, she refuses, causing him to terminate the deal. Holding steadfast to her highest value, the protection of her unborn child, she gets up to leave. The cartel member relents and tries the cocaine himself. Using savvy negotiating skills, she clears her husband's debt, becomes the sole distributor of the Tijuana cartel's product in the United States, and has the principal witness in her husband's court case assassinated.

After her husband's trial is dismissed due to the death of this witness, Helena resumes her former life. Unconcerned about her husband's business practices, she hosts a party for her son at their house in the final scene. Her story concludes rather ambivalently, however, as a DEA officer, whose partner was killed as a result of Helena's plot to have the witness murdered, plants a bug in the family's household. Viewers are consequently left wondering if Helena's choices will ultimately have negative ramifications for her and her family. Though the outcome for Helena is uncertain, it is clear that the business of drug trafficking will continue with or without the Ayala family.

A Moral Life

In the preceding section, we presented a mostly descriptive account of the moral choices made by *Traffic*'s three main characters. In this section, we analyze and assess those choices to understand the film's unique rhetoric of conscience and attendant border politics. To appreciate the consequentiality of that rhetoric, however, it is necessary to consider briefly the nature of conscience, how it is articulated, and why it matters. Conscience is a complex and challenging concept that has been a central concern of philosophers in the West since before Plato. Our understanding of the concept is grounded in the work of rhetorical scholar Michael Hyde, who draws his inspiration primarily from the philosophical work of Martin Heidegger and Emmanuel Levinas. For Hyde, conscience is characterized by three features: its Other-directedness, its interruptive and destabilizing effect on Being, and its intrinsic rhetoricity.

Hyde asserts that *conscience* or the "call for responsible thought and action" (*Life-Giving Gift* 45) originates in the "'face-to-face' encounter between the self and other" (*Call of Conscience* 8) in the "lived space of our everyday being-with-others" ("Matter of Heart" 87). From a psychoanalytic perspective, a person's Being or sense of Self (an "I") is constituted in relation to an Other (a symbolic "not-me"). When one acknowledges the Other and experiences oneself as seen through the Other, the relationship is intersubjective. By contrast, when one fails to acknowledge the Other or acts without care, concern, or thought for the well-being of the Other, one acts without conscience. To act purely out of self-interest is to fail to hear or consciously to ignore the (call of the) Other. Sounding a similar note, Tzvetan Todorov explains, "Moral life is a constitutive dimension of the intersubjective world," adding that "moral action par excellence is 'caring.' Through caring, the 'I' has as its goal the well-being of the 'you' (whether singular or multiple)" (286, 287).

Acknowledging the Other (i.e., responding to the call for recognition) is necessarily a calling into question of the Self, a de(con)struction and interruption of "self-assurance"—of the certitude of Self (Hyde and Rufo 5). Given the co-constitutive nature of Self and Other, the call of the Other is a recognition of difference, of the plurality of humanity, and thus "essentially the call of Being" (Hyde, *Life-Giving Gift* 45). The temporality of existence ensures that Being is never stable or finished. Consequently, one is always already involved in the process of (un)becoming, always being summoned by the Other. "Standing exposed to the face of the other," Hyde and Rufo explain, "the self is called out of itself, out of its preoccupation with its personal wants and priorities . . . the taken-for-granted routines and rituals that make up one's rule-governed, everyday social encounters" (16, 3). The call of the Other is felt most acutely in moments of *anxiety*, which "[disrupt] a person's conditioned and typical ways of understanding and inhabiting the world" (Hyde, *Life-Giving Gift* xiii).

Anxiety prevails at times of great disturbance and uncertainty—when "the taken-for-granted function of the world of know-how experiences an interruption" (Hyde, *Life-Giving Gift* 45). It is this interruption that issues forth the call of conscience, a call that is fundamentally rhetorical (Hyde, *Call of Conscience* 10; Hyde and Rufo 2). The presence of pain, suffering, disease, death, and/or (social) destruction that summons us to be responsible, ethical, and accountable can take a variety of forms. But one of the most potent is narrative, for "storytelling is . . . a moral activity that seeks to turn 'suffering into testimony,' and that offers itself as a response" (Hyde and Rufo 11). Thus, films that take up significant social issues and the anxieties they evoke have the capacity to function as powerful rhetorics of conscience. Such is the case with *Traffic,* a film that works to attune spectators to the tragedies of drug culture on both sides of the US-Mexico border. In enlisting viewers to acknowledge and sympathize with the Other, the film models and advocates a particular way of being-with-others.

As we noted in the introduction, *Traffic* both homogenizes and demonizes Mexico, stereotyping the country and its people as corrupt, barbaric, lawless, and threatening (see Wood 760). Film scholars have—justifiably—been overwhelmingly critical of this representation. But in their zeal to decry this image, they have largely ignored how it is deployed and functions rhetorically in the film. *Traffic* invokes these common perceptions and stereotypes not for the purpose of endorsing them, but for the purpose of deconstructing them and advancing a transborder politics. So, let us return to *Traffic's* three central characters and examine their specific moral actions.

Javier and his actions function as a cinematic trope—an invitation to hear the voice of the Other and to respond to the call of conscience. As with all of the film's main characters, Javier is a border crosser. He comes to the United States not to sell out Mexico, but to humanize it, to ask DEA agents (and viewers) to acknowledge the pain and suffering on the "other" side of the border. Appealing on behalf of Mexico's children, Javier tells the DEA agents, "The US needs to take an interest in Tijuana now." Javier's rhetoric is an indictment of self-interested and self-righteous US policies that reductively treat the United States as the sole site of human tragedy in the drug trade—an innocent victim of Mexico's drug cartels. Javier's appeal for recognition, for acknowledgment, is made all the more compelling because Javier is, as one critic has observed, "the closest character *Traffic* has to a hero . . . [and] the highest in terms of moral integrity" (Shaw 214). In identifying with Javier, viewers are asked to acknowledge the Other (side of the border), to exercise thought and compassion for future generations of children in Mexico, and consequently to question their nationalistic sense of self.

Though Judge Wakefield also spends time on both sides of the US-Mexico border, the borders he struggles with have far more to do with racialized spaces/bodies and the boundaries of public versus private than with national borders. Early in the film, Robert conceives of drug trafficking as a "faceless" public problem that can be solved through good policy and adequate enforcement. But as he is forced to confront his daughter's drug addiction and the way it has laid siege to her body, his perspective and politics shift. As Hyde and Rufo explain, "The broken body is an interruption to itself, as well as to others; it presents discomfort . . . to those who witness its dysfunction" (11). Caroline's drug-ravaged body reframes the drug problem for Robert and the audience as personal. Near the end of the film, as Wakefield in his role as Drug Czar begins to lay out his ten-point plan to "win the war on drugs," he has a moment of conscience, stops, and then says, "If there is a war on drugs, then many of our families are the enemy. And I don't know how you wage war on your own family."

Ultimately, Robert resigns his position and joins his wife in support of their daughter. His transformation from public official (and absent father) to private citizen (and concerned parent) coincides with a shift in the film from the depiction of drugs and addiction as a faceless, urban "black problem" to a familial, suburban transracial problem. Caroline's privileged, white body turned vulnerable, contaminated body is a synecdoche that rhetorically issues forth the call of conscience, saying, I am the body of the Other and I am yours. The story of Robert and his daughter invites spectators to turn the gaze inward, to consider their own complicity in social ills. Among the faces seeking acknowledgment in *Traffic* are those of family and friends. The moral message of Robert's story—that social justice begins at home by *hearing* the call of those closest to us—is evident in his final words: "My name is Robert. And my wife, Barbara, and I are here to support our daughter, Caroline. And we're here to listen."

In contrast to Javier and Robert who live on opposite sides of the US-Mexico border, Helena lives on the border itself—on the limen. For Turner, "Liminal entities are neither here nor there; they are betwixt and between the positions assigned and arrayed by law, custom, convention, and ceremonial" (95). Helena exists in an ambiguous state between the sepia-toned lawlessness of Mexico and the blue-hued legal institutions of the United States. Consequently, her moral choices and her border politics are themselves ambiguous. As Turner elaborates, "The attributes of liminality or liminal *personae* ('threshold people') are necessarily ambiguous, since this condition and these persons elude or slip through the network of classifications that normally locate states and positions in cultural space" (95). Understanding Helena's (a)moral choices, then, is challenging, for her choices do not articulate a clear, unified set of motives. Helena's actions sound a cautionary note about conscience, about how easy it is to slide from care and concern for others into self-serving and self-interested choices.

When Helena's son is kidnapped, her decision to take over her husband's drug business is framed empathetically for viewers, perhaps because it seems to be other-directed. She is acting out of genuine concern for her son. But when she arranges to have the principal witness in her husband's trial murdered, her motives no longer appear selfless. Helena's action in this regard, the film suggests, has less to do with Carlos and more to do with her unwillingness to sacrifice her lavish lifestyle. Thus, it is precisely because of her inability to think and act in a transborder way—to cross class boundaries—that she begins to make morally bereft choices. Helena's unwillingness to affirm and acknowledge the Other, whether it be the witness in her husband's trial or those of lower economic means, allows her to "justify" an unconscionable act such as murder. Explains Todorov, "evil has always consisted of denying someone his or her right to be fully human" (289). That *Traffic* would have spectators reject Helena's moral choices is signified by the strong contrast between the way her narrative ends and the manner in which Javier's and Robert's narratives end. Whereas their stories end with a sense of hope and possibility, Helena's narrative ends with a sense of impending reprisal. Through narrative juxtaposition, then, the film articulates a clear preference for Javier's and Robert's moral choices over Helena's. One important, if unintended, political consequence of this preference is that the film codes efforts to combat the drug trade as a principally masculine endeavor—a perspective that admittedly risks perpetuating a model of moral agency rooted in hegemonic masculinity.

Conclusion: Conscience and Citizenship

Steven Soderbergh's film *Traffic* stories one of the deepest anxieties of the contemporary moment—that of the US-Mexico drug trade. At the heart of this social anxiety are the border and its porousness. As Michelle Brown explains in her reading of *Traffic,* "Crossings become the central gesture in the film's most ambitious project, the incorporation of the trajectories of numerous individual lives and deaths into one larger social narrative that transcends geopolitical boundaries. This use of borders as the film's essential framing device is a crucial theoretical maneuver in that whereas the frontier implies a state center and a unidirectional movement of power, borders are permeable, perpetually being traversed, and thus tend to have a decentering effect" (20). The decentering effect described by Brown arises as the film's three primary characters traverse national, racial, and class borders—crossings that expose them (and, by extension, the audience) to difference and suffering, that elicit a call for acknowledgment, and that destabilize their sense of self. The stories of these characters' border crossings operate rhetorically to promote a transborder conscience—one that seeks "not to combat drugs by prohibition but through . . . caring for young people who need it" (dell'Agnese 215). As with perhaps any moralizing rhetoric, the discourse of *Traffic* has both laudable and disconcerting dimensions.

On the positive side, *Traffic* posits that in our everyday lives we have a duty to act with conscience—to act with an awareness of, consideration for, and responsiveness to Others, namely children. In short, the film advocates acting intersubjectively or as beings-with-others. On this count, we might say, quoting Hyde, that the film's "rhetoric demonstrates its 'physicianship' as it helps to promote reasoned judgment and civic virtue and thereby lends itself to the task of enriching the moral character of a people's communal existence" (*Call of Conscience* 13). For *Traffic*, the call to conscience is closely connected to the notion of borders and to a willingness to cross them, to "see" the world from the "other" side. Through the story of Helena, the film also tells a cautionary tale about what happens when we lose sight of our being-with-others. The ideology underlying each of its stories is one of individual agency. So, while *Traffic* sees little possibility for progress in the drug war on a systemic level, it does insist that individuals, acting in good conscience, can make a difference. That having been said, *Traffic* ignores the way that one's material conditions of existence, along with structural inequalities in power, may severely limit the scope and influence of individual action.

Moreover, the film's message of individual agency, though uplifting, poses a number of significant political limitations and challenges, especially with regard to "agentive citizenship" (Berlant, "Theory" 398). According to Lauren Berlant, the reformulation of citizenship as one involving personal and private acts (rather than civil acts) aimed primarily at protecting the innocent, specifically children, reflects an ever-expanding conservative political ideology (*Queen Goes to America* 3, 5) and "mediated dispersal of critical national identifications" ("Theory" 398). For Berlant and Michael Warner, "replacing state mandates for social justice with a privatized ethics of responsibility, charity, atonement, and 'values'" (554) erodes the public sphere, absolves the state of social responsibility, and undermines collective agency. Lee Edelman concurs, noting that the figure of "the Child" in mediated political discourses (like *Traffic*, for instance) serves to reproduce the existing social order (3, 11). For Edelman, the image of the Child does not refer "to the lived experiences of any historical [i.e., actual] children" (11); rather, it is a rhetorical trope conjured in popular political discourses to foreclose debate about social policy. Who, after all, does not want to protect and preserve the future for our children? The image of the Child does more than simply truncate political debate, however; it also limits the horizon of acceptable political ideas and discourses by suggesting that social policies motivated by any alternative telos are unworthy of our consideration (Edelman 11). Consequently, while concern for the Other (as articulated through the figure of the Child) promotes individual conscience, its pervasive invocation in political discourse "serves to regulate political discourse—to prescribe what will *count* as a political discourse" (Edelman 11).

In light of Berlant's and Edelman's concern that the increasing privatization of citizenship through popular political discourses that locate "the Child as the emblem of futurity's unquestioned value and purpose" (Edelman 4) may (re)affirm the political status quo, rhetorical critics would be well advised to approach seemingly progressive films like *Traffic* with a high degree of caution and skepticism. Developing an ethical border politics is no easy matter, then. So, perhaps it is apropos that a film concerned with a subject as complex, contentious, and contradictory as drug trafficking would in the end model a politics that is equally complex, contentious, and contradictory.

12

Decriminalizing Illegal Immigration

Immigrants' Rights through the Documentary Lens

Anne Teresa Demo

The first documentary to address the issue of illegal immigration aired in 1976 on KNBC-TV in Los Angeles. *The Unwanted* earned three regional Emmys including awards for best writing and best current affairs special. In 1997, the documentary was rereleased by the National Latino Communications Center and described by *LA Weekly* as a "haunting time capsule that reminds us of the same problems we face today" (qtd. on back cover of *The Unwanted*). Although the problems depicted in the documentary continue to be relevant, the film's tone and perspective on illegal immigration would be jarring to contemporary viewers acculturated to cable and network news coverage of the issue. In comparison to the demonization of unauthorized immigrants in shows like *Lou Dobbs Tonight* and the adulation of border patrol agents in series like the National Geographic Channel's *Border Wars,* the KNBC documentary (produced by José Luis Ruiz and written by Frank del Olmo) revealed both the frustration of immigration agents and humiliation of undocumented immigrants. This narrative balance is reflected in the documentary's closing argument: "Neither of the two main characters in this drama, the illegal alien or the immigration officer, is a villain or a hero. They are both victims. Trapped in a system that does not work and they are trying to make the best of an impossible situation." Whereas *The Unwanted* was unique in its balanced indictment of border control policy in the 1970s, the documentaries on illegal immigration produced since 2000 attempt to counterbalance the exclusionary discourse that defines contemporary mainstream cable and broadcast media outlets. As this chapter will show, these documentaries reveal an emerging pattern of representation that seeks to decriminalize unauthorized immigrants and challenge the border as the exclusive site for negotiating the relationship between illegal immigration and civic identity, thus suggesting a potential turning point in border rhetorics.

The use of documentaries as an advocacy and organizing tool has been well documented for activists in the Chicano rights, anti-globalization, and human rights movements. By the mid-1970s, the Chicano rights movement had already embraced the documentary format, producing over forty-two documentaries between 1967 and 1980. The focus of these works ranged from histories of the Chicano movement to socioeconomic problems faced by Chicanos. Although immigration control policy was not dealt with directly, films like *The Trail North* (1984) and *In the Shadow of the Law* (1988) addressed the experiences of families living illegally in the US (Maciel 152). In the years prior to the historic passage of the North American Free Trade Agreement (NAFTA), various anti-NAFTA interest groups (from environmentalists and labor unions to feminists and religious organizations) produced over twenty-six documentaries about NAFTA and border-related issues (Fox 58). These films illuminated the economic context that fosters illegal immigration and tended to reinforce stereotypes with what Claire Fox describes as "stock shots of the 'poor but dignified people'" and the border as "seamy and lawless" (61–62). As the ensuing discussion of the social documentary tradition reveals, the enthusiastic embrace of video advocacy by human rights activists contributed to major developments in media activism and, importantly, a dramatic increase in the number of documentaries that foreground the perspective of unauthorized immigrants.[1]

Although immigrants' rights advocates may have a limited voice in the mainstream media, their growing presence in the documentary film market is evident in the twenty-two projects produced since 1996, with the majority (twenty) produced between 2001 and 2010. Eight of the documentaries were broadcast nationally on HBO, the Sundance Channel, PBS (including on its non-fiction film series *POV*), or MTV: *9500 Liberty* (2010); *In the Shadow of the Raid* (2010); *Which Way Home* (2009); *Crossing Arizona* (2006); *Mexico—Death in the Desert—June 4, 2004* (2004); *Farmingville* (2003); *The Sixth Section* (2003); and *The Ballad of Esequiel Hernández* (2008). Eleven documentaries were screened widely at prominent film festivals and universities: *New World Border* (2001); *Death on a Friendly Border* (2001); *Mojados: Through the Night* (2004); *El Inmigrante* (2005); *Rights on the Line* (2005); *Wetback: The Undocumented Documentary* (2005); *Walking the Line* (2006); *The Wall* (2009); *The Other Side of Immigration* (2009); *The Least of These* (2009); and *Swift Justice: Illegal Immigration in America* (2009). Three were screened on a more limited basis to local community groups and distributed to universities and organizations such as the American Friends Service Committee Lending Library: *The 800 Mile Wall* (2009); *The Time Has Come! An Immigrant Community Stands Up to the Border Patrol* (1996); and *Ties That Bind: Stories behind the Immigration Controversy* (1996).

The purpose of this chapter is to address a gap in the literature on border rhetorics and suggest an alternative lens for future advocacy efforts. Despite the noteworthy scholarship on contemporary pro-immigrant arguments, most of the border rhetorics literature has focused on the verbal and visual modes of nativist and enforcement-first arguments. The most extensive work on pro-immigrants' rights arguments has dealt with advocates seeking to defeat particular legislative initiatives at the state and national level, specifically, the 1994 Save Our State initiative in California (also known as Proposition 187), the Personal Responsibility and Work Opportunity Reconciliation Act of 1996, and House Resolution 4437 (Border Protection, Antiterrorism, and Illegal Immigration Control Act of 2005).[2] In their book on Proposition 187 rhetoric, Kent Ono and John Sloop conclude that the majority of anti-187 arguments reflected nativist assumptions such as "constructions of immigrants as economic units, anxiety about contagion, and faith in a trustworthy and equitable state" (159). More problematically, the authors found that anti-187 rhetoric often relied on belittling rhetorical strategies that would "construct an infantile, innocent, and therefore passive immigrant subject" (158–59). In contrast, Lynn Fujiwara delineates the limited success of arguments made on behalf of "immigrants worthy of sympathy" in activist campaigns responding to the Personal Responsibility and Work Opportunity Reconciliation Act of 1996, which denied food stamp and social security benefits to noncitizens (Fujiwara 91). Addressing the potential for activism after 9/11, Fujiwara concludes that pro-immigrant activists face an "impenetrable anti-immigrant public and Congress" and an "economic and political climate of threat and terror" that makes pro-immigrant arguments exceedingly difficult (99). Finally, the emerging scholarship on the 2006 pro-immigrant protests has focused on modes of organizing rather than the specific arguments advanced on behalf of unauthorized immigrants. For example, the spring 2009 special issue of *Latino Studies* on undocumented immigrants features two articles on the 2006 marches, but the essays emphasize organizational communication and media frames over the specific arguments used to humanize and/or decriminalize undocumented immigrants (Baker-Cristales; Gonzalez).

In contrast, this project surveys the twenty documentaries produced between 2001 and 2010 that incorporate an immigrants' rights perspective.[3] The purpose of this chapter is to assess the recurrent visual and narrative strategies used to make immigrants' rights arguments in the medium that, over the past decade, offered the greatest potential for diverse and far-reaching critiques of US immigration enforcement policies. A number of the twenty documentaries examined for this chapter have been reviewed in the popular press and academic journals; however, no scholarly work has examined the documentaries as an emerging genre or examined the films diagnostically to identify what pro-immigrant arguments are most and least prevalent. The analysis that follows focuses on the most prominent story-structure across the documentaries. More than half of the films examined employ a conflict-driven narrative that contests the criminality of illegal immigration by contrasting portraits of the immigrant laborer sacrificing for his family and the alienated Anglos promoting tougher immigration enforcement. These films provide an important counterimage to mainstream media depictions of unauthorized immigrants and a challenge to the logic of border militarization but stop short of explicitly framing border enforcement policy as a human rights issue. In what follows, I analyze how the conflict-driven documentaries challenge the criminalization of immigrants through key charter-types, including the immigrant as laborer, provider, and neighbor as well as the alienated Anglo and ambivalent lawmen. The chapter closes by addressing how evolutions in the content and form of immigrants' rights advocacy may inform future border rhetorics.

Contesting Illegality

Documentaries on illegal immigration share the singular focus on immigrants and illegality that has defined mainstream immigration coverage since the 1980s. Not surprisingly, documentaries approach these subjects in radically different ways. Although mainstream media and documentary accounts both situate the undocumented immigrant as their central protagonist, documentaries privilege the testimony of individual immigrants over those who speak about them as a multitude. Within the past decade, arguments that foreground the perspective of unauthorized immigrants have been largely relegated to Spanish-language media, English-language newspapers (during spikes in immigration coverage), and alternative media (Akdenizli). Yet, a study of immigration news coverage since the 1980s noted a long-term trend toward framing the undocumented immigrant as "the protagonist of the [immigration] drama, exercising his will over the nation" (Suro). The emphasis on authorized immigrants to the exclusion of other stakeholders, such as employers and consumers, within immigration news coverage over the past two decades is well established (Suro 12). That said, even as immigration coverage frames unauthorized immigrants as key agents in the unfolding immigration context, the reporting also privileges statements from policy-makers and advocates on both sides of the issue over the testimony of unauthorized immigrants. As a result, immigration news often characterizes unauthorized immigrants as having agency without voice. The most egregious example of this paradox in reporting is former CNN anchor Lou Dobbs, whose hour-long show *Lou Dobbs Tonight* once had over

1.7 million viewers nightly. Watchdog groups such as Fairness and Accuracy in Reporting (FAIR) and the Southern Poverty Law Center, as well as more centrist organizations like the Brooking Institution, have criticized Dobbs for his alarmist portrait of unauthorized immigrants as a threat to US sovereignty and a danger to the safety and health of American citizens.[4] While his descriptions clearly present unauthorized immigrants with agency, his show and much of the mainstream English-language press privilege anti-amnesty and pro-restriction voices, so much so that the Brookings Institution characterized the battle for public opinion over the 2007 Senate immigration bill as "entirely one-sided" (qtd. in Suro 42). The media bias toward policy insiders and controversial voices limits the potential for immigrants' rights advocates working with authorized immigrants on a day-to-day basis to reach key decision-makers and shape public opinion. As a result, immigrants' rights advocates have increasingly turned to video advocacy as an alternative way to impact immigration policy by either producing their own project or featuring previously produced documentaries in their outreach programs. Such projects foreground the testimony of undocumented immigrants and the citizen surrogates who speak on their behalf. These perspectives introduce competing frames of interpretation that reveal the distortions in media and government accounts of immigration as a criminal activity and national security threat. In exposing why criminalization is an insufficient framework for approaching the contemporary immigration context, the documentaries also lay the foundation for challenging the national security paradigm that currently governs immigration enforcement. Through the lens of the documentaries, illegal immigration is framed as an economic problem resulting from US trade policy with Mexico and as a humanitarian problem that separates families and jeopardizes the lives of undocumented immigrants who risk everything to enter the United States.

Although the mainstream media coverage of immigration normalizes associations between immigration and illegal behavior, the documentaries examined for this project display multiple strategies that trouble the association (Cisneros, "Contaminated Communities"; Waldman et al.). These narrative strategies often reflect legal tactics used in deportation and removal hearings. In an analysis of cases involving three Central American community organizations that offered legal services to undocumented immigrants, anthropologist Susan Bibler Coutin identified three rationales that were successful in contesting the prosecution of Section 8, Title 1325 of US Code, "improper entry by alien." First, defendants in legal hearings challenged the illegality of improper entry by arguing either that immigration was a "necessity, to escape political violence" or that "it is not illegal to seek a job or support one's family" (23). Documentaries on illegal immigration that include an immigrants' rights perspective rarely cite the fear of persecution as a rationale for illegal immigration and instead base their justification almost exclusively on economic grounds. Second, defendants in legal hearings also contested their status as "illegal" by compiling evidence that shows their de facto membership in US society through histories of law-abiding actions, family ties, and community involvement (23). This rationale is generally limited to conflict-driven documentaries set in the interior United States, whereas the need for work to support a family is a common rationale across the documentaries. Finally, challenges to "the very grounds on which law and illegality are distinguished" occurred when US actions were deemed culpable in creating political and economic conditions that made life in their country of origin untenable (23). Nearly all the films reference the role of international trade (from NAFTA to domestic sugar subsidies) in stimulating illegal immigration; however, two documentaries foreground these issues: *New World Border* and *The Other Side of Immigration*. These films are also distinct from the other documentaries on illegal immigration because they do not employ a conflict- or journey-driven story structure but function more as investigative documentaries. Based on over seven hundred interviews with residents from high-emigration towns in rural Mexico, *The Other Side of Immigration* is particularly noteworthy because the film introduces audiences to immigrant-laborers who only reluctantly seek employment in the United States because their livelihoods in Mexico have been stripped away by US agricultural subsidies. The perspectives offered by the film suggest that the cause of illegal immigration is not lax border enforcement but unfair trade practices and visa programs that disadvantage low-skilled workers from Mexico. The solution is not expanded policing but a guest-worker program that will allow Mexicans to work in the United States legally on a temporary but renewable basis. Within such a framework, economic programs function as the centerpiece of immigration policy, not enforcement initiatives.

Despite the nuanced economic analysis of *The Other Side of Immigration*, the complex relationship between immigration and trade policy is difficult to foreground in conflict- or journey-driven story structures. In conflict-driven documentaries, the wide cast of characters necessary to dramatize immigration controversies makes it difficult to provide the necessary context for understanding the interrelationship between US trade policy and illegal immigration. Similarly, journey-driven storylines foreground the suffering and sacrifices of individuals who cross illegally for access to jobs that will support the workers' families living in rural Mexico and Central American countries like Nicaragua, Honduras, and Guatemala. The narrative identification with particular immigrants and immigrant families in the journey-driven documentaries comes at a cost, however, as the economic context for their sacrifice is often unarticulated.

In comparison, all the documentaries that incorporate a pro-immigrant perspective challenge the illegality associated with "improper entry" with testimony from immigrants who justify their actions on familial needs. The pervasiveness of this appeal across the twenty documentaries and diverse ways that the subject positions of worker and provider are coupled indicate a significant shift from the way the immigrant subject was depicted in pro-immigrant arguments expressed during the 1990s, which generally accepted the language of illegality and logic of criminalization (Ono and Sloop 80, 122–23). Though the length and particular word choice may change depending on the film, the sentiment expressed by "Jaime" in Swift Justice is representative of the immigrants interviewed in other films: "The reasons I did this is because I want to work for my family. I don't want my family to suffer, and I also want to try to get my family ahead without asking for help from the government. Unfortunately I came to this country without documents. I started working at Swift in 1999. When I started working at Swift I had two jobs. I also worked in the fields so that my whole family could get ahead. I worked at Swift for seven years until this happened and they caught us." Unlike pro-immigrant arguments from the 1990s that distinguish the innocence of immigrant children from the culpability of their parents, the documentaries produced between 2001 and 2010 challenge the very notion that coming "without documents" is a crime, and, in so doing, challenge a narrow definition of citizenship. Regardless of story structure, testimony from immigrants consistently echoes key American values such as the desire to work hard and provide for the family to minimize the illegality associated with improper entry. The Swift Justice interview with Jaime is unique in that it also directly counters a common concern associated with illegal immigration—the expanding government doles—and provides evidence of a good employment record and strong family ties, both traits associated with good citizenship. Although the unauthorized immigrants interviewed are most often men, testimony from wives, children, and clergy further redeems the male immigrant worker by also emphasizing his role as the family provider (Ono and Sloop 93–95). Just as organizations such as the National Association of Hispanic Journalists have argued for terms that humanize ("undocumented worker") over terms that suggest criminality and suspicion ("illegal alien"), testimony that equates undocumented workers with family providers neutralizes mainstream portraits of unauthorized immigrants as a threat or suspect.

The tendency to associate illegality with people rather than actions is countered most in conflict-driven documentaries set in the interior United States. These films not only dramatize examples of de facto citizenship once in the United States but also document the adverse community effects when immigrants depart due to either Immigration and Customs Enforcement (ICE) raids or perceived hostility by the community. For example, a subplot within *Farmingville* is the attempt to establish an advocacy group of immigrant day laborers, Human Solidarity, that will provide support to undocumented workers and contribute to the community by volunteering to care for local soccer fields. Footage of immigrants cleaning the fields and hosting soccer tournaments edited with upbeat guitar instrumentals provides an uplifting counterpoint to the tension of community meetings and protests. In the final five minutes of the film, footage from the Human Solidarity Soccer Tournament is intercut with an interview with one of the group's leaders, who explains the value of soccer as a mobilizing tool: "Now we work together with the Americans who let us use their fields. They see that, besides working, we want to laugh, we want to play sports. We want them to see that we are real people." By connecting the story of the group's volunteerism with scenes of organized sport, the film provides a productive counterimage to the loitering day laborer menacing street corners. More importantly, the footage of immigrants caring for community fields provides proof that, despite their legal status, these unauthorized immigrants have embraced key principles of citizenship such as community involvement. Indeed, one subtheme of *Farmingville, The Sixth Section,* and *9500 Liberty,* all films that aired nationally, is a definition of citizenship based not on legal status but civic contribution. As a result, these films not only challenge the criminalization of immigration but also make a case for expanding "conditions of membership in the national political community" (De-Chaine, this volume).

In addition to the civic contribution of unauthorized immigrants, *Farmingville* and other documentaries set in the interior United States correlate the economic growth of communities with the presence of unauthorized immigrants. The devastating economic impact of losing a significant immigrant population is a key subplot for *In the Shadow of the Raid* and *9500 Liberty.* The documentary short *In the Shadow of the Raid* traces the economic collapse of Postville, Iowa, following the May 2008 ICE raid of Agriprocessors Inc., a kosher slaughterhouse and meat-packing plant. Although the film also addresses the economic impact of the lost remittances to Guatemala, the central focus is Postville during the boom-time before the raid and the economic collapse that followed the mass deportations and voluntary exodus. The effect, as one remaining resident notes, was catastrophic: "They call it a ghost town now. Everyone's gone." Intercutting interviews with an economist, citizen-activist, and small-business owner, *9500 Liberty* provides a comprehensive portrait of the economic impact of pro-enforcement legislation on a northern Virginia suburb. Economist Stephen Fuller anchors the sequence of interviews with the big-picture view, "The slowdown in the economy is happening because of a national slow-down in the economy. In Prince William County, they made it worse by targeting a portion of their low-income population, making it feel less welcome. They took that spending power, that tax-generating power, that economic benefit, out of the solution." Interviews with the citizen-activist and small-business owner then capture the economic impact at more micro-levels: "My grandson has lost all of his friends. I mean literally everyone in the neighborhood that he used to play with except for one child has left. . . . I should have fifty customers today and I had fifteen or eighteen all day." This sequence not only demonstrates the irrelevance of legal status when considering the value of unauthorized immigrants as consumers who enrich communities but also introduces the potential for seeing unauthorized immigrants as good neighbors, which would help facilitate support for immigration reforms that include a pathway to citizenship. As a whole, such depictions seek to dissociate illegal behavior with immigrants. The documentaries further contest the expanding criminalization of immigration with portraits of border vigilantes and commentary from law enforcement officers that challenge the correspondence of enforcement with security and justice.

Reframing Immigration Crimes: Alienated Anglos and Ambivalent Lawmen

The central antagonist in documentaries on illegal immigration is not the immigration enforcement agent but the alienated Anglo citizen. Conflict-driven documentaries feature alienated Anglos as central characters (leaders of local pro-enforcement campaigns) and peripheral figures (for example, unnamed citizens making statements at community forums and characters identified by name but in few scenes). Of the Anglos depicted across the documentaries, pro-enforcement activists get the most screen time. Among this group, vigilantes play a particularly important role in contesting the dominant notion of illegality in immigration contexts. Films such as *Rights on the Line, Crossing Arizona, El Inmigrante,* and *Walking the Line,* which document the efforts of border militia groups, frame vigilante actions as not only more unlawful than illegal entry but also less liable for prosecution. More generally, the conflict-driven documentaries reverse the binary that defines conventional immigration coverage, presenting unauthorized immigrants as victims and presenting abuse by citizen vigilantes as the relevant crime.

Films that address vigilante activity make the most sustained case for proenforcement rhetoric as an incitement to violence; however, even films focused on civic activism suggest a causal relationship between pro-enforcement campaigns and anti-immigrant hate crimes. *Farmingville* not only begins and ends with references to violence against immigrant laborers but also documents the minor abuses experienced by citizens who in some way support immigrant laborers, either by hiring or renting to them. One of the film's key moral lessons is that hatred is spread both geographically and generationally. The film closes by underscoring this lesson with title cards that confirm fears expressed in earlier scenes, that a parent's hateful words will yield a child's violent deeds: "On July 5, 2003 a Mexican family home in Farmingville was firebombed." "Four Sachem High School students were arrested and charged with hate crimes and arson." In this context of the violent crime detailed in films like *Farmingville, The Ballad of Esequiel Hernández,* and *El Inmigrante,* violations of immigration codes appear benign and victimless.

The most threatening characters across the documentaries are members of border militias and vigilante groups. Intending to obscure differences between pro-enforcement campaigns and anti-immigration extremism, the films present vigilante actions as morally reprehensible and unlawful. Despite questions about their own lawfulness, leaders from civilian militia and border vigilante groups like the Minuteman Project have been prominent figures in mainstream media coverage of illegal immigration. In his analysis of the Minuteman Project, anthropologist Leo Chavez has found that following their April 2005 national call to patrol the US-Mexico border, "the Minuteman Project established itself as a voice in the public debate over immigration, a voice reporters would now routinely seek out for responses to immigration-related stories" (*Latino Threat,* 146). In particular, Chris Simcox, founder of the Minuteman Civil Defense Corps and a key organizer for the April 2005 Minuteman Project event, has appeared on major broadcast and cable news networks to comment on immigration issues nearly three hundred times since January 1, 2006.[5] Simcox is a key protagonist in *Rights on the Line, Crossing Arizona,* and *Walking the Line* and a secondary character in *El Inmigrante* and *Wetback: The Undocumented Documentary*. Such films function as an important counter-discourse to both the mainstream media image of Simcox as a credible source and immigration as criminal act.

All five films document Simcox's zeal apprehending migrants and his bravado on patrol in ways that undermine his mainstream credibility. A Southern Poverty Law Center review that focuses on four of the films describes Simcox as "giddy with excitement" in scenes with captured migrants as he "paws through their belongings" and "goads them in a feigned Mexican accent," saying, "'See, I told you! No mas! Vigilantes get you, man!'" (Buchanan). In a scene from *Walking the Line,* captured migrants sit with their heads bowed waiting for border patrol as Simcox clicks his digital camera, saying, "Aw, don't be shy, guys. You'll be in my newspaper this week!" Although Simcox's swagger in such scenes would potentially appeal to some enforcement-first viewers, his obvious enjoyment in the act of exercising power over cowering migrants may encourage others to wonder about the migrants' treatment by vigilantes when cameras are not rolling. *Crossing Arizona* dramatizes Simcox's extremism by crosscutting footage of border patrol with Simcox on patrol. In the concluding contrast, an unnamed border patrol agent is shown distributing water to apprehended migrants while stating that "90 percent of these people probably have no outstanding records. . . . Most of them are good people just here for a job." As the last word is uttered, the border patrol door shuts and the film cuts to lone Simcox in the desert with his back to the camera, stating, "It takes a lot of restraint for Americans to not sit out here with guns. I have nothing against immigrants as long as you come in legally . . . but these people are coming and just spitting on our citizenship, just trampling on it, cheapening it." Thus, the footage of Simcox on patrol in *Crossing Arizona* and the other feature-length documentaries introduces a darker side to the media persona Simcox cultivated as a retired kindergarten teacher and impassioned citizen organizing a group akin to a "neighborhood watch."

Rights on the Line directly challenges the connotations of criminality attached to unauthorized immigrants by foregrounding the constitutional and human rights violations perpetrated by vigilantes. Importantly, this discussion revolves around Simcox rather than the Minuteman Project volunteers. The film features footage of Simcox detaining migrants (footage that also appears in *Walking the Line*) and an interview in which he addresses the issue of migrant abuse directly: "Let's look at the facts: no immigrant, illegal or legal, coming across that border has ever been harmed by an American citizen. There is not a documented account since 1976. There are, have been some wild allegations but there is not one victim." This twenty-second clip is countered with a minute-long montage of incident reports and direct testimony documenting abuses such as citizen volunteers threatening migrants with guns and dogs, pulling them by their hair, and using physical force while detaining migrants for the border patrol. One indicator of the film's success linking border militia groups to human rights violations is a 2005 resolution requiring authorities to monitor and report all vigilante activity, which received unanimous support from the Austin City Council after a screening of the film. The film's critique of the criminalization of immigration also mobilized immigration rights activists in San Elizario, Texas, to create a video that was submitted as testimony to the state capitol regarding the unconstitutionality of traffic checkpoints operated by local sheriffs as immigration checkpoints (Rios). In the conflict-driven documentaries, representatives of local law enforcement not only rebuke vigilante actions and extremism but also warn of hasty and injudicious approaches to immigration enforcement.

Documentaries on illegal immigration that incorporate pro-immigrant perspectives draw on clergy and immigration rights activists to make more sweeping critiques of the dominant enforcement paradigm; however, local law enforcement officers provide powerful indictments of specific immigration enforcement practices. The 2010 documentary *9500 Liberty* chronicles a prolonged controversy over a law requiring police in Prince William County, Virginia, to detain anyone officers have "probable cause" to suspect as an unauthorized immigrant. Although the film focuses on the polarizing effect of pro-enforcement activists and politicians seeking to pass the "probable cause" ordinance, interviews with US citizens detained by police describe the experience as racial profiling and a constitutional violation. In footage from a public hearing about the ordinance, Chief of Police Charlie Deane warns, "Prince William County, which over the past two decades has established an outstanding reputation for inclusion, will be painted as a racist community intent on driving out a single population." This clip is followed by an interview with Chief Deane that addresses the larger enforcement implications: "You cannot keep a community safe unless the majority of the community has trust in the police and will call, will bear witness when they need to, so it is vital that we retain the trust of all elements of the community." Such critiques are in some ways more powerful than individual challenges to an ordinance's constitutionality because they provide a rationale for challenging the expanding criminalization of immigration on the grounds of community safety.

The dilemmas created by federal enforcement policies made without consulting local officials form a subtheme within conflict-driven documentaries on illegal immigration that further undermines the national security framework for immigration enforcement. Within these storylines, the federal leadership responsible for instituting enforcement policy are framed as politically driven, impractical, and largely incompetent. The 2009 documentary *The Wall* documents the failures and unintended consequences of the 2006 Secure Border Fence Act, which called for the construction of over seven hundred miles of fencing along the US-Mexico border. The film addresses the diverse stakeholders affected by the fence construction, from the unauthorized immigrants forced to seek more perilous routes to enter the US to the citizens whose property was threatened by government claims of eminent domain. Interviews with local leaders, particularly law enforcement officials, dramatize how political pressure for a high mile-count resulted in a rush to construction and lack of consultation with locals. Sheriffs from Yuma and Nogales, Arizona, address the lack of coordination in explicit ways throughout the film with comments such as "when they are down here, they don't tell anyone" and "we, and by we, I think I'm talking about people in the field including Border Patrol to some point, are not familiar with what their plan is." As the film shows, this lack of consultation had costly results when a barrier constructed by US Border Patrol impeded floodwaters during a July 2008 storm, causing over $8 million in damages to Nogales businesses. The deadly consequences of bypassing local law enforcement are chronicled in *The Ballad of Esequiel Hernández,* which recounts the shooting of an eighteen-year-old American by a four-person Marine unit deployed to the US-Mexico border to monitor drug trafficking. The *POV* documentary draws on interviews with law enforcement officers from diverse branches of government (Marine Corps, US Border Patrol, FBI, and Justice Department) not only to rebuke the conduct of this deployment, particularly the lack of consultation with local law enforcement, but also to question the value of border militarization more generally.

Conclusion

Evidence of the expanding criminalization of immigration over the last decade abounds in the growing number of interior state ordinances related to immigration, the rise of partnerships between local law enforcement and ICE, and the booming immigration detention industry. In this context, immigrants' rights advocates have turned to new modes of organizing and advocacy. This chapter examines one medium of advocacy, the documentary, and assesses how the twenty films produced since 2001 challenge the criminalization of immigration through three primary characterizations. Most importantly, testimony from unauthorized immigrants works to minimize the illegality associated with improper entry and provides humanizing details about immigrants' family ties and community connections that challenge the propriety of applying a national security paradigm to immigration. Footage of alienated Anglo activists reveals how the logic of criminalizing immigration could mobilize extremism and breed violence, from vandalism and simple assault to murder. Interviews with law enforcement officers establish important critiques of the rapidly expanding web of immigration enforcement on the basis of community concerns such as public safety and economic development. Thus, instead of conceding the issue of illegality, the documentaries exhibit diverse strategies for directly contesting it and challenging definitions of citizenship and civic belonging based only on legal status.

In addition to challenging the logic of criminalization, the documentaries also suggest that the geography of immigration debates may be shifting. Of the twenty documentaries examined, five films are set in the interior United States, three of which were produced after 2009. The US-Mexico border clearly constitutes the sine qua non of immigration enforcement; however, the dramatic population growth of a low-wage, Spanish-speaking workforce in historically Anglo communities indicates a tectonic shift in the landscape of US border rhetorics. Interior states like Colorado, Georgia, North Carolina, and Oklahoma have been polarized by new immigration patterns. Unlike border communities, which historically have had a more symbiotic relationship with Mexico and moderate tolerance for Spanish speakers, the small towns and city suburbs that now serve as hypergrowth destinations feel acutely threatened by the changes that new immigrants bring to their communities. The level of fear associated with the demographic changes in these communities is evidenced by draconian measures such as the Oklahoma Taxpayer and Citizen Protection Act of 2007, which made it a felony to "transport, move, . . . conceal, shelter or harbor" an illegal immigrant. Additionally, unlike the border communities that rely on US Customs and Border Patrol agents who specialize in immigration enforcement protocols, communities in the interior United States have little recourse for federal enforcement and have therefore increasingly sought to pass state and city ordinances that allow local police and sheriffs to enforce immigration laws. Such ordinances have, in the words of one Tulsa city official, "caused a lot of confusion, inconsistency and fear, mainly in the Hispanic community" (Huus). In addition to differences in community and enforcement responses to illegal immigration, the employment record and

civic ties that unauthorized immigrants establish in communities far removed from the border alter the range of arguments available to advocates
on either side of the issue. As this chapter shows, communities new to the
immigration debate will certainly draw from the existing landscape of border rhetorics but also introduce unexpected twists and turns in local and national disputes over how communities respond to and enforce immigration.

In 2010, for the first time, the Academy Awards nominations for Best Feature Documentary included a film that dealt with the issue of illegal immigration from Mexico. The critically acclaimed HBO documentary *Which
Way Home* chronicles the perilous journey of unaccompanied children traveling across Mexico into the United States in search of their parents living
in the country illegally. Although the film was not awarded the Academy
Award, the efforts of filmmakers and activists over the last decade suggest
a building momentum for video advocacy as a tool for change within the
immigrants' rights movement. With national legislative debates over comprehensive immigration reform on the horizon, the stories of why undocumented immigrants journey to the US and how their lives unfold once
here must be part of the national conversation. These living stories, depicted
through the documentary lens and on YouTube channels, provide a fuller
vision of the tired and poor tending our fields and constructing our homes.
In seeing and embracing their stories, we enrich our own.

Notes

1. The terminology used in the debates over immigration is almost as contested as the policies. In September 2009, the National Association of Hispanic
Journalists (NAHJ) called for the news media to refrain from using the term
"illegal" as a noun because the term "criminalizes the person rather than the
actual act of illegally entering, residing in the US without documents" (US
Census Bureau). Following this call, I use the term "unauthorized immigrant"
to indicate foreign nationals who immigrate to the United States without au-
thorization. The term best encompasses the administrative violation of improper entry and is also used by the US Census Bureau and the Department of
Homeland Security (US Census Bureau).

2. Proposition 187 sought to prohibit undocumented workers from accessing state social services. The proposed law was passed by California voters in
1994 by a margin of nearly 59 percent but was found to be unconstitutional by
the state courts after a lengthy appeals process (Ono and Sloop). In 1996, US
president Bill Clinton signed into law both the Personal Responsibility and
Work Opportunity Reconciliation Act (PRWORA) and the Illegal Immigra-

tion Reform and Immigrant Responsibility Act (IIRIRA). IIRIRA offered sweeping changes in immigration enforcement such as the creation of a Department of Homeland Security program that allows local law enforcement to perform immigration enforcement functions. Although PRWORA focused on welfare reforms such as new work requirements, the law also ruled that "nearly all non-citizen immigrants would be ineligible for Supplemental Security Income" (Fujiwara 79). House Resolution 4437 (Border Protection, Antiterrorism, and Illegal Immigration Control Act of 2005) was never passed by the Senate and prompted the mass immigration reform protests in spring 2006 across the country.

3. This chapter is part of a larger project that examines how documentaries challenge the "War on Terror" pretext that justifies affiliating border control and national security. In addition to the analysis of decriminalization featured herein, the larger in-progress project examines how graphic accounts of the perilous journeys of unauthorized immigrants provide an alternative framework for conceptualizing terror.

4. The most infamous statements include Dobbs's description of Mexican immigrants as an "army of invaders" in an episode aired on March 31, 2006, and his claim that "the invasion of illegal aliens is threatening the health of many Americans" through "deadly imports of diseases like leprosy and malaria," which aired on April 14, 2005 (qtd. in Suro 42).

5. A LexisNexis search of "Chris Simcox" on TV and radio broadcasts after January 1, 2006, identified 320 news transcripts.

13
The Ragpicker-Citizen

Toby Miller

This chapter juggles multiple determinations and overdeterminations, keeping the interrelationships of state, capital, people, environment, and discourse in tension. My method draws on work done to forward a new communication studies that differs from aesthetic criticism based on interpretation and identity, as per much of media and cultural studies; scientistic service to militarism, business, policing, and the professions (q.v. mainstream communication research); and the neoliberal embrace of bourgeois economics undertaken by prelates of the creative industries (Miller, "'Step Away'"; Miller, "Media Studies 3.0"; Miller, "A Future for Media Studies"). The project necessitates a radical contextualization of the shifts and shocks of institutions and rhetorics. Such an approach combines political economy, ethnography, and textual analysis, weaving its way across commentary, fiction, statistics, poetry, law, science, and history to construct a materialist account of political-economic transformations and myths, in this case at the Mexico-US border. It delves into cultural citizenship to address policy and rights as well as structure and spectacle (Miller, *Cultural Citizenship*; De-Chaine, "Bordering the Civic Imaginary"; Robertson).

Let's begin with four quotations. They come from both famous and less well-known sources: "[F]oul and adventures-seeking dregs of the bourgeoisie, there were vagabonds, dismissed soldiers, discharged convicts, runaway galley slaves, sharpers, jugglers, lazzaroni, pickpockets, sleight-of-hand performers, gamblers, procurers, keepers of disorderly houses, porters, literati, organ grinders, rag pickers, scissors grinders, tinkers, beggars—in short, that whole undefined, dissolute, kicked-about mass" (Marx 63). The quotation above is Marx's description of "sub-proletariat" classes living outside conventional government and commerce in nineteenth-century France (Oppenheimer). Such people continue to pose "problems" for critics and fellow residents:

> The community in question occupied a tract of land at the foot of the mesa. Above it hunkered the remains of *Reciclaje Integral,* a deserted smelting and battery recycling plant. For years the residents of Vista Nueva had reported skin ulcers, respiratory ailments, birth defects. A number of children had died. . . . When it became apparent that

charges would be brought against him in a Mexican court, however, the owner, an American, simply filed for bankruptcy in Mexico, left the factory as it stood, and withdrew across the border, where he continued to prosper. . . . He lived in a million-dollar house somewhere in San Diego County while his deserted plant continued to poison the residents of Vista Nueva. (Nunn 25)

This second quotation comes from Kem Nunn's surfing mystery novel, *Tijuana Straits,* a complex story of violence, misunderstanding, difference, sacrifice, and redemption on and across the Mexican-US border, under the sign of *maquiladoras* and their deadly, rancorous impact on occupational and residential health and safety. The seeming villain of the novel is himself a victim of the systematic exploitation of workers, who move between ragpicking, employment, and drug use in a desperate cycle. The world it describes is like the one Marx sought to explain—a liminal life in terms of both physical borders and metaphorical exclusions.

A modern equivalent world has been textualized by some of its occupants/activists:

The National Coalition of Electronic Industry Workers, declares that five years after the publication of the Electronic Industry Code of Conduct: the same companies that signed the Code are the ones violating the human labor rights. The Code states (part A-7) that the signing companies should respect the workers' freedom of association. This right, in our Federal Labor Law, is constantly violated. We recall two recent cases. The first one: the dismissal of more than 10 workers of Flextronics, only because they demanded transparency on the issue of profit shares. The second case was the dismissal of Aureliano Rosas Suárez, Omar Manuel Montes Estrada y Vicente de Jesús Rodríguez Roa, sacked because they demanded their right to have their wages leveled. They also worked for the company Flextronics. We inform the International Electronic Industry that the members of the National Coalition of Electronic Industry Workers will continue to use this mask as a symbol of our repression. But the coalition will continue demanding and defending our human labor rights. (Centre for Reflection and Action on Labour Issues 28)

This third quotation comes from a group of masked activists who protest labor conditions. These anonymous protestors have made periodic media appearances since 2007, drawing attention to the employment agencies that govern the casualized world of electronics workers in Mexican assembly plants. The coalition represents workers whose rights are not respected by corporate capital, a civil-society voice that is organic to current and former workers on the line (unions exist, but are basically inactive). Their identities are secret in order to protect the employment of themselves and their friends and relatives.

The final opening quotation is from Luis Alberto Urrea, a ficto-critical writer who blends sociological observation, roman à clef,[1] and ethnography in his searing account of cultural difference and destruction. "*Maquis,* of course, are binational or multinational factories. They sit on their bulldozed hills like raw-concrete forts, and the huts of the peasants ring their walls. Some of them have Japanese names on them, some of them have American names. All along Tijuana's new high-tech highway, *el Periférico,* you can see them up there, receding into the hazy distance. Headstones for the graveyard of American union labor" (Urrea 25). Urrea wryly notes that Mexican progressives have dubbed the Mexico-US western border region *Palestijuas* (Tijuana-Palestine) (5).

My particular focus here is the culture industries and their environmental impact on citizens, especially impoverished ones. This crystallizes at the border, where historic loss is spectacularized and US cultural production is logocentrically interdependent on its excluded other. We often think of the cultural sector as relatively positive in its environmental impact by comparison with mining or agriculture, or we think of the media as conduits of information about the environment rather than polluters. The reality is that they are environmental participants, frequently with very negative effects. The media index the complex relationship of these bordering nations, both as sites of production and as textual encounters. Given the fear expressed by so many *Yanquis* of so many Mexicans, and the extraordinary history of structural inequality between the two countries, this opens up culture to politics in a way that is both material and symbolic.

Consider Hollywood's greatest global triumph of the last century, Fox's *Titanic* (directed by James Cameron, 1997). Much of it was shot in a giant water tank in Mexico. Studio owner Rupert Murdoch approvingly cited the number of workers invisibly employed in making the film: "This cross-border cultural co-operation is not the result of regulation, but market forces. It's the freedom to move capital, technology and talent around the world that adds value, invigorates ailing markets, creates new ones." Even as it played this self-aggrandizing clip, National Public Radio reported that Fox was asking the Mexican government for financial incentives (ctd. by Miller et al.).

Titanic was a screen testimony to the 1994 North American Free Trade Agreement/Tratado de Libre Comercio (NAFTA/TLC), which has seen offshore film and television production in Mexico increase thanks to easy shipment of film stock and special-effects equipment, especially for low-budget shoots. During the making of *Titanic,* the national film studio Churubusco was renovated and a National Film Commission established, with satellites across the country that offered *Yanqui* moguls trips in governors' helicopters amid other services. Mexico's new film union set up shop in Los Angeles to reassure industry mavens of its cooperativeness and to remain up to date on US pay rates—in order to undercut them. Restoring Mexico to the Hollywood map gained James Cameron the Order of the Aztec Eagle from a grateful government. Meanwhile, local Mexican production spiraled downwards, from 747 films in the decade prior to the agreement/tratado to 212 in the decade after (Maxwell and Miller, "Film and Globalization").

There is a cruel irony to this globalization of cultural labor: people submerged in the credits to *Titanic* (or not listed at all) supposedly benefited from the textualization of a boat sunk by invisible ice and business bombast eighty years earlier. During filming, the village of Popotla was cut off from the sea and local fisheries by a walled movie *maquiladora,* built to keep citizens away. Fox's chlorination of surrounding seawater decimated sea urchins, which locals had long fished, and reduced overall fish levels by a third. The cost of the film could have provided safe drinking water to 600,000 people for a year (Miller et al. 165). The Popotlanos demonstrated their environmental critique of this situation by decorating the wall with rubbish to ridicule the filmmakers, calling for *mariscos libre* ("freedom for shellfish") ("Popotla vs. Titanic"; Coombe and Herman). The Popotlanos' view of Cameron's putatively green, pro-indigenous, anti-imperialist credentials (*Avatar,* 2009) is not yet on record. Nor is their view of the way that Hollywood's private bureaucracy proudly boasts of the fact that its earliest studio owners had been ragpickers in New York (Motion Picture Association of America).

This submersion through fetishization and its impact on the environment and workers is a jumping-off point for considering border issues from mixed perspectives, both theoretical and empirical. Drawing on earlier work (Miller, *Cultural Citizenship*; Maxwell and Miller, "Green Smokestacks?"; Maxwell and Miller, "Talking Rubbish"), I examine *maquiladora* workers and ragpickers or *recicladores* as border subjects, liminal figures in terms of social legitimacy and conventional citizenship. The backdrop is the manufacture of television sets and the transnational dumping of electronic waste (e-waste) in Latin America and elsewhere by the United States and other countries.

I place *maquiladora* workers and ragpickers together, despite their differences, for three reasons: there is mobility between the two sectors; both are affected by the environmental impact of electronics assembly and disassembly; and they share the missing, fetishized aspects of most cultural analysis—physical assembly and disassembly, versus the ever-popular topics of textual morphology and consumer use. The term "ragpicker" is a global one that is used by scholars, activists, and governments everywhere—you can read it in your local newspaper if you live in the global South—so I ultimately favor its use as my key concept.

The International Division of Labor and *Maquiladoras*

Life-cycle models of international products suggest that they are initially made and consumed in the center, in a major industrial economy, then exported to the periphery, and finally produced and consumed "out there," once technology is standardized and savings can be made on the labor front. Folker Fröbel and his collaborators have christened this trend the New International Division of Labor (NIDL). The old IDL had kept labor costs down through the formal and informal slavery of colonialism (the trade in people and indentureship) and expropriation of cheap raw materials, with value added in the metropole. Successful action by the working class at the center eventually redistributed income there downwards. The response from capital was to export production, with an increasing focus on young women workers.

There are approximately 61,000 multinational corporations worldwide, with links to 900,000 firms. These multinationals look for state incentives, weak labor organization and protection, docile labor, minimal environmental regulation, favorable exchange rates, low wages, and sparse human-rights enforcement. By the mid-1980s, so many had found these jewels that the value of offshore production by multinationals began to exceed trade between states (Miller et al.).

Mexican *maquiladoras* exemplify the NIDL. They opened their doors in the mid-1960s, when a *bracero* (guest-worker) program between Mexico and the United States was terminated. Then the Mexican state introduced import-tax exemptions to stimulate in-bond input assembly, and Washington permitted duty-free return of assembled components that had originated north of the border. What began as a temporary initiative became of massive economic significance during the 1980s and 1990s. In 1993, *maquiladora* exports amounted to US $21.9 billion; in 2000, the figure was US $79.5 billion. The *maquiladoras'* proportion of Mexico's overall exports grew from 37.8 percent in 1995 to 47.1 percent in 2006, when they employed upwards of 1.2 million people, a labor force generated through the migration of poor rural people to the north. There was no equivalent growth in social services, education, public health, housing, and water (Carrillo and Zárate; Mendoza; Reygadas; Baram). The key instrument of this exploitation has been NAFTA/TLC. Since the treaty's adoption, trade between the United States and Mexico has grown without an equitable distribution of wealth or economic development. The junction of the two countries sees "greater income disparity . . . than at any other major commercial border in the world" (Jacott, Reed, and Winfield).

Women have long been at the forefront of the *maquiladoras'* electronic-labor process and its environmental impact. For instance, when RCA moved its radio and TV plants from Camden to Bloomington to Ciudad Juarez, in search of ever-cheaper costs, company elders sought a workforce of young, unmarried women. This strategy had little to do with biology (aka the docile and nimble-fingered girls found in management prayer books). Rather, it was about an ideology of gendered control, with domination (Cowie 17–18; Maxwell and Miller, "Green Smokestacks?"; Kalm).

The gendered nature of this employment has been accompanied by violence. Human Rights Watch disclosed the numerous misogynistic assaults and discrimination against *maquiladoras* in 1996. Matters have hardly improved. The Centre for Reflection and Action on Labour Issues (CEREAL) interviewed thousands of workers in 2008 and 2009 across the Mexican electronics sector. Its subsequent report revealed systematic sexual harassment and fundamental exploitation; one reads telling stories of each female employee preparing over one hundred central-processing units an hour in factories, where they are classified as "temporary" so their employers can elude regulations and deals that govern full-time labor (Centre for Reflection and Action on Labour Issues; Paterson).

Then there is the environment. The 1983 La Paz Agreement on Cooperation for the Protection and Improvement of the Environment in the Border Area/Convenio entre los Estados Unidos Mexicanos y los Estados Unidos de América sobre cooperación para la protección y mejoramiento del medio ambiente between Mexico and the United States mandates that *maquiladora* waste return to where the relevant multinational corporation is domiciled. But despite that accord and NAFTA/TLC's environmental and labor protections, the *maquilas* have ushered in and maintained low wages, labor-law violations, and exposure to unhealthy chemicals and gases—a toxic life in every sense. Enforcement has been lax, and statistics about environmental side effects of production and the flow of contaminated goods are spotty (the anecdotal evidence is appalling) (Simpson 166–67).

The 1992 Basel Convention on the Control of Transboundary Movements of Hazardous Wastes and Their Disposal prohibits international transportation of hazardous material, even between non-signatories of the accord (the United States) and signatories (Mexico). But powerful polluters like Japan, Canada, and the US engage in "venue shopping," seeking out dumping grounds wherever feasible. They justify such actions on a neoliberal basis, invoking the doctrines of comparative advantage and the notion that every nation has a certain amount of e-waste it can bear. California alone shipped about twenty million pounds of e-waste in 2006 to various nations, including Mexico (Lee). Such waste is one of the biggest sources of heavy metals and toxic pollutants. It causes grave environmental and health concerns, stemming from the potential seepage of noxious chemicals, gases, and metals into landfills, water sources, and salvage yards. Much e-waste recycling is done by preteen young girls, ragpickers who work without protection to pull apart outmoded First World televisions and computers. The remains are dumped in landfills (Maxwell and Miller, "Green Smokestacks?").

Television Sets

. . . are dangerous. I remember them exploding when I was a child. Some got so hot they were known as "curtain-burners." But TV remains popular. In 2007, 207.5 million sets were sold around the globe, of which 56 percent were old-style, fat-screen televisions. The estimated number for 2011 is 245.5 million, with one-third being fat-screen and the remainder the newer, leaner flat-screen. Regulators favor digital broadcast systems, the cost of sets has dropped, and their uptake has increased, all with little regard for electricity consumption—up to 250 watts per hour (Miller, *Television Studies* 175–89).

Television is responsible for monumental environmental despoliation, despite claims that as one of the culture industries it helps form a post-smokestacks utopia. Like electronic production more generally, TV relies on exorbitant water use and carcinogens. Most color sets use cathode-ray tubes (CRTs), which send electrons from cesium cathodes into high-voltage electrodes that project onto phosphorescent screens and emit radiation to illuminate phosphors. CRTs are made of zinc, copper, cesium, cadmium, silver, and lead. Major environmental problems occur when they are created and when they are thrown away, because their components seep into underground water at both stages, leaving a base history of heavy metals and toxic chemicals. This situation worsened with the 2009 transition to digital broadcasting in the United States, when many outdated analog sets, perhaps the hardest of devices to recycle, were discarded (Conner and Williams; Puzzanghera).

Major TV manufacturers in Mexico have included Sanyo, Sony, Samsung, JVC, Hitachi, and Panasonic; in 2001, twenty thousand people were employed making over 10 million televisions, "soldering, inserting screws, connecting wires, testing, inspecting, painting, and packaging" (García and Simpson 150). Tijuana became "TV Capital of the World." But lower wages, energy costs, and taxes saw the People's Republic of China, Thailand, Malaysia, and the Socialist Republic of Viet Nam competing for the NIDL. Whereas Mexico accounted for 30.42 percent and China 18.5 percent of television-set and video-equipment exports to the United States in 2002, by 2006, the proportions were virtually equal (35.07 percent compared to 34.76 percent). *Maquiladora* employment fell from 2000 to 2003, and the global recession, evident by 2008, slashed employment and investment. The nearly two hundred companies that assembled electronics in Mexico decreased production by almost 40 percent from mid-2008. Sony, for instance, announced the closure of a TV plant in 2009, with the loss of six hundred positions, and sold its Mexican interests to the notorious Foxconn in 2010, which has seen numerous suicides at a Chinese factory making iPhones and iPads. The *maquiladora* slide slowed in 2009 as firms looked to cut the time wasted exporting parts and importing sets across the Pacific, but this did not restore pre-recession production or jobs: 144 plants closed in the twelve months prior to October 2009, and 122 new ones opened (Centre for Reflection and Action on Labour Issues; Mendoza; García and Simpson; Moore; Barboza; Gaffney; Mari Castañeda; NOTIMEX).

It's not as though labor costs were high across the border. Mexican *maquiladora* wages consistently declined from 1993 to 2006, while productivity increased. Two full-time workers in a Mexican plant receive just two-thirds of the pay needed to support a family of four, prior to medical and educational expenses, and employees are denied collective-bargaining rights and legal protection of privacy, health, and safety. Notably, the people who make these gadgets can't afford to purchase them—a flat-screen TV costs less in San Diego than where it is made, in Tijuana, because tariff-free manufactures there are strictly for export ("Where Is 'Away'?").

Maquiladora warehouses, managers, and researchers are generally based in San Diego. Components are imported to Mexico from there, in addition to Germany, Korea, Japan, Taiwan, Malaysia, and Thailand. Put another way, so-called high value is created in the United States and elsewhere, with the dangerous, dull, and poorly remunerated work done across the border. In response, vigorous civil-society groups remind authorities of their responsibilities and encourage direct citizen activism, notably Las Voces de la Maquila, the Colectivo Chilpancingo Pro Justicia Ambiental, the Environmental Health Coalition, and Greenpeace (García and Simpson; Simpson). But mainstream economic analyses focus on foreign direct investment, local employment, and technology transfer, largely ignoring pollution, exploitation, and gender relations (see Mendoza) and the *New York Times* headlines TV-set manufacture as "A Boom across the Border" (Malkin). For such approaches, "*maquiladora* diseases . . . that bloom in wombs and spinal columns" (Urrea 12) are no doubt negative externalities, to be considered—if at all—in a calculus of Paretian optimality.[2]

Of course, manufacturing television sets is only one part of Mexico's electronics production. Hewlett-Packard, Hitachi, IBM, Nokia, Siemens, Phillips, and Motorola all have businesses there, not to mention such subcontractors as Foxconn, Solectron, Flextronics, and Jabil Circuit. Mexico is also Latin America's second-biggest consumer of electronics, and itself accumulates 100,000 or 180,000 tons of electronic waste each year, depending on whether you believe activists, commercial TV, academia, or progressive journalism (Greenpeace; Guadarrama; Moguel; Enciso).

The people who deal with this waste are as liminal as the border itself. Like other global fringe-dwellers who have circled both modernity and postmodernity, they are crucial yet often invisible contributors to material and mythological life.

Ragpickers

The *ur*-figure in myths of modernity was the decidedly immaterial *flâneur*, whose roving gentlemanly eye viewed the city with a mixture of distraction and immersion. But another person, also on the street, could ill afford such gazes and glances. This was the ragpicker, an intensely practical *bricoleur* for whom recycling was a way of life.[3] Itinerant ragpickers are actually hardy perennials, supplying raw materials to cultural industries from Gutenberg to the Internet. Perhaps 1 percent of people in the global South live this way—approximately 15 million people worldwide (Medina; da Silva et al., "World at Work").

Before the Spanish invasion, Mexico had many *pepenadores*—people who managed waste. Their policies and practices were disrupted by the conquest, which saw more and more urban dross accumulate over three centuries as commodification took hold and put an end to rural recycling norms (Medina 130; Braudel 296). As in pre-industrial European towns, the anxious rich condemned the "odor of crowded bodies" and the "rising tide of excrement and rubbish." Ragpickers typified urban untouchables: "sewermen, gut dressers, knackers, drain cleaners, workers in refuse dumps, and dredging gangs" (Corbin 53, 114, 115, 145–46). Removal meant the *displacement* of waste, but not its *elimination*. As a living, malodorous reminder of urban filth, the lowly ragpicker foiled bourgeois fantasies of cleanliness that depended on "escape from and rejection of a primitive agricultural system now in a state of crisis" (Calvino 113).

By the nineteenth century, urban dross/modernity was stimulating art that expressed the ambivalence and ambiguity of garbage—a sign of both progress and abjection. You can read about it in Charles Dickens, E. T. A. Hoffmann, and Émile Zola, among others (Moser; Dorde Cuvardic García). In his poem "Le Vin des Chiffoniers" ("The Ragpickers' Wine"), Charles Baudelaire famously portrayed these pioneering recyclers as defenders of the poor and enemies of the rich, poetlike in their *bricolage* (141–42). Vincent van Gogh called The Hague's city dump "a paradise for the artist" (qtd. in Hughes), while Manet's *Ragpicker* trudged disconsolately toward refuse he could not refuse.

There was a public-policy corollary of ragpicker art. Karl Polanyi referred to this as "the discovery of society"—that moment in the nineteenth-century transformation of capitalism when Marx's "kicked-about mass" referred to earlier came to be marked as part of the social—and hence deserving of aid and inclusion—critique and exclusion. Their well-being was incorporated into collective subjectivity as a right, a problem, a statistic, and a law, juxtaposed to the self-governing worker or owner. When merged with class activism and philanthropic moralism, the positive side of this statistical pauperization was that society was held to be simultaneously more and less than the promises and precepts of the market. Ragpickers derived a certain visibility by being made into statistical problems in need of resolution.

But they remain abject. In the e-waste era, ragpickers are statistical and managerial problems in terms of public health, income, self-sufficiency, and so on. Indian ragpickers, who number in the hundreds of thousands, suffer a historically unprecedented prevalence of low hemoglobin, high monocyte and eosinophil counts, gum disease, diarrhea, and dermatitis.[4] In Brazil, where it's estimated that there are half a million ragpickers, extraordinary levels of physiological disorder and psychological distress are reported. Epidemiological studies find ragpicking at fault for polluting the surrounding environments, and seek to outlaw the practice (da Silva, Fassa, and Kriebel; Ray et al.; Mukherjee et al.). Such research is diligent, sophisticated, and concerned about forgotten, exploited workers in the gray economy; but it may further marginalize and deny a voice to folks whose lives are complex to study, comprehend, and represent.

Mexican e-waste ragpickers are frequently former employees or family members of *maquiladora* workers. They operate beyond taxation, labor laws, and police by collecting, separating, cataloging, and selling materials from spurned consumer and business products that have made their way to rubbish dumps and low-income areas. Most ragpickers do not earn wages from employers; nor are they in registered cooperatives or small businesses. As we have seen, this informality also characterizes the *maquiladoras,* which use temporary-employment agencies to hire workers who are never deemed full-time and hence lack organization and rights (Medina vii, 1, 128; Paterson).

The wider background to their story is structural adjustment, peddled by the World Bank, the International Monetary Fund, the World Trade Organization, and the sovereign states that dominate them. This neoliberal clerisy encouraged the global South to turn away from subsistence agriculture and toward tradable goods. Neoliberalism has urged and capitalism has driven chaotic urban growth, as per Mexico City's sprawling deterioration and regeneration. The result is an "informal working class" that is generally disarticulated from political activity and nongovernment organizations, because it lacks monetary and cultural capital and organizational heft. In a sign that ragpickers remain embarrassing embodiments of post-industrial "progress," Baudelaire's poem is translated on the World Bank's PovertyNet website to moralize about sub-proletarian decadence that uses wine to salve the pain of poverty. Not surprisingly, the World Bank and its kind show no interest in actually engaging ragpickers; they want to transform them from a distance (Harriss; Gidwani; Medina ix). Ragpickers themselves seek a dignified recognition of their contribution plus material improvements to their lives, as Fernando Solanas's 2005 documentary, *Dignity of the Nobodies,* tellingly shows.

The narrower background to ragpickers' lives is local public policy, which has militated against them by mandating that they forge perverse alliances with exploitative middle-"man" brokers even as they remain outside the law: the Mexican case saw quasi-formalization of the informal sector under the *clientelismo* of the Partido Revolucionario Institucional, which ran national and rural politics for decades through a mixture of electoral popularity, corruption, and international networks (Medina ix, 133; Guillermoprieto).

What can be done to aid these formal and informal workers, and movement between the categories? Could citizenship rights be of help?

Citizenship

The last two hundred years of modernity have produced three zones of citizenship, with partially overlapping but also distinct historicities. These zones are the political (conferring the right to reside and vote); the economic (the right to work and prosper); and the cultural (the right to know and speak). They correspond to the French Revolutionary cry "*liberté, égalité, fraternité*" ("liberty, equality, solidarity") and the Argentine left's contemporary version "*ser ciudadano, tener trabajo, y ser alfabetizado*" ("citizenship, employment, and literacy") (Martín-Barbero 9). The first category concerns political rights; the second, material interests; and the third, cultural representation (Miller, *Cultural Citizenship*). They have normally assumed the capacity to appeal to national jurisdictions. For people working in the shadow of the NIDL on behalf of multinational corporations, and with the particularly perverse structural inequality of Mexican-US history and geography, citizenship is both desirable and frustrating.

Many US progressives lament what they see as race-blind cultural politics in Latin America, claiming that the utopias of *mestizaje* preclude locals from adopting the supposedly superior understanding of environmental justice as a product of racial discrimination as opposed to socio-economic difference (Simpson 156–57 exemplifies this position). This is a false dichotomy, because such ways of understanding and dividing society have interlocked attitudes, values, norms, and interpersonal and social relations. But the dichotomy is a powerful tendency in the US academy and its civil society. Both have been slow to learn from theory and analysis that emanate from the global South.

And it is in Latin America that we see the successful mobilization of ragpickers' citizenship rights: in 2009, Colombia's Constitutional Court ruled that they are entrepreneurs, thus permitting them to tender for waste-management concessions from local government. That decision formalized their status, decriminalized their actions, protected their livelihood from shifts in state policy that had shut down dumps, and offered them franchises if they created conventional firms. Cali-based ragpickers were pioneers in establishing cooperatives, and held the world's first global conference of their colleagues in 2008, including Brazilian ragpickers, whose work is now recognized by the labor ministry ("Muck"). This represents one of those fascinating transformations from social problem to social boon, as ragpickers shift from being regarded as unpleasant, odoriferous embodiments of abjection to model citizens of sustainable development and targets of the contemporary development discourse of microcredit.

That change was achieved by combining political, economic, and cultural citizenship—drawing on the law to change economic and legal conditions and cultural links to act collectively. The next step is to do so transnationally. Consider these precedents:

> As workers and communities outside of Silicon Valley began to discover this "dark side of the chip," they also began to come together to confront its "clean" image. Community and worker based movements began to emerge in other countries—PHASE II in Scotland, Asia Monitor Resource Centre in Hong Kong, TAVOI in Taiwan, CEREAL in Mexico, etc. as the grassroots efforts began to grow into a global movement. Many of these groups are now working together internationally through various networks to develop worker training on occupational health and safety, to clean up and prevent air and water pollution, to press the electronics industry to phase out use of the most toxic chemicals. (Smith)

Several options for regulating multinational corporations and the challenges they pose trans-territorially for citizen action present themselves: "soft law [protocols of international organizations], hard law [nationally based legislation], codes of conduct [transnational norms], and voluntary self-regulation" (Baram). But the latest critical research suggests that these strategies have not secured a nexus between "the transfer of technology" and the transfer of "practices for using it safely" (Baram). That would necessitate universal standards of health and safety across sites, from the post-industrial core to the manufacturing periphery, in addition to contractual deals between multinationals and their hosts (Ferus-Comelo; Schatan and Castilleja). Guidance must come from a blend of political, economic, and cultural citizenship, with an awareness of the New International Division of Labor. In the case of border workers, there is a special need for coordination across a line that is as semipermeable, traumatic, and exploitative. Our border communication research needs to be as nimble as they are so we can juggle political economy, ethnography, and textual analysis and work with the relevant parties.

Notes

Thanks for ideas and sources to Mari Castañeda, Jorge Castillo, Rick Maxwell, Luis Reygadas, Luis Alberto Urrea; to two anonymous manuscript reviewers for suggestions; and to the editor for his encouragement and patience.

1. A roman à clef is a novel with a code that conceals the fact that it is drawn from real life.

2. Paretian optimality is a doctrine from the social sciences that says that the best possible outcome is one that "satisfices" rather than satisfies; in other words, it allocates goods among people in ways that do not affect anyone adversely but may not be technically best for any given individual.

3. A *bricoleur* combines objects to make new, surprising meanings.

4. Monocytes and eosinophil are white blood cells.

Afterword

Border Optics

John Louis Lucaites

As I drive from my home near Indianapolis to my office in Bloomington, I cross three county lines, all duly marked with official signs. As I approach the university I pass the gates that separate the campus from the town that surrounds it on all sides. Traffic markers declare a "school zone" (when children are present). Once in my private office I open a three-day-old newspaper and come across two stories on the same page: the one below the fold tells the story of Japanese internment on Bainbridge Island, Washington, in 1942 under the title "A Wall to Remember"; the one above the fold reports on Texas governor Rick Perry's Houston prayer rally with the headline "Rally Raises Questions Anew of the Boundaries of Perry's Faith." Logging in to my computer, I am informed that my firewall needs to be updated. Several hours later I sit in a conference room with deans and colleagues from other departments where the sometimes rigid disciplinary differences that purport to distinguish and legitimize our expertise as professors of communication, English, history, sociology, and political science come into tension with one another as we deliberate the propriety of inviting a politically controversial speaker to campus. At lunch a friend and I debate the possibility that local congressional districts will be gerrymandered to produce favorable election outcomes for one party or another. Back in my car on the way home I find myself somewhat disoriented by detour signs that have me driving on what would otherwise be the wrong side of the road. As I enter the suburban subdivision in which I reside, I notice a surveyor marking the line between the lot on which my house sits and the plot of land immediately to the north. When I ask him what he is doing, he tells me that my neighbor is preparing to install a "privacy barrier" (aka a fence).

We live our civic lives amidst all manner of borders and boundaries. Some are obvious and announce themselves as such; others are spoken or otherwise symbolized but generally unremarked upon, hidden behind layers of metaphors and formal conventions that imply a degree of normalcy that betokens the natural or the ordinary. Most tend to be seen but go unnoticed, observed only in the breach as we become habituated to—and, truth to tell, rely upon—their presence. Some are benign, and others more intrusive. But, and here is the key point, they all indicate some degree of human volition and, as such, mark a power dynamic central to, if not characteristic of, modern liberal societies.

There is something ironic about this power dynamic, for modern liberal societies are underwritten by notions of individual and civic freedom and liberty, but borders and boundaries are, by definition and in practice, designed to limit and constrain. They rely upon and thus demonstrate a sense of sovereignty, but only as they manifest the hubris of absolute control which, of course, we know to be a fantasy: indeed, a very condition of their existence appears to be the inevitability of their failure (Wendy Brown). And yet, it seems, we can't live without them, a troubled and troubling nod to their allegedly social and political normality. And the question is, how might we constructively and creatively acknowledge and manage this conundrum?

The chapters in this volume invite consideration of the notion of "border rhetorics" as what I will call an optic for how we might proceed. As the *OED* reminds us, in the sixteenth century an "optic" was understood to be an "instrument or device; constructed to assist vision" ("Optic," def. A4), but in contemporary times it has also taken on the meaning of a "particular way of interpreting or experiencing something" ("Optic," def. B2c). I mean to conflate these two definitions here so as to suggest the sense in which "border rhetorics" operate as a theory (derived from the Greek *theorein*, "a way of seeing") that coaches our ability *to observe* and evaluate the borders and boundaries that constitute our civic life and that might otherwise remain invisible or go unnoticed, treated as altogether natural, ordinary, and apolitical. The key is in noting that the emphasis is on the *act of seeing* as a primary mode of civic behavior. Understood as an optic, in other words, border rhetorics offer one avenue for engaging the question, what might it mean "to see" or "to be seen" as a citizen.

The tension between "seeing" and "being seen" as a citizen underscores the essentially embodied, performative dimension of civic life. As civic performance, citizenship relies upon one's capacity as both agent and spectator, enacting the demands of civic life for the benefit of others to witness or observe—if not judge, while also viewing the world through the eyes of the citizen (see Hariman and Lucaites; Azoulay). What border rhetorics call attention to is the sense in which "seeing" and "being seen" are not simply metaphors for a representational process, but actively and performatively constitute the very terms of our identities in a multitude of palpably visible ways. The case study that animates this volume is very much to the point, perhaps after the model of a representative anecdote for the problems and possibilities of border rhetorics generally understood.

The physical border between the United States and Mexico—itself a symbolic, cartographic contrivance of modern governance—has rarely been in question, but, as the range of chapters here demonstrate, that boundary is not so easily reduced to a static mark in the ground. This fact has not mitigated efforts to reify such geographical borders by visibly marking them with fences and sentries (underwritten by laws and statutes). Such labors, both physical and judicial, are obvious performances of national sovereignty, acts central no doubt to what anthropologist James C. Scott characterizes as "seeing like a state," but as history shows, such spectacles by themselves ultimately do little to alter the actual flow of peoples or goods from one side to the other. What they are designed to keep out always finds its way in, and what is being contained always finds a way to leak or leach out. What they do, however, is to adjust the citizen's optic so that what one is invited to see are literally "patriots" and "criminals." And seeing this way inevitably entails a rhetoric of "being seen" that legitimates subsequent behavior and action, fortifying and reinforcing the obsessive paranoia and fear of the alien that led to the building of the walls and the posting of sentries in the first place. It is one more event in a cycle of state-driven violence that filters our perception and blinds us from seeing more humane solutions to our problems.

National and cultural borders, of course, rarely exist without borderlands, zones of liminality that straddle what purportedly is bounded in and out and thus complicate, if not altogether confound, the impulse to rigid logics of inclusion and exclusion. The borderlands between the United States and Mexico serve as potent inventional resources for challenging the ways in which we see ourselves and the other in terms of a simple and purified national imaginary of "white" natives and "brown" aliens, while potentially enabling us to re-envision a more productive and fungible civic life that sees and is seen with cultural and political magnanimity. Or not. But more, and again as the case studies here demonstrate with care and clarity, such borders and borderlands are best understood as extending beyond any simple or singular sense of physical location (i.e., the geographical boundary between the United States and Mexico), situating the entailments of the "US-Mexican frontier" in a wide array of local and national economies and mediated contexts. We find them in international treaties and laws, but also as they circulate on websites, in movies—both commercial and otherwise—photographs, poetry, and even in our trash. And in every instance they stand as testimony to our current civic life, however one wants to evaluate the outcome.

D. Robert DeChaine concludes his introduction to this volume by noting that the time has come "to treat the rhetoricity of borders seriously." The point is very well taken, and it extends well beyond our otherwise considerable concern with the US–Mexico border. Rhetoric is first and foremost about our civic life. Each generation, it seems, is destined to reimagine the manner and implications of rhetoric (or, perhaps more properly, the rhetorics) for its own times. We currently sit at a transitional moment in our history where the borders and boundaries of our civic life are being challenged as never before, both from within and from without the dominant culture, both from home and from abroad. The resources needed to engage these challenges to civic life—whether they concern the boundaries between the United States and Mexico, or red and blue states, or urban and suburban residents, or rich and poor, or gay and straight—need to be seen anew. It is time to begin to think of rhetoric as a way of seeing and being seen, of the implications of such a rhetoric as a performative mode of being, and of border rhetorics as a powerful optic for understanding a chief problematic of contemporary public culture and civic life.

Suggested Readings

The following is a brief list of suggested readings for the study of border rhetorics. Readers who are new to the field may find these texts to be a useful starting point for further exploration.

Aizura, Aren Z. "Of Borders and Homes: The Imaginary Community of (Trans)-Sexual Citizenship." *Inter-Asia Cultural Studies* 7.2 (2006): 289–309. Print.

Anderson, Benedict. *Imagined Communities: Reflections on the Origin and Spread of Nationalism.* London: Verso, 1983. Print.

Anzaldúa, Gloria. *Borderlands/La Frontera: The New Mestiza.* San Francisco: Aunt Lute, 1987. Print.

Beasley, Vanessa B., ed. *Who Belongs in America?: Presidents, Rhetoric, and Immigration.* College Station: Texas A&M UP, 2006. Print.

Butler, Judith. *Undoing Gender.* New York: Routledge, 2004. Print.

Calafell, Bernadette Marie. "Disrupting the Dichotomy: 'Yo Soy Chicana/o?' In the New Latina/o South." *Communication Review* 7.2 (2004): 175–204. Print.

———. *Latina/o Communication Studies: Theorizing Performance.* New York: Peter Lang, 2007. Print.

Calafell, Bernadette Marie, and Fernando Delgado. "Reading Latina/o Images: Interrogating *Americanos." Critical Studies in Media Communication* 21.1 (2004): 1–21. Print.

Carrillo Rowe, Aimee. "Whose 'America'? The Politics of Rhetoric and Space in the Formation of US Nationalism." *Radical History Review* 89 (2004): 115–34. Print.

Chávez, Karma R. "Border (In)Securities: Normative and Differential Belonging in LGBTQ and Immigrant Rights Discourse." *Communication and Critical/Cultural Studies* 7.2 (2010): 136–55. Print.

Chavez, Leo R. *Covering Immigration: Popular Images and the Politics of the Nation.* Berkeley: U of California P, 2001. Print.

————. *The Latino Threat: Constructing Immigrants, Citizens, and the Nation*. Stanford, CA: Stanford UP, 2008. Print.

Cisneros, J. David. "Contaminated Communities: The Metaphor of 'Immigrant as Pollutant' in Media Representations of Immigration." *Rhetoric and Public Affairs* 11.4 (2008): 569–602. Print.

————. "(Re)Bordering the Civic Imaginary: Rhetoric, Hybridity, and Citizenship in *La Gran Marcha*." *Quarterly Journal of Speech* 97.1 (2011): 26–49. Print.

DeChaine, D. Robert. "Bordering the Civic Imaginary: Alienization, Fence Logic, and the Minuteman Civil Defense Corps." *Quarterly Journal of Speech* 95.1 (2009): 43–65. Print.

————. "Imagined Immunities: Border Rhetorics and the Ethos of Sans Frontièrisme." *Interdisciplinarity and Social Justice: Revisioning Academic Accountability*. Ed. Joe Parker, Ranu Samantrai, and Mary Romero. Ithaca: State U of New York P, 2010. 261–85. Print.

Delgado, Fernando P. "Chicano Movement Rhetoric: An Ideographic Interpretation." *Communication Quarterly* 43 (1995): 446–54. Print.

Demo, Anne Teresa. "Sovereignty Discourse and Contemporary Immigration Politics." *Quarterly Journal of Speech* 91.3 (2005): 291–311. Print.

Flores, Lisa A. "Constructing National Bodies: Public Argument in the English-Only Movement." *Argument at Century's End: Reflecting on the Past and Envisioning the Future*. Ed. Thomas A. Hollihan. Annandale, VA: National Communication Association, 2000. 436–45. Print.

————. "Constructing Rhetorical Borders: Peons, Illegal Aliens, and Competing Narratives of Immigration." *Critical Studies in Media Communication* 20.4 (2003): 362–87. Print.

Flores, Lisa A., and Marouf A. Hasian Jr. "Returning to Aztlán and La Raza: Political Communication and the Vernacular Construction of Chicano/a Nationalism." *Politics, Communication, and Culture*. Ed. Alberto González and Dolores V. Tanno. Thousand Oaks, CA: Sage, 1997. 186–203. Print.

Fox, Claire F. *The Fence and the River: Culture and Politics at the US-Mexico Border*. Minneapolis: U of Minnesota P, 1999. Print.

Hasian, Marouf, Jr., and Fernando Delgado. "Trials and Tribulations of Racialized Critical Rhetorical Theory: Understanding the Rhetorical Ambiguities of Proposition 187." *Communication Theory* 8.3 (1998): 245–70. Print.

Holling, Michelle A. "Patrolling National Identity, Masking White Supremacy: The Minuteman Project." *Critical Rhetorics of Race*. Ed. Michael Lacy and Kent A. Ono. New York: New York UP, 2011. 98–116. Print.

Luibhéid, Eithne, and Lionel Cantú Jr., eds. *Queer Migrations: Sexuality, US Citizenship, and Border Crossings*. Minneapolis: U of Minnesota P, 2005. Print.

McKinnon, Sara L. "Citizenship and the Performance of Credibility: Audiencing Gender-Based Asylum Seekers in US Immigration Courts." *Text and Performance Quarterly* 29.3 (2009): 205–221. Print.

Miller, Toby. *Cultural Citizenship: Cosmopolitanism, Consumerism, and Television in a Neoliberal Age.* Philadelphia: Temple UP, 2007. Print.

Moraga, Cherríe, and Gloria Anzaldúa, eds. *This Bridge Called My Back: Writings by Radical Women of Color.* New York: Kitchen Table, 1981. Print.

Muñoz, José Esteban. *Disidentifications: Queers of Color and the Performance of Politics.* Minneapolis: U of Minnesota P, 1999. Print.

Nevins, Joseph. *Operation Gatekeeper: The Rise of the "Illegal Alien" and the Making of the US-Mexico Boundary.* New York: Routledge, 2002. Print.

Ngai, Mae M. *Impossible Subjects: Illegal Aliens and the Making of Modern America.* Princeton, NJ: Princeton UP, 2004. Print.

Ono, Kent A., and John M. Sloop. *Shifting Borders: Rhetoric, Immigration, and California's Proposition 187.* Philadelphia: Temple UP, 2002. Print.

Palczewski, Catherine. "*Bodies,* Borders, and Letters: Gloria Anzaldúa's 'Speaking in Tongues: A Letter to 3rd World Women Writers.'" *Southern Communication Journal* 62 (1996): 1–16. Print.

Rodriguez, Néstor P. "The Social Construction of the US-Mexico Border." *Immigrants Out! The New Nativism and the Anti-Immigrant Impulse in the United States.* Ed. Juan F. Perea. New York: New York UP, 1997. 223–43. Print.

Saldívar, José David. *Border Matters: Remapping American Cultural Studies.* Berkeley: U of California P, 1997. Print.

Schmidt Camacho, Alicia. *Migrant Imaginaries: Latino Cultural Politics in the US-Mexico Borderlands.* New York: New York UP, 2008. Print.

Shome, Raka. "Whiteness and the Politics of Location: Postcolonial Reflections." *Whiteness: The Communication of Social Identity.* Ed. Thomas K. Nakayama and Judith N. Martin. Thousand Oaks, CA: Sage, 1999. 107–128. Print.

Vila, Pablo. *Border Identifications: Narratives of Religion, Gender, and Class on the US-Mexico Border.* Austin: U of Texas P, 2005. Print.

Works Cited

Abrahams, Ray. *Vigilant Citizens: Vigilantism and the State.* Cambridge, UK: Polity, 1998. Print.

Acuña, Rodolfo. *Occupied America: A History of Chicanos.* 3rd ed. New York: HarperCollins, 1988. Print.

Agamben, Giorgio. *Homo Sacer: Sovereign Power and Bare Life.* Trans. Daniel Heller-Roazen. Stanford, CA: Stanford UP, 1998. Print.

———. *The State of Exception.* Trans. Kevin Attell. Chicago: U of Chicago P, 2005. Print.

A.G.L., Mrs. Letter to the editor. *Sentinel* (Corpus Christi, TX), 12 Mar. 1948: 2. Print.

Ahmed, Sara. "Affective Economies." *Social Text* 22.2 (2004): 117–39. Print.

———. *The Cultural Politics of Emotion.* New York: Routledge, 2004. Print.

Aizura, Aren Z. "Of Borders and Homes: The Imaginary Community of (Trans)-Sexual Citizenship." *Inter-Asia Cultural Studies* 7.2 (2006): 289–309. Print.

Akdenizli, Banu. "News Coverage of Immigration 2007: A Political Story, Not an Issue, Covered Episodically." *Project for Excellence in Journalism* 2008. Web. 1 Mar. 2010.

Alexander, Bryant Keith. *Performing Black Masculinity: Race, Culture, and Queer Identity.* Lanham, MD: Altamira, 2006. Print.

———. "Performing Culture in the Classroom: An Instructional (Auto)Ethnography." *Text and Performance Quarterly* 19 (1999): 307–331. Print.

Allsup, V. Carl. "Delgado v. Bastrop I.S.D." *Handbook of Texas Online.* Texas State Historical Association. Web. 8 June 2010.

Alvarez, Robert R. "The Mexican-US Border: The Making of an Anthropology of Borderlands." *Annual Review of Anthropology* 24 (1995): 447–70. Print.

"Am an American Day Observance Set for Sunday." *Sentinel* (Corpus Christi, TX), 14 May 1948: 1. Print.

Anderson, Benedict. *Imagined Communities: Reflections on the Origin and Spread of Nationalism.* London: Verso, 1983. Print.

Andreas, Peter. *Border Games: Policing the US-Mexico Divide.* Ithaca: Cornell UP, 2000. Print.

——. "Redrawing the Line: Borders and Security in the Twenty-First Century." *International Security* 28.2 (2003): 78–111. Print.

Angus, Ian. "The Politics of Common Sense: Articulation Theory and Critical Communication Studies." *Communication Yearbook* 15 (1992): 535–70. Print.

Anzaldúa, Gloria. *Borderlands/La Frontera: The New Mestiza.* San Francisco: Aunt Lute, 1987. Print.

Appadurai, Arjun. "Global Ethnoscapes: Notes and Queries for a Transnational Anthropology." *Recapturing Anthropology: Working in the Present.* Ed. Richard G. Fox. Santa Fe, NM: School of American Research, 1991. 191–210. Print.

Archibold, Randal C. "Arizona Enacts Stringent Law on Immigration." *New York Times,* n.p. Web. 10 June 2010.

——. "Scathing Report on Border Security Is Issued." *New York Times,* 18 Sept. 2009, late ed.: A21. Print.

——. "The Two Sides Intersect in Immigration Debate." *New York Times,* 30 May 2010: A14. Print.

Arizona Peace Officers Standards and Training Board. "Implementation of the 2010 Arizona Immigration Laws Statutory Provisions for Peace Officers." *AZPOST Recommended Minimum Course of Training on Arizona Immigration Laws,* June 2010. Web. 2 Aug. 2010.

Arizona State Senate. "Fact Sheet for S.B. 1070." *Senate Research.* 2010. Web. 3 Aug. 2010.

Arondekar, Anjali. "Border/Line Sex: Queer Postcolonialities, or How Race Matters outside the United States." *Interventions: The International Journal of Postcolonial Studies* 7.2 (2005): 236–50. Print.

Asen, Robert. "A Discourse Theory of Citizenship." *Quarterly Journal of Speech* 90 (2004): 189–211. Print.

Associated Press. "Environmental Rules Waived for Border Fence." MSNBC. com. 15 Jan. 2007. Web. 1 Feb. 2010.

Azoulay, Ariella. *The Civil Contract of Photography.* New York: Zone Books, 2008. Print.

"Background." Amigos de las Mujeres de Juárez. n.d. Web. 25 May 2011.

Baker-Cristales, Beth. "Mediated Resistance: The Construction of Neoliberal Citizenship in the Immigrant Rights Movement." *Latino Studies* 7 (2009): 60–82. Print.

Balibar, Etienne. "The Nation Form: History and Ideology." *Race Critical Theo-*

ries: Text and Context. Ed. Philomena Essed and David T. Goldberg. Malden, MA: Blackwell, 2002. 220–30. Print.

The Ballad of Esequiel Hernández. Directed by Kieran Fitzgerald. PBS, 2007. DVD.

Baram, Michael. "Globalization and Workplace Hazards in Developing Nations." *Safety Science* 47.6 (2009): 756–66. Print.

"Barbecue, Fiesta at Kingsville to Climax School Fund Drive." *Sentinel* (Corpus Christi, TX), 28 May 1948: 1. Print.

Barboza, David. "String of Suicides Continues at Electronics Supplier in China." *New York Times,* 26 May 2010: B10. Print.

Barrett, James R., and David Roediger. "Inbetween Peoples: Race, Nationality and the 'New Immigrant' Working Class." *Journal of American Ethnic History* 16 (1997): 3–45. Print.

Basel Action Network and Silicon Valley Toxics Coalition. *Exporting Harm: The High-Tech Trashing of Asia,* 2002. Print.

Baudelaire, Charles. *Les Fleurs du Mal.* Paris: Gallimard, 1972. Print.

Beard Rau, Alia, Ginger Rough, and J. J. Hensley. "Arizona Immigration Law: State to Appeal Injunction." *Arizona Republic,* 28 July 2010. Web. 23 Aug. 2010.

Beasley, Vanessa B., ed. *Who Belongs in America?: Presidents, Rhetoric, and Immigration.* College Station: Texas A&M UP, 2006. Print.

Beckham, Jack M., II. "Border Policy/Border Cinema: Placing *Touch of Evil, The Border,* and *Traffic* in the American Imagination." *Journal of Popular Film and Television* 33 (2005): 130–41. Print.

Berlant, Lauren. *The Queen of America Goes to Washington City: Essays on Sex and Citizenship.* Durham, NC: Duke UP, 1997. Print.

———. "The Theory of Infantile Citizenship." *Public Culture* 5 (1993): 395–410. Print.

Berlant, Lauren, and Michael Warner. "Sex in Public." *Critical Inquiry* 24 (1998): 547–66. Print.

Bernazzoli, Richelle M., and Colin Flint. "Embodying the Garrison State? Everyday Geographies of Militarization in American Society." *Political Geography* 29 (2010): 157–66. Print.

Berson, Robin Kadison. *Young Heroes in World History.* Westport, CT: Greenwood, 1999. Print.

Bhabha, Homi K. *The Location of Culture.* New York: Routledge, 1994. Print.

Bibler Coutin, Susan. "Contesting Criminality: Illegal Immigration and the Spatialization of Legality." *Theoretical Criminology* 9.1 (2005): 5–33. Print.

Blackwelder, Julia Kirk. "Emma Tenayuca, Vision and Courage." *The Human*

Tradition in Texas. Ed. Ty Cashion and Jesús F. de la Teja. Wilmington, DE: Scholarly Resources, 2001. 191–208. Print.

Bosniak, Linda. *The Citizen and the Alien: Dilemmas of Contemporary Membership.* Princeton, NJ: Princeton UP, 2006. Print.

Brady, Mary Pat. *Extinct Lands, Temporal Geographies: Chicana Literature and the Urgency of Space.* Durham, NC: Duke UP, 2002. Print.

———. "The Homoerotics of Immigration Control." *Scholar and Feminist Online* 6.3 (2008). Web. 24 Sept. 2010.

Braudel, Fernand. *Capitalism and Material Life, 1400–1800.* Trans. Miriam Kochan. New York: Harper Colophon, 1973. Print.

Brewer, Jan. "Statement by Governor Jan Brewer on Senate Bill 1070." *Office of the Governor,* 23 Apr. 2010. Web. 23 Aug. 2010.

Brokaw, Chet. "S. Dakota Files Brief Supporting Arizona Immigration Law." *Azcentral.com.* 13 July 2010. Web. 16 July 2010.

Brouwer, Daniel, and Aaron Hess. "Making Sense of 'God Hates Fags' and 'Thank God for 9/11': A Thematic Analysis of Milbloggers' Responses to Reverend Fred Phelps and the Westboro Baptist Church." *Western Journal of Communication* 77 (2007): 69–90. Print.

Brown, Michelle. "Mapping Discursive Closings in the War on Drugs." *Crime Media Culture* 3 (2007): 11–29. Print.

Brown, Wendy. *Walled States, Waning Sovereignty.* New York: Zone Books, 2010. Print.

Buchanan, Susy. "Starring Role." *Southern Poverty Law Center Intelligence Report,* 2006. Web. 1 Mar. 2010.

Buchanan, Susy, and David Holthouse. "Shoot, Shovel, Shut Up." *Southern Poverty Law Center Intelligence Report,* 2007. Web. 31 Jan. 2010.

"Budget FY 2009—Department of Homeland Security." Washington, DC, 2009. Budget Brief. White House Office of Management and Budget. Web. 1 Feb. 2010.

Buelna, Enrique M. "The Mexican Question: Mexican Americans in the Communist Party, 1940–1957." *Center for Research on Latinos in a Global Society,* Working Paper 14. U of California, Irvine, 1999. Print.

Bush, George W. "Address to the Nation on Immigration Reform." 15 May 2006. Web. 20 Aug. 2010.

———. "The President's News Conference with President Vincente Fox of Mexico and Prime Minister Paul Martin of Canada in Waco, Texas." *Weekly Compilation of Presidential Documents* 509 (23 Mar. 2005): 509–517. Print.

Butler, Judith. *Precarious Life: The Powers of Mourning and Violence.* New York: Verso, 2006. Print.

———. *Undoing Gender.* New York: Routledge, 2004. Print.

Calafell, Bernadette Marie. "Disrupting the Dichotomy: 'Yo Soy Chicana/o?' In the New Latina/o South." *Communication Review* 7.2 (2004): 175–204. Print.

———. *Latina/o Communication Studies: Theorizing Performance*. New York: Peter Lang, 2007. Print.

———. "Mocking Mexicans for Profit." *Latino Studies* 4 (2006): 162–65. Print.

———. "Performing the Responsible Sponsor: Everything You Never Wanted to Know about Immigration Post-9/11." *Latina/o Communication Studies Today*. Ed. Angharad Valdivia. New York: Peter Lang, 2008. 69–89. Print.

Calafell, Bernadette Marie, and Fernando Delgado. "Reading Latina/o Images: Interrogating *Americanos*." *Critical Studies in Media Communication* 21.1 (2004): 1–21. Print.

Calderón, Roberto, and Emilio Zamora. "Manuela Solis Sager and Emma Tenayuca: A Tribute." *Chicana Voices: Intersections of Class, Race, and Gender*. Ed. Teresa Córdova, et al. Austin, TX: National Association for Chicano Studies, 1990. 30–41. Print.

Calvino, Italo. *The Road to San Giovanni*. Trans. Tim Parks. New York: Vintage International, 1994. Print.

"Canvassing Ends in Fund Drive by Local Clubs." *Sentinel* (Corpus Christi, TX), 12 Mar. 1948: 1. Print.

Carrillo, Jorge, and Robert Zárate. "The Evolution of Maquiladora Best Practices: 1965–2008." *Journal of Business Ethics* 88.2 (2009): 335–48. Print.

Carrillo Rowe, Aimee. *Power Lines: On the Subject of Feminist Alliances*. Durham, NC: Duke UP, 2008. Print.

———. "Whose 'America'? The Politics of Rhetoric and Space in the Formation of US Nationalism." *Radical History Review* 89 (2004): 115–34. Print.

Castañeda, Alejandra. "Roads to Citizenship: Mexican Migrants in the United States." *Latinos and Citizenship: The Dilemma of Belonging*. Ed. Suzanne Oboler. New York: Palgrave Macmillan, 2006. 143–65. Print.

Castañeda, Mari. "Television Set Production in the Era of Digital TV." *Companion to Media Production Studies*. Ed. Vicki Mayer. Malden, MA: Blackwell. In press.

Castillo, Debra A., María Gudelia Rangel Gómez, and Armando Rosas Solís. "Violence and Transvestite/Transgender Sex Workers in Tijuana." *Gender Violence at the US-Mexico Border: Media Representation and Public Response*. Ed. Héctor Domínguez-Ruvalcaba and Ignacio Corona. Tucson: U of Arizona P, 2010. 15–34. Print.

Ceccarelli, Leah. "History of the 'Frontier of Science' Metaphor." Western States Communication Association annual conference, Monterey, CA, 2011. Unpublished conference paper. Print.

Centre for Reflection and Action on Labor Issues. *Labor Rights in a Time of Crisis: Third Report on Working Conditions in the Mexican Electronics Industry,* 2009. Print.

Chacón, Justin Akers, and Mike Davis. *No One Is Illegal: Fighting Racism and State Violence on the US-Mexico Border.* Chicago: Haymarket, 2006. Print.

Charland, Maurice. "Constitutive Rhetoric: The Case of *Peuple Québécois.*" *Quarterly Journal of Speech* 73 (1987): 133–50. Print.

Chávez, Karma R. "Border (In)Securities: Normative and Differential Belonging in LGBTQ and Immigrant Rights Discourse." *Communication and Critical/ Cultural Studies* 7.2 (2010): 136–55. Print.

———. "Coalitional Politics and Confronting the Constructions of Queers and Migrants in the State of Arizona." Doctoral Dissertation. Arizona State University, 2007. Print.

———. "Embodied Translation: Dominant Discourse and Communication with Migrant Bodies-as-Text." *Howard Journal of Communications* 20 (2009): 18–36. Print.

———. "Spatializing Gender Performativity: Ecstasy and Possibilities for Livable Life in the Tragic Case of Victoria Arellano." *Women's Studies in Communication* 33.1 (2010): 1–15. Print.

Chavez, Leo R. *Covering Immigration: Popular Images and the Politics of the Nation.* Berkeley: U of California P, 2001. Print.

———. *The Latino Threat: Constructing Immigrants, Citizens, and the Nation.* Stanford, CA: Stanford UP, 2008. Print.

Chin, Gabriel J., et al. "A Legal Labyrinth: Issues Raised by Arizona Senate Bill 1070." *Georgetown Immigration Law Journal* 25 (2010): 47–92. Print.

Christian, Barbara. "The Race for Theory." *Making Face, Making Soul: Haciendo Caras.* Ed. Gloria Anzaldúa. San Francisco: Aunt Lute, 1990. 335–45. Print.

Cisneros, J. David. "Contaminated Communities: The Metaphor of 'Immigrant as Pollutant' in Media Representations of Immigration." *Rhetoric and Public Affairs* 11.4 (2008): 569–602. Print.

———. "Latina/os and Party Politics in the California Campaign against Bilingual Education: A Case Study in Argument from Transcendence." *Argumentation and Advocacy* 45.3 (2009): 115–34. Print.

———. "(Re)Bordering the Civic Imaginary: Rhetoric, Hybridity, and Citizenship in *La Gran Marcha.*" *Quarterly Journal of Speech* 97.1 (2011): 26–49. Print.

Clare, Eli. *Exile and Pride: Disability, Queerness, and Liberation.* Cambridge, MA: South End P, 1999. Print.

Cohn, Marjorie. "Arizona Legalizes Racial Profiling." *Jurist,* 27 Apr. 2010. Web. 3 Sept. 2010.

Conley, Donovan, and Greg Dickenson. "Textural Democracy." *Critical Studies in Media Communication* 27.1 (2010): 1–7. Print.

Conner, Teri L., and Ronald W. Williams. "Identification of Possible Sources of Particulate Matter in the Personal Cloud Using SEM/EDX." *Atmospheric Environment* 38.31 (2004): 5305–10. Print.

Conquergood, Dwight. "Performing as a Moral Act: Ethical Dimensions of the Ethnography of Performance." *Literature in Performance: A Journal of Literary and Performing Art* 5 (1985): 1–13. Print.

———. "Rethinking Ethnography: Towards a Critical Cultural Politics." *The Sage Handbook of Performance Studies*. Ed. D. Soyini Madison and Judith Hamera. Thousand Oaks, CA: Sage, 2006. 351–65. Print.

Coombe, Rosemary, and Andrew Herman. "Trademarks, Property, and Propriety: The Moral Economy of Consumer Politics and Corporate Accountability in the World Wide Web." *DePaul Law Review* 50.2 (2000): 597–632. Print.

Corbin, Alain. *The Foul and the Fragrant: Odor and the French Social Imagination*. Cambridge, MA: Harvard UP, 1986. Print.

Corey, Frederick C. "The Personal: Against the Master Narrative." *The Future of Performance Studies: Visions and Revisions*. Ed. Sheron J. Dailey. Annandale, VA: National Communication Association, 1998. 249–53. Print.

———. "On Possibility." *Text and Performance Quarterly* 26 (2006): 330–32. Print.

Cornelius, Wayne A. "Death at the Border: The Efficacy and Unintended Consequences of US Immigration Control Policy." *Population and Development Review* 27 (2001): 661–85. Print.

Cornelius, Wayne A., and Idean Salehyan. "Does Border Enforcement Deter Unauthorized Immigration? The Case of Mexican Migration to the United States of America." *Regulation and Governance* 1 (2007): 139–53. Print.

Corona, Ignacio. "Over Their Dead Bodies: Reading the Newspapers on Gender Violence." *Gender Violence at the US-Mexico Border: Media Representation and Public Response*. Ed. Héctor Domínguez-Ruvalcaba and Ignacio Corona. Tucson: U of Arizona P, 2010. 105–127. Print.

Corona, Ignacio, and Héctor Domínguez-Ruvalcaba. "Gender Violence: An Introduction." *Gender Violence at the US-Mexico Border: Media Representation and Public Response*. Ed. Héctor Domínguez-Ruvalcaba and Ignacio Corona. Tucson: U of Arizona P, 2010. 1–12. Print.

Cotera, Marta. "Among the Feminists: Racist Classist Issues—1976." *Chicana Feminist Thought: The Basic Historical Writings*. Ed. Alma García. New York: Routledge, 1997. 213–20. Print.

———. "Our Feminist Heritage." *Chicana Feminist Thought: The Basic Historical Writings*. Ed. Alma García. New York: Routledge, 1997. 41–44. Print.

Cowie, Jefferson. *Capital Moves: RCA's Seventy-Year Quest for Cheap Labor*. New York: New Press, 2001. Print.

Crenshaw, Kimberly. "Mapping the Margins: Intersectionality, Identity Politics, and Violence against Women of Color." *Stanford Law Review* 43.6 (1991): 1241–99. Print.

Crossing Arizona. Directed by Joseph Mathew and Dan DeVivo. Cinema Guild, 2006. DVD.

Currah, Paisley. "Stepping Back, Looking Outward: Situating Transgender Activism and Transgender Studies—Kris Hayashi, Matt Richardson, and Susan Stryker Frame the Movement." *Sexuality Research and Social Policy* 5 (2008): 93–105. Print.

da Silva, Marcelo Cozzensa, Anaclaudia Gastal Fassa, and David Kriebel. "Minor Psychiatric Disorders among Brazilian Ragpickers: A Cross-Sectional Study." *Environmental Health* 5 (2006). Web. 1 Aug. 2010.

da Silva, Marcelo Cozzensa, Anaclaudia Gastal Fassa, C. E. Siquiera, and David Kriebel. "World at Work: Brazilian Ragpickers." *Occupational and Environmental Medicine* 62.10 (2005): 736–40. Print.

Davenport, Paul, and Amanda Lee Myers. "Jan Brewer Admits She Was Wrong about Beheadings." *Associated Press,* 4 Sept. 2010. Web. 14 Sept. 2010.

Davidmann, Sara. "Beyond Borders: Lived Experiences of Atypically Gendered Transsexual People." *Transgender Identities: Towards a Social Analysis of Gender Diversity.* Ed. Sally Hines and Tam Sanger. London: Routledge, 2010. 186–303. Print.

Death on a Friendly Border. Directed by Rachel Antell. Filmakers Library, Inc., 2001. DVD.

DeChaine, D. Robert. "Affect and Embodied Understanding in Musical Experience." *Text and Performance Quarterly* 22.2 (2002): 79–98. Print.

———. "Bordering the Civic Imaginary: Alienization, Fence Logic, and the Minuteman Civil Defense Corps." *Quarterly Journal of Speech* 95.1 (2009): 43–65. Print.

———. "Imagined Immunities: Border Rhetorics and the Ethos of Sans Frontièrisme." *Interdisciplinarity and Social Justice: Revisioning Academic Accountability.* Ed. Joe Parker, Ranu Samantrai, and Mary Romero. Ithaca: State U of New York P, 2010. 261–85. Print.

Declaration Alliance. "Minuteman Civil Defense Corps Mission Statement." Minuteman Civil Defense Corps Headquarters. Web. 31 Jan. 2010.

Delgado, Fernando P. "Chicano Movement Rhetoric: An Ideographic Interpretation." *Communication Quarterly* 43 (1995): 446–54. Print.

dell'Agnese, Elena. "The US-Mexico Border in American Films: A Political Geography Perspective." *Geopolitics* 10 (2005): 204–221. Print.

De Los Santos, Al. Letter to the editor. *Sentinel* (Corpus Christi, TX), 5 Mar. 1948: 2. Print.

DeLuca, Kevin. "Articulation Theory: A Discursive Grounding for Rhetorical Practice." *Philosophy and Rhetoric* 32 (1999): 334–48. Print.

Demo, Anne Teresa. "The Afterimage: Immigration Policy after Elián." *Rhetoric and Public Affairs* 10.1 (2007): 27–49. Print.

———. "Sovereignty Discourse and Contemporary Immigration Politics." *Quarterly Journal of Speech* 91.3 (2005): 291–311. Print.

Department of Homeland Security Budget in Brief. Washington, DC: Department of Homeland Security, 2004. Print.

Derrida, Jacques. *Dissemination.* Chicago: U of Chicago P, 1981. Print.

DiBranco, Alex. "6 in 10 Migrant Women Raped Seeking a Better Life." Change .org, 17 May 2010. Web. 11 Apr. 2011.

Doty, Roxanne L. "States of Exception on the Mexico-US Border: Security, 'Decisions,' and Civilian Border Patrols." *International Political Sociology* 1 (2007): 113–37. Print.

Douglas, Mary. *Natural Symbols: Explorations in Cosmology.* London: Routledge, 1996. Print.

Du Bois, W. E. B. *The Souls of Black Folk.* New York: Vintage Books, 1990. Print.

Dunmire, Patricia L. "'9/11 Changed Everything': An Intertextual Analysis of the Bush Doctrine." *Discourse and Society* 20.2 (2009): 195–222. Print.

———. "Preempting the Future: Rhetoric and Ideology of the Future in Political Discourse." *Discourse and Society* 16.4 (2005): 481–513. Print.

Dunn, Timothy J. "Border Militarization via Drug and Immigration Enforcement: Human Rights Implications." *Social Justice* 28.2 (2001): 7–30. Print.

———. *The Militarization of the US-Mexico Border, 1978–1992: Low-Intensity Conflict Doctrine Comes Home.* Austin: U of Texas P, 1996. Print.

Ebert, Roger. Review of *Traffic,* directed by Steven Soderbergh. *Chicago-Sun Times,* 1 Jan. 2001. Web. 26 July 2010.

Edelman, Lee. *No Future: Queer Theory and the Death Drive.* Durham, NC: Duke UP, 2005. Print.

Editorial. *Sentinel* (Corpus Christi, TX), 5 Mar. 1948: 2. Print.

Editorial. *Sentinel* (Corpus Christi, TX), 12 Mar. 1948: 2. Print.

Editorial. *Sentinel* (Corpus Christi, TX), 2 Apr. 1948: 2. Print.

Editorial. *Sentinel* (Corpus Christi, TX), 23 Apr. 1948: 2. Print.

Egan, Timothy. "Wanted: Border Hoppers. And Some Excitement." *New York Times,* 1 Apr. 2005: A14. Print.

The 800 Mile Wall. Directed by John Carlos Frey. Gatekeeper Productions, 2009. DVD.

Elder, Larry. "Minutemen: Don't Call Us Vigilantes." WorldNetDaily, 14 Apr. 2005. Web. 31 Aug. 2010.

El Inmigrante: Life and Death Crossing the United States Mexico Border. Directed by David Eckenrode, John Eckenrode, and John Sheedy. 6512 Productions and Impala Roja, 2005. DVD.

"Emma Tenayuca." *La Voz de Esperanza* 12.7 (Sept. 1999), 2–19. Print.

Enciso, Angélica. "México Genera Cada Año Hasta 180 Mil Toneladas de Basura Electronica." *La Jornada,* 24 Dec. 2007. Web. 1 Aug. 2010.

Enloe, Cynthia. *Does Khaki Become You? The Militarisation of Women's Lives.* London: Pluto, 1983. Print.

———. *Globalization and Militarism: Feminists Make the Link.* Lanham, MD: Rowman and Littlefield, 2007. Print.

———. *Maneuvers: The International Politics of Militarizing Women's Lives.* Berkeley: U of California P, 2000. Print.

Enoch, Jessica. "Survival Stories: Feminist Historiographic Approaches to Chicana Rhetorics of Sterilization Abuse." *Rhetoric Society Quarterly* 35.3 (Summer 2005): 5–30. Print.

Eschbach, Karl, Jacqueline Hagan, Néstor Rodriguez, Ruben Hernandez-Leon, and Stanley Bailey. "Death at the Border." *International Migration Review* 33.2 (1999): 430–54. Print.

Falcón, Sylvanna. "Rape as a Weapon of War: Advancing Human Rights for Women at the US–Mexico Border." *Social Justice* 28.2 (2001): 31–50. Print.

Farmingville. Directed by Carlos Sandoval and Catherine Tambini. Camino Bluff Productions and New Video Group, 2004. DVD.

Faulkner, Sandra L. *Poetry as Method: Reporting Research through Verse.* Walnut Creek, CA: Left Coast P, 2010. Print.

Faulkner, Sandra L., Bernadette Calafell, and Diane Grimes. "Hello Kitty Goes to College: Poems about Harassment in the Academy." *Poetic Inquiry: Vibrant Voices in the Social Sciences.* Ed. Monica Prendergast, Carl Leggo, and Pauline Sameshima. Rotterdam: Sense Publishers, 2009. 187–208. Print.

Feagin, Joe R. "Old Poison in New Bottles: The Deep Roots of Modern Nativism." *Immigrants Out! The New Nativism and the Anti-Immigrant Impulse in the United States.* Ed. Juan F. Perea. New York: New York UP, 1997. 13–43. Print.

Feinberg, Leslie. *Drag King Dreams.* Berkeley, CA: Seal, 2006. Print.

———. "Transgender Warrior: Leslie Feinberg." 2010. Web. 10 July 2010.

Fernández, Valeria. "Long before SB 1070 Arizona Put Squeeze on Immigrants." *New America Media, News Report,* 29 July 2010. Web. 23 Aug. 2010.

Ferus-Comelo, Anibel. "Mission Impossible?: Raising Labor Standards in the ICT Sector." *Labor Studies Journal* 33.2 (2008): 141–62. Print.

Flores, Lisa A. "Constructing Citizens: Narratives of Patriotism and National Identity." Paper presented at Annual Meeting of the Western States Communication Association, Feb. 2005. Print.

———. "Constructing National Bodies: Public Argument in the English-Only Movement." *Argument at Century's End: Reflecting on the Past and Envisioning the Future.* Ed. Thomas A. Hollihan. Annandale, VA: National Communication Association, 2000. 436–45. Print.

———. "Constructing Rhetorical Borders: Peons, Illegal Aliens, and Competing Narratives of Immigration." *Critical Studies in Media Communication* 20.4 (2003): 362–87. Print.

———. "Creating Discursive Space through a Rhetoric of Difference: Chicana Feminists Craft a Homeland." *Quarterly Journal of Speech* 82 (1996): 142–56. Print.

Flores, Lisa A., and Marouf A. Hasian Jr. "Returning to Aztlán and La Raza: Political Communication and the Vernacular Construction of Chicano/a Nationalism." *Politics, Communication, and Culture.* Ed. Alberto González and Dolores V. Tanno. Thousand Oaks, CA: Sage, 1997. 186–203. Print.

Foley, Neil. *The White Scourge: Mexicans, Blacks, and Poor Whites in Texas Cotton Culture.* Berkeley: U of California P, 1999. Print.

Forrestal, Frank, and Gabriela Moreno. "220 Workers Arrested in Swift Raids Are Charged with 'Identity Theft.'" *The Militant* 71.3, 22 Jan. 2007. Web. 15 Apr. 2007.

Foucault, Michel. *Power/Knowledge: Selected Interviews and Other Writings, 1972–1977.* Ed. Colin Gordon. Trans. Colin Gordon, Leo Marshall, John Mepham, and Kate Soper. New York: Pantheon, 1980. Print.

———. *"Society Must Be Defended": Lectures at the Collége de France, 1975–1976.* New York: Picador, 2003. Print.

Fox, Claire F. *The Fence and the River: Culture and Politics at the US-Mexico Border.* Minneapolis: U of Minnesota P, 1999. Print.

Frankenberg, Ruth. "'When We Are Capable of Stopping, We Begin to See': Being White, Seeing Whiteness." *Names We Call Home: Autobiography on Racial Identity.* Ed. Becky Thompson and Sangeeta Tyagi. New York: Routledge, 1996. 2–17. Print.

Franklin, Aretha. "A Rose Is Still a Rose." Arista Records, 1998. CD.

Freire, Paulo. *Pedagogy of the Oppressed.* New York: Continuum, 1990. Print.

Fröbel, Folker, Jürgen Heinrichs, and Otto Kreye. *The New International Division of Labour: Structural Unemployment in Industrialised Countries and Industrialisation in Developing Countries.* Trans. Pete Burgess. Cambridge: Cambridge UP, 1982. Print.

Frosch, Dan. "Report Faults Treatment of Women Held at Immigration Centers." *New York Times,* 20 Jan. 2009. Web. 11 Apr. 2011.

Fujiwara, Lynn H. "Immigrants Rights Are Human Rights: The Reframing of Immigrant Entitlement and Welfare." *Social Problems* 52.1 (2005): 79–101. Print.

Gaffney, Sean. "Rise in Maquiladora Jobs May Signal Wider Rebound." *The Monitor,* 7 Jan. 2010. Web. 1 Aug. 2010.

Gales, Tammy. "'Diversity' as Enacted in US Immigration Politics and Law: A Corpus-Based Approach." *Discourse and Society* 20.2 (2009): 223–40. Print.

García, Arnoldo. "National Security and Vigilantes Put the US–Mexico Border 'Under Siege.'" *Network News: National Network for Immigrant and Refugee Rights* (Spring 2005): 7–9. Print.

García, Connie, and Amelia Simpson. "Community-Based Organizing for Labor Rights, Health, and the Environment." *Challenging the Chip: Labor Rights and Environmental Justice in the Global Electronics Industry.* Ed. Ted Smith, David A. Sonnenfeld, and David Naguib Pellow. Philadelphia: Temple UP, 2006. 150–60. Print.

García, Dorde Cuvardic. "El *Trapero:* El *Otro Marginal* en la Historia de la Literatura y de la Cultura Popular." *Káñina: Revista de las Artes y Letras* 31.1 (2007): 217–27. Print.

García, Mario T. *Mexican Americans: Leadership, Ideology, and Identity, 1930–1960.* New Haven, CT: Yale UP, 1989. Print.

García Canclini, Néstor. *Hybrid Cultures: Strategies for Entering and Leaving Modernity.* Minneapolis: U of Minnesota P, 1995. Print.

Garner, Steve. *Whiteness: An Introduction.* New York: Routledge, 2007. Print.

Geis, Sonya. "Minuteman Project in Turmoil over Financial Allegations." *Washington Post,* 13 Mar. 2007: A3. Print.

Gerstein, Josh. "Bush Pardons Few in Final Hours." *Politico,* 18 Jan. 2009. Web. 31 Aug. 2010.

Gibbs, Nancy. "The New Frontier/La Nueva Frontera: A Whole New World." *Time* 11 June 2001: 36–48. Print.

Gidwani, Vinay K. "Subaltern Cosmopolitanism as Politics." *Antipode* 38.1 (2006): 7–21. Print.

"GI Forum Meeting Slated Tonight at Lamar School." *Sentinel* (Corpus Christi, TX),. 2 Apr. 1948: 1. Print.

Gilchrist, Jim. "An Essay by Jim Gilchrist." *Georgetown Immigration Law Journal* 22 (2008): 415–28. Print.

Gilot, Louie. "Sentence Handed to Border Agents; Free Until Jan. 17." *El Paso Times,* 20 Oct. 2006. Web. 31 Jan. 2010.

Goldstein, Eric L. *The Price of Whiteness: Jews, Race, and American Identity.* Princeton: Princeton UP, 2006. Print.

Gómez-Peña, Guillermo. "Border Hysteria and the War against Difference." *TDR: The Drama Review* 52.1 (2008): 196–203. Print.

Gonzalez, Alfonso. "The 2006 Mega Marchas in Greater Los Angeles: Counterhegemonic Moment and the Future of El Migrante Struggle." *Latino Studies* 7 (2009): 30–59. Print.

González, Gabriela. "Carolina Munguía and Emma Tenayuca: The Politics of Benevolence and Radical Reform." *Frontiers* 24 (2003): 200–229. Print.

Greene, Ronald W. "The Concept of Global Citizenship in Michael Hardt and

Antonio Negri's *Empire:* A Challenge to Three Ideas of Rhetorical Mediation." *Rhetorical Democracy: Discursive Practices of Civic Engagement.* Ed. Gerard A. Hauser and Amy Grim. Mahwah, NJ: Lawrence Erlbaum, 2004. 165–71. Print.

Greenpeace. "Tóxicos en la Producción y Basura Electronica (e-waste)." n.d. Web. 1 Aug. 2010.

Greg L. "Help Save Manassas Wednesday." *Black Velvet Bruce Li,* 27 Jan. 2009. Web. 16 July 2010.

Grewal, Inderpal. *Transnational America: Feminisms, Diasporas, Neoliberalisms.* Durham, NC: Duke UP, 2005. Print.

Gross, Ariela J. "Texas Mexicans and the Politics of Whiteness." *Law and History Review* 21.1 (2003): 195–205. Print.

Guadarrama, Rafael H. " 'Reciclotrón,' Este Fin de Semana en el Valle de México." *Once TV Mexico Noticias,* 28 Jan. 2010. Web. 1 Aug. 2010.

Guglielmo, Thomas A. *White on Arrival: Italians, Race, Color, and Power in Chicago, 1890–1945.* New York: Oxford UP, 2003. Print.

Guillermoprieto, Alma. "Letter from Mexico City." *New Yorker,* 17 Sept. 1990: 93. Print.

Gutiérrez, David G. *Walls and Mirrors: Mexican Americans, Mexican Immigrants, and the Politics of Ethnicity.* Berkeley: U of California P, 1995. Print.

Hahner, Leslie. "Practical Patriotism: Camp Fire Girls, Girl Scouts, and Americanization." *Communication and Critical/Cultural Studies* 5 (2008): 113–34. Print.

Hall, Stuart. "On Postmodernism and Articulation: An Interview with Stuart Hall." Ed. Lawrence Grossberg. *Journal of Communication Inquiry* 10 (1986): 45–60. Print.

———. *Stuart Hall: Representation and the Media.* Produced and directed by Sut Jhally. Media Education Foundation, 1997. VHS.

Hammerback, John C., and Richard J. Jensen. "Ethnic Heritage as Rhetorical Legacy: The Plan of Delano." *Quarterly Journal of Speech* 80 (1994): 53–70. Print.

Hanczor, Robert. "Articulation Theory and Public Controversy: Taking Sides over *NYPD Blue.*" *Critical Studies in Mass Communication* 14 (1997): 1–31. Print.

Hannity, Sean, and Alan Colmes. "Interview with James Gilchrist." *Fox News: Hannity and Colmes,* 25 Jan. 2005. Web. 20 Aug. 2010.

Hardt, Michael, and Antonio Negri. *Empire.* Cambridge, MA: Harvard UP, 2000. Print.

———. *Multitude: War and Democracy in the Age of Empire.* New York: Penguin, 2004. Print.

Hardy, Gayle J. "Emma Tenayuca." *American Women Civil Rights Activists: Biobibliographies of Sixty-eight Leaders, 1825–1992.* Jefferson, NC: McFarland, 1993. 375–78. Print.

Hariman, Robert, and John Louis Lucaites. *No Caption Needed: Iconic Photographs, Public Culture, and Liberal Democracy.* Chicago: U of Chicago P, 2007. Print.

Harriss, John. "Middle-Class Activism and the Politics of the Informal Working Class: A Perspective on Class Relations and Civil Society in Indian Cities." *Critical Asian Studies* 38.4 (2006): 445–65. Print.

Hasian, Marouf, Jr., and Fernando Delgado. "Trials and Tribulations of Racialized Critical Rhetorical Theory: Understanding the Rhetorical Ambiguities of Proposition 187." *Communication Theory* 8.3 (1998): 245–70. Print.

Henderson, Mae G. "Introduction: Borders, Boundaries, and Frame(work)s." *Borders, Boundaries, and Frames: Essays in Cultural Criticism and Cultural Studies.* Ed. Mae G. Henderson. New York: Routledge, 1995. 1–30. Print.

Hendricks, Tyche. "The Human Face of Immigration Raids in Bay Area Arrests of Parents Can Deeply Traumatize Children Caught in the Fray, Experts Argue." *San Francisco Chronicle,* 27 Apr. 2007, final ed.: A1. Print.

Hill Collins, Patricia. *Black Feminist Thought: Knowledge, Consciousness, and the Politics of Empowerment.* New York: Routledge, 2000. Print.

Holling, Michelle A. "Patrolling National Identity, Masking White Supremacy: The Minuteman Project." *Critical Rhetorics of Race.* Ed. Michael Lacy and Kent A. Ono. New York: New York UP, 2011. 98–116. Print.

——. "Retrospective on Latin@ Rhetorical-Performance Scholarship: From 'Chicano Communication' to 'Latina/o Communication'?" *Communication Review* 11 (2008): 293–322. Print.

Holman Jones, Stacy. "Autoethnography: Making the Personal Political." *The Sage Handbook of Qualitative Research,* 3rd ed. Ed. Norman K. Denzin and Yvonna S. Lincoln. Thousand Oaks, CA: Sage, 2005. 763–91. Print.

Holthouse, David. "Ruckus on the Right." *Southern Poverty Law Center,* 15 Aug. 2006. Web. 20 Aug. 2010.

House Bill 2162. 49th Leg. 2nd sess. (30 Apr. 2010). Print.

Hughes, Robert. "The Urban Poet." *Time,* 9 Sept. 1985. Web. 1 Aug. 2010.

Human Rights Watch. *No Guarantees: Sex Discrimination in Mexico's Maquiladora Sector.* 1 Aug. 1996, B806. Web. 7 Sept. 2010.

Huneke, Anya. "Vermont Couple Says Border Patrol Ruined Their Wedding." *NECN:* n.p. Web. 10 June 2010.

Huntington, Samuel. *Who Are We? The Challenges to America's National Identity.* New York: Simon and Schuster, 2004. Print.

Huus, Kari. "Turmoil in Tulsa: The Illegal Immigration Wreck." MSNBC.com, 17 July 2007. Web. 1 Mar. 2010.

Hyde, Michael J. *The Call of Conscience: Heidegger and Levinas, Rhetoric and the Euthanasia Debate*. Columbia: U of South Carolina P, 2001. Print.

———. *The Life-Giving Gift of Acknowledgment*. West Lafayette, IN: Purdue UP, 2006. Print.

———. "A Matter of Heart: Epideictic Rhetoric and Heidegger's Call of Conscience." *Heidegger and Rhetoric*. Ed. Daniel M. Gross and Ansgar Kemmann. Albany: State U of New York P, 2005. 81–104. Print.

Hyde, Michael J., and Ken Rufo. "The Call of Conscience, Rhetorical Interruptions, and the Euthanasia Controversy." *Journal of Applied Communication Research* 28.1 (2000): 1–23. Print.

Ignatiev, Noel. *How the Irish Became White*. New York: Routledge, 1995. Print.

Immigration Policy Center. "Q&A Guide to Arizona's New Immigration Law: What You Need to Know about the New Law and How It Can Impact Your State." *American Immigration Council,* June 2010. Web. 2 Aug. 2010.

Inda, Jonathan Xavier. "Performativity, Materiality, and the Racial Body." *Latino Studies Journal* 11.3 (2000): 74–99. Print.

———. *Targeting Immigrants: Government, Technology, and Ethics*. Malden, MA: Blackwell, 2006. Print.

In the Shadow of the Raid. Directed by Greg Brosnan and Jennifer Szymaszek. MCO Film Works, 2010. DVD.

"In Solidarity." *Time Out New York*: n.p. Web. 14 June 2010.

Ivie, Robert L. "Fighting Terror by Rite of Redemption and Reconciliation." *Rhetoric and Public Affairs* 10.2 (2007): 221–48. Print.

Ivie, Robert L., and Oscar Giner. "More Good, Less Evil: Contesting the Mythos of National Insecurity in the 2008 Presidential Primaries." *Rhetoric and Public Affairs* 12.2 (2009): 279–301. Print.

Jacobson, Matthew Frye. "Becoming Caucasian: Vicissitudes of Whiteness in American Politics and Culture." *Identities* 8.1 (2001): 83–104. Print.

———. *Whiteness of a Different Color: European Immigrants and the Alchemy of Race*. Cambridge, MA: Harvard UP, 1999. Print.

Jacobson, Robin Dale. *The New Nativism: Proposition 187 and the Debate over Immigration*. Minneapolis: U of Minnesota P, 2008. Print.

Jacott, Marisa, Cyrus Reed, and Mark Winfield. *The Generation and Management of Hazardous Wastes and Transboundary Hazardous Waste Shipments between Mexico, Canada and the United States Since 2004: A 2004 Update*. Austin: Texas Center for Policy Studies, 2004. Print.

Jensen, Richard J., and John C. Hammerback. "'No Revolutions Without Poets': The Rhetoric of Rodolfo 'Corky' Gonzáles." *Western Journal of Speech Communication* 44 (1982): 72–91. Print.

———. "Radical Nationalism among Chicanos: The Rhetoric of José Angel Gutiérrez." *Western Journal of Speech Communication* 44 (1980): 191–202. Print.

Jimenez, Maria. *Humanitarian Crisis: Migrant Deaths at the US-Mexico Border.* San Diego: American Civil Liberties Union and Mexico's National Commission of Human Rights, 2009. Print.

Johnson, Julia R., Archana Pathak Bhatt, and Tracey O. Patton. "Dismantling Essentialisms in Academic Organizations: Intersectional Articulation and Possibilities of Alliance Formation." *Communicating Within/Across Organizations.* Ed. Brenda J. Allen, Lisa A. Flores, and Mark P. Orbe. Washington, DC: National Communication Association, 2004. 21–50. Print.

Johnson, Kevin R. "An Essay on Immigration, Citizenship, and US/Mexico Relations: The Tale of Two Treaties." *Southwestern Journal of Law and Trade in the Americas* 5 (1998): 121–40. Print.

———. "Free Trade and Closed Borders: NAFTA and Mexican Immigration to the United States." *University of California Davis Law Review* 27 (1993–94): 937–78. Print.

———. "How Racial Profiling in America Became the Law of the Land: United States v. Brignoni-Ponce and Whren v. United States and the Need for Truly Rebellious Lawyering." *Georgetown Immigration Law Journal* 98 (2010): 1005–77. Print.

Kalm, Sara. "Emancipation or Exploitation? A Study of Women Workers in Mexico's Maquiladora Industry." *Statsveteskaplig Tidskrift* 104.3 (2001): 225–58. Print.

Kandinsky, Wassily. *Concerning the Spiritual in Art.* Trans. M. T. H. Sadler. Mineola, NY: Dover, 1977. Print.

Kanellos, Nicolás. Reprint of *The Mexican Question in the Southwest. Herencia: The Anthology of Hispanic Literature of the United States.* Ed. Nicolás Kanellos. Oxford, UK: Oxford UP, 2002. 156–62. Print.

Kaplan, Caren. "Precision Targets: GPS and the Militarization of US Consumer Identity." *American Quarterly* 58.3 (2006): 693–714. Print.

Kymlicka, Will, and Wayne Norman. "Return of the Citizen: A Survey of Recent Work on Citizenship Theory." *Theorizing Citizenship.* Ed. Ronald Beiner. New York: State U of New York P, 1995. 283–322. Print.

Laclau, Ernesto, and Chantal Mouffe. *Hegemony and Socialist Strategy: Towards a Radical Democratic Politics.* London: Verso, 2001. Print.

Lady Gaga. "Speechless." *The Fame Monster.* Interscope Records, 2009. CD.

Langellier, Kristin M. "Personal Narrative, Performance, Performativity: Two or Three Things I Know for Sure." *Text and Performance Quarterly* 19 (1999): 125–44. Print.

———. "Voiceless Bodies, Bodiless Voices: The Future of Personal Narrative Performance." *The Future of Performance Studies: Visions and Revisions.* Ed. Sheron J. Dailey. Annandale, VA: National Communication Association, 1998. 207–213. Print.

Langellier, Kristin M., and Eric Peterson. *Storytelling in Daily Life: Performing Narrative.* Philadelphia, PA: Temple UP, 2004. Print.

The Least of These. Directed by Clark Lyda and Jesse Lyda. Glasshouse Productions, 2009. DVD.

Lee, Mike. "Our Electronic Waste Is Piling Up Overseas." *San Diego Union-Tribune,* 19 June 2007: A1. Print.

Lefebvre, Henri. *The Production of Space.* 1974. Oxford: Blackwell, 1991. Print.

Lindlof, Thomas, and Bryan Taylor. *Qualitative Communication Research Methods.* Thousand Oaks, CA: Sage, 2002. Print.

Lister, Ruth. "Citizenship: Towards a Feminist Synthesis." *Feminist Review* 57 (1997): 28–48. Print.

Lugo-Lugo, Carmen R., and Mary K. Bloodsworth-Lugo. "475° from September 11." *Cultural Studies* 24.2 (2010): 234–55. Print.

Luibhéid, Eithne. *Entry Denied: Controlling Sexuality at the Border.* Minneapolis: U of Minnesota P, 2002. Print.

———. "Introduction: Queering Migration and Citizenship." *Queer Migrations: Sexuality, US Citizenship, and Border Crossings.* Ed. Eithne Luibhéid and Lionel Cantú Jr. Minneapolis: U of Minnesota P, 2005. ix–xlvi. Print.

"LULAC Attorney Sees Segregation Case on Way to Chief Court." *Sentinel* (Corpus Christi, TX), 16 Jan. 1948: 1, 6. Print.

Lundberg, Christian. "Enjoying God's Death: The Passion of the Christ and the Practices of an Evangelical Public." *Quarterly Journal of Speech* 95.4 (2009): 387–411. Print.

Lyall, James Duff. "Vigilante State: Reframing the Minuteman Project in American Politics and Culture." *Georgetown Immigration Law Journal* 23 (2009): 257–91. Print.

Maciel, David. *El Bandoloer, El Poncho, y La Raza.* Mexico: Conaculta, 2000. Print.

Mackie, Vera. "The Trans-sexual Citizen: Queering Sameness and Difference." *Australian Feminist Studies* 16.2 (2001): 185–92. Print.

Madison, D. Soyini, and Judith Hamera. "Performance Studies at the Intersections." *The Sage Handbook of Performance Studies.* Ed. D. Soyini Madison and Judith Hamera. Thousand Oaks, CA: Sage, 2006. xi–xxv. Print.

Magnet, Shoshana. "Bio-Benefits: Technologies of Criminalization, Biometrics and the Welfare System." *Surveillance: Power, Problems, and Politics.* Ed. Sean P. Hier and Josh Greenberg. Seattle: U of Washington P, 2010. 169–83. Print.

———. "Using Biometrics to Re-Visualize the Canada-US Border." *Lessons from the Identity Trail: Anonymity, Privacy, and Identity in a Networked Society.* Ed. Ian Kerr, Valerie Steeves, and Carole Lucock. Oxford, UK: Oxford UP, 2009. Print.

Malkin, Elisabeth. "A Boom across the Border." *New York Times,* 26 Aug. 2004. Web. 7 Sept. 2010.

Manalansan, Martin F. *Global Divas: Filipino Gay Men in the Diaspora.* Durham, NC: Duke UP, 2003. Print.

———. "Migrancy, Modernity, Mobility: Quotidian Struggles and Queer Diasporic Intimacy." *Queer Migrations: Sexuality, US Citizenship, and Border Crossings.* Ed. Eithne Luibhéid and Lionel Cantú Jr. Minneapolis: U of Minnesota P, 2005. 146–60. Print.

Martín-Barbero, Jesús. "Introducción." *Imaginarios de Nación: Pensar en Medio de la Tormenta.* Ed. Jesús Martín-Barbero. Bogotá: Ministerio de Cultura, 2001. 7–10. Print.

Marx, Karl. *The Eighteenth Brumaire of Louis Bonaparte.* Trans. Daniel De Leon. Mountain View: New York Labor News, 2003. Print.

Massey, Doreen. *Spatial Divisions of Labor: Social Structures and the Geography of Production.* London: Macmillan, 1984. Print.

Massumi, Brian. *Parables for the Virtual: Movement, Affect, Sensation.* Durham, NC: Duke UP, 2002. Print.

"Mathis Object of GI Forum—LULAC Heat." *Sentinel* (Corpus Christi, TX), 28 May 1948: 4. Print.

Maxwell, Richard, and Toby Miller. "Film and Globalization." *Communications Media, Globalization and Empire.* Ed. Oliver Boyd-Barrett. Eastleigh, UK: John Libbey, 2006. 33–52. Print.

———. "Green Smokestacks?" *Feminist Media Studies* 8.3 (2008): 324–29. Print.

———. "Talking Rubbish: Green Citizenship, Media, and the Environment." *Climate Change and the Media.* Ed. Tammy Boyce and Justin Lewis. New York: Peter Lang, 2009. 17–27. Print.

McCarthy, Todd. Review of *Traffic,* directed by Steven Soderbergh. *Variety* 12 Dec. 2000. Web. 8 Dec. 2011.

McClintock, Anne. *Imperial Leather: Race, Gender, and Sexuality in the Colonial Contest.* New York: Routledge, 1995. Print.

McGee, Michael Calvin. "The 'Ideograph': A Link between Rhetoric and Ideology." *Quarterly Journal of Speech* 66 (1980): 1–16. Print.

———. "In Search of 'The People': A Rhetorical Alternative." *Quarterly Journal of Speech* 61 (1975): 235–49. Print.

McKinnon, Sara L. "Citizenship and the Performance of Credibility: Audiencing Gender-Based Asylum Seekers in US Immigration Courts." *Text and Performance Quarterly* 29.3 (2009): 205–221. Print.

Medina, Martin. *The World's Scavengers: Salvaging for Sustainable Consumption and Production*. Lanham, MD: AltaMira, 2007. Print.

Meier, Matt S., and Feliciano Ribera. *Mexican Americans/American Mexicans: From Conquistadors to Chicanos*. Rev. ed. New York: Hill and Wang, 1993. Print.

Mendoza, Jorge Eduardo. "The Effect of the Chinese Economy on Mexican Maquiladora Employment." *International Trade Journal* 24.1 (2010): 52–83. Print.

"Mesa Day Labor Protests through September." Minuteman Civil Defense Corps Headquarters, 2006. Web. 31 Jan. 2010.

Mexico—Death in the Desert—June 4, 2004. Directed by Claudine LoMonaco and Mary Spicuzza, *Frontline*, 2004, http://www.pbs.org/frontlineworld.

Midwest Coalition to Reduce Immigration. "About Midwest Coalition to Reduce Immigration." *Midwest Coalition to Reduce Immigration,* 1 May 2011. Web. 9 May 1999.

Miller, Toby. *Cultural Citizenship: Cosmopolitanism, Consumerism, and Television in a Neoliberal Age*. Philadelphia: Temple UP, 2007. Print.

———."A Future for Media Studies: Cultural Labour, Cultural Relations, Cultural Politics." *How Canadians Communicate III: Contexts of Canadian Popular Culture*. Ed. Bart Beaty, Derek Briton, Gloria Filax, and Rebecca Sullivan. Edmonton: Athabasca UP, 2010. 35–53. Print.

———. "Media Studies 3.0." *Television and New Media* 10.1 (2009): 5–6. Print.

———. "'Step Away from the Croissant': Media Studies 3.0." *The Media and Social Theory*. Ed. David Hesmondhalgh and Jason Toynbee. London: Routledge, 2008. 213–30. Print.

———. *Television Studies: The Basics*. London: Routledge, 2010. Print.

Miller, Toby, Nitin Govil, John McMurria, Richard Maxwell, and Ting Wang. *Global Hollywood 2*. London: British Film Institute, 2005. Print.

Mirandé, Alfredo. *Gringo Justice*. Notre Dame, IN: U of Notre Dame P, 1987. Print.

Mirrlees, Tanner. "Historicizing US Imperial Culture." *Communication Review* 11.2 (2008): 176–91. Print.

Mitchell, Gordon R. "Public Argument Action Research and the Learning Curve of New Social Movements." *Argumentation and Advocacy* 40 (2004): 209–225. Print.

Miyoshi, Masao. "A Borderless World? From Colonialism to Transnationalism and the Decline of the Nation-State." *Critical Inquiry* 19.4 (1993): 726–51. Print.

Moguel, Guillermo J. Román. *Diagnóstico Sobre la Generación de Basura Electrónica en México.* Mexico City: Instituto Nacional de Ecología, 2007. Print.

Mojados: Through the Night. Directed by Tommy Davis. Vanguard Cinema, 2004. DVD.

Montejano, David. *Anglos and Mexicans in the Making of Texas, 1836–1986.* Austin: U of Texas P, 1987. Print.

Montini, E. J. "What Part of Distortion Doesn't Brewer Understand?" AZCentral .com, 23 June 2010. Web. 5 Oct. 2010.

Moon, Dreama. "White Enculturation and Bourgeois Ideology: The Discursive Production of 'Good (White) Girls.'" *Whiteness: The Communication of Social Identity.* Ed. Thomas K. Nakayama and Judith N. Martin. Thousand Oaks, CA: Sage, 1999. 177–97. Print.

Moon, Dreama G., and Garry L. Rolison. "Communication of Classism." *Communicating Prejudice.* Ed. Michael L. Hecht. Thousand Oaks, CA: Sage, 1998. 122–35. Print.

Moore, Malcolm. "Four Suicide Attempts in a Month at Foxconn, the Makers of the iPad." *Daily Telegraph,* 7 Apr. 2010. Web. 7 Sept. 2010.

Moraga, Cherríe. *The Last Generation.* Boston: South End P, 1993. Print.

———. *Loving in the War Years: Lo Que Nunca Pasó Por Sus Labios,* 2nd ed. Boston: South End, 2000. Print.

Moraga, Cherríe, and Gloria Anzaldúa, eds. *This Bridge Called My Back: Writings by Radical Women of Color.* New York: Kitchen Table, 1981. Print.

Moreno, Sylvia. "For Residents of Arizona Border Town, Towers Are Unwelcome Eyes in the Sky." *Washington Post,* 10 June 2007, suburban ed.: A03. Print.

Morgensen, Scott Lauria. "Settler Homonationalism: Theorizing Settler Colonialism within Queer Modernities." *GLQ* 16.1 (2010): 105–131. Print.

Moser, Walter. "Garbage and Recycling: From Literary Theme to Mode of Production." *Other Voices: The eJournal of Cultural Criticism* 3.1, May 2007. Web. 7 Sept. 2010.

Moss, Kirby. *The Color of Class: Poor Whites and the Paradox of Privilege.* Philadelphia: U of Pennsylvania P, 2003. Print.

Motion Picture Association of America. *The Economic Impact of the Motion Picture and Television Industry on the United States.* Washington, DC, 2009. Print.

"Muck and Brass Plates." *Economist,* 13 June 2009: 44. Print.

Mukherjee, Sanjukta, with Central Department for Development Studies, Tribhuvan University. *Child Ragpickers in Nepal: A Report on the 2002–2003 Baseline Survey.* Bangkok: International Labour Organization, 2003. Print.

Muñoz, José Esteban. *Cruising Utopia: The Then and There of Queer Futurity.* New York: New York UP, 2009. Print.

———. *Disidentifications: Queers of Color and the Performance of Politics.* Minneapolis: U of Minnesota P, 1999. Print.

———. "Feeling Brown: Ethnicity and Affect in Ricardo Bracho's 'The Sweetest Hangover (and Other STDs).'" *Theatre Journal* 52.1 (2000): 67–79. Print.

Muñoz, Vic, and Ednie Kaeh Garrison. "Transpedagogies: A Roundtable Dialogue." *Women's Studies Quarterly* 36 (2008): 288–308. Print.

Murillo, Enrique, Jr. "Mojado Crossing along Neoliberal Borderlands." *Postcritical Ethnography: An Introduction.* Ed. George W. Noblit, Susana Y. Flores, and Enrique G. Murillo. Creskill, NJ: Hampton, 2004. 155–79. Print.

Nakayama, Thomas K., and Robert L. Krizek. "Whiteness: A Strategic Rhetoric." *Quarterly Journal of Speech* 81 (1995): 291–309. Print.

Nevins, Joseph. *Operation Gatekeeper: The Rise of the "Illegal Alien" and the Making of the US-Mexico Boundary.* New York: Routledge, 2002. Print.

Newman, David. "The Lines That Continue to Separate Us: Borders in Our 'Borderless' World." *Progress in Human Geography* 30 (2006): 143–61. Print.

New World Border. Directed by Casey Peek. Peek Media, 2001. DVD.

Ngai, Mae M. *Impossible Subjects: Illegal Aliens and the Making of Modern America.* Princeton, NJ: Princeton UP, 2004. Print.

Nicholas, Peter, and Robert Salladay. "Governor Praises 'Minuteman' Campaign." *Los Angeles Times,* 29 Apr. 2005: B1. Print.

NietoGomez, Anna. "Chicana Feminism." *Chicana Feminist Thought: The Basic Historical Writings.* Ed. Alma Garcia. New York: Routledge, 1997. 52–57. Print.

9500 Liberty. Directed by Annabel Park and Eric Byler. Democracy Alliance, 2010. DVD.

NOTIMEX. "22 Maquiladoras Closed in 2009 Due to the Economic Crisis." *Maquila Portal* 24 Feb. 2010. Web. 7 Sept. 2010.

Nuñez-Neto, Blas. *Border Security: The Role of the US Border Patrol. CRS Report for Congress.* Washington, DC: Congressional Research Service, 2008. Print.

Nunn, Kem. *Tijuana Straits: A Novel.* New York: Scribner, 2005. Print.

Ochoa O'Leary, Anna. "Close Encounters of the Deadly Kind: Gender, Migration, and Border (in)Security." *Migration Letters* 5.2 (2008): 111–21. Print.

Oklahoma State Legislature. Bill 1804: Oklahoma Taxpayer and Citizen Protection Act of 2007. *Tulsa World Online.* Web. 1 Mar. 2010.

Omi, Michael, and Howard Winant. *Racial Formation in the United States: From the 1960s to the 1990s.* 2nd ed. New York: Routledge, 1994. Print.

"One of the Foremost Decisions Rendered Recently: Dr. Garcia." *Sentinel* (Corpus Christi, TX), 18 June 1948: 1. Print.

Ono, Kent A. "From Nationalism to Migrancy: The Politics of Asian American Transnationalism." *Communication Law Review* 5.1 (2005): 1–17. Print.

Ono, Kent A., and John M. Sloop. *Shifting Borders: Rhetoric, Immigration, and California's Proposition 187*. Philadelphia: Temple UP, 2002. Print.

Oppenheimer, Martin. "The Sub-Proletariat: Dark Skins and Dirty Work." *Critical Sociology* 4.2 (1974): 7–20. Print.

"Optic." *The Oxford English Dictionary*. Defs. A4, B2c. Web. 3 Aug. 2011.

Orozco, Cynthia E. *No Mexicans, Women, or Dogs Allowed: The Rise of the Mexican American Civil Rights Movement*. Austin: U of Texas P, 2009. Print.

The Other Side of Immigration. Directed by Roy Germano. Team Love LLC, 2009. DVD.

Ott, Brian L. "The Visceral Politics of *V for Vendetta*: On Political Affect in Cinema." *Critical Studies in Media Communication* 27.1 (2010): 29–54. Print.

Ó Tuathail, Gearóid. *Critical Geopolitics: The Politics of Writing Global Space*. Minneapolis: U of Minnesota P, 1996. Print.

Palczewski, Catherine. "*Bodies,* Borders, and Letters: Gloria Anzaldúa's 'Speaking in Tongues: A Letter to 3rd World Women Writers.'" *Southern Communication Journal* 62 (1996): 1–16. Print.

Parekh, Bhikhu. "What Is Multiculturalism?" *Multiculturalism: A Symposium on Democracy in Culturally Diverse Societies*. Dec. 1999. Web. 10 Apr. 2008.

Paterson, Kent. "Temping Down Labor Rights: The Manpowerization of Mexico." *Corpwatch,* 6 Jan. 2010. Web. 7 Sept. 2010.

Pathak, Archana A. "Being Indian in the US : Exploring the Hyphen as an Ethnographic Frame." *International and Intercultural Communication Annual* 31 (2008): 175–96. Print.

Payan, Tony. *The Three U.S.-Mexico Border Wars: Drugs, Immigration, and Homeland Security*. Westport, CT: Praeger Security International, 2006. Print.

Pelias, Ronald J. "Performative Writing as Scholarship: An Apology, an Argument, an Anecdote." *Cultural Studies <=> Critical Methodologies* 5 (2005): 415–24. Print.

Pérez, Kimberlee, and Dustin B. Goltz. "Treading across Lines in the Sand: Performing Bodies in Coalitional Subjectivity." *Text and Performance Quarterly* 30 (2010): 247–68. Print.

Peters, Katherine McIntire. "Ig: Secure Border Initiative Lacks Effective Oversight." Government Executive, 10 July 2009. Web. 24 Sept. 2010.

Pickering, Sharon. "Border Narratives: From Talking Security to Performing Borderlands." *Borders, Mobility and Technologies of Control*. Ed. Sharon Pickering and Leanne Weber. New York: Springer, 2006. 45–62. Print.

Polanyi, Karl. *The Great Transformation: The Political and Economic Origins of Our Time*. Boston: Beacon, 2001. Print.

Pollock, Della. "Performative Writing." *The Ends of Performance*. Ed. Peggy Phelan and Jill Lane. New York: New York UP, 1998. 73–103. Print.

"Popotla vs. Titanic." n.d. Web. 7 Sept. 2010.

Porton, Richard. Review of *Traffic*, directed by Steven Soderbergh. *Cineaste* 23 (2001): 41–43. Print.

Projansky, Sarah, and Kent A. Ono. "Strategic Whiteness as Cinematic Racial Politics." *Whiteness: The Communication of Social Identity*. Ed. Thomas K. Nakayama and Judith N. Martin. Thousand Oaks, CA: Sage, 1999. 149–74. Print.

Puar, Jasbir K. *Terrorist Assemblages: Homonationalism in Queer Times*. Durham, NC: Duke UP, 2007. Print.

Puar, Jasbir K., and Amit S. Rai. "Monster, Terrorist, Fag: The War on Terrorism and the Production of Docile Patriots." *Social Text* 20 (2002): 117–48. Print.

Puzzanghera, Jim. "High-Tech TV Upgrades Will Create Low-Tech Trash." *Los Angeles Times*, 24 May 2007: C1, C6. Print.

Quiroz, Anthony. *Claiming Citizenship: Mexican Americans in Victoria, Texas*. College Station, TX: Texas A&M UP, 2005. Print.

Rasmussen, Birgit Brander, et al. "Introduction." *The Making and Unmaking of Whiteness*. Ed. Birgit Brander Rasmussen et al. Durham, NC: Duke UP, 2001. 1–24. Print.

Ray, Manas Ranjan, Gopeshwar Mukherjee, Sanghita Roychowdhury, and Twisha Lahiri. "Respiratory and General Health Impairments of Ragpickers in India: A Study in Delhi." *International Archives of Occupational and Environmental Health* 77.8 (2004): 595–98. Print.

Reimers, David M. *Unwelcome Strangers: American Identity and the Turn against Immigration*. New York: Columbia UP, 1998. Print.

Reygadas, Luis. *Ensamblando Culturas: Diversidad y Conflicto en la Globalización de la Industria*. Barcelona: Editorial Gedisa, 2002. Print.

Riccardi, Nicholas. "Thousands Protest in Arizona; the Rally Is by Far the Largest since an Immigration Law Was Signed in April." *Los Angeles Times*, 30 May 2010: A16. Print.

Rice, Jenny Edbauer. "The New 'New': Making a Case for Critical Affect Studies." *Quarterly Journal of Speech* 94.2 (2008): 200–212. Print.

Rights on the Line: Vigilantes on the Border. Directed by Ray Ybarra. American Friends Service Committee, American Civil Liberties Union, and Witness, 2005. DVD.

Rigsby, Enrique D. "African American Rhetoric and the 'Profession.'" *Western Journal of Communication* 57 (1993): 191–99. Print.

Rios, Pedro. "*Rights on the Line* Impact." E-mail to Anne Teresa Demo, 24 Mar. 2010.

Rips, Geoffrey. "Living History: Emma Tenayuca Tells Her Story." *Texas Observer* 28 (1983): 9. Print.

Rivera-Servera, Ramon H. "Exhibiting Voice/Narrating Migration: Performance-Based Curatorial Practice in *¡Azucar! The Life and Music of Celia Cruz.*" *Text and Performance Quarterly* 29.2 (2009): 131–48. Print.

Robertson, Craig. *The Passport in America: The History of a Document.* Oxford, UK: Oxford UP, 2010. Print.

Rodriguez, Joe G. Letter to the editor. *Sentinel* (Corpus Christi, TX), 23 Apr. 1948: 2. Print.

Rodriguez, Néstor P. "The Social Construction of the US-Mexico Border." *Immigrants Out! The New Nativism and the Anti-Immigrant Impulse in the United States.* Ed. Juan F. Perea. New York: New York UP, 1997. 223–43. Print.

Roediger, David R. *The Wages of Whiteness: Race and the Making of the American Working Class.* New York: Verso, 1991. Print.

———. *Working toward Whiteness: How America's Immigrants Became White.* New York: Basic Books, 2005. Print.

Rojecki, Andrew. "Rhetorical Alchemy: American Exceptionalism and the War on Terror." *Political Communication* 25.1 (2008): 67–88. Print.

Romero, Fernando. *Hyper-Border: The Contemporary US-Mexico Border and Its Future.* New York: Princeton Architectural P, 2008. Print.

Rosaldo, Renato. "Cultural Citizenship, Inequality, and Multiculturalism." *Race, Identity, and Citizenship: A Reader.* Ed. Rodolfo D. Torres, Louis F. Mirón, and Jonathan Xavier Inda. Malden, MA: Blackwell, 1999. 253–61. Print.

———. *Culture and Truth: The Remaking of Social Analysis.* Boston: Beacon, 1989. Print.

Rosas, Gilberto. "The Managed Violences of the Borderlands: Treacherous Geographies, Policeability, and the Politics of Race." *Latino Studies* 4.4 (2006): 401–418. Print.

Ross, Susan Dente. "In the Shadow of Terror: The Illusive First Amendment Rights of Aliens." *Communication Law and Policy* 6.1 (2001): 75–122. Print.

Rubio-Goldsmith, Raquel, et al. *The "Funnel Effect" & Recovered Bodies of Unauthorized Migrants Processed by the Pima County Office of the Medical Examiner, 1990–2005.* Tucson: University of Arizona Binational Migration Institute, 2006. Print.

Ruiz, Vicki L. *From out of the Shadows: Mexican Women in Twentieth-Century America.* New York: Oxford UP, 1998. Print.

———. "South by Southwest: Mexican Americans and Segregated Schooling, 1900–1950." *OAH Magazine of History* 15.2 (2001): 23–27. Print.

Saldívar, José David. *Border Matters: Remapping American Cultural Studies.* Berkeley: U of California P, 1997. Print.

"Same Educational Opportunity Basic Reason for Organization." *Sentinel* (Corpus Christi, TX), 18 June 1948: 1. Print.

Sanchez, Jennifer, Dawn House, and Kristen Moulton. "Federal Raid Puts Families in Limbo: Immigration Agents Looking for Stolen IDs Detain Scores in Hyrum." Immigration Solidarity Network, 13 Dec. 2006. Web. 5 Aug. 2007.

Sandoval, Chela. "Dissonant Globalizations, Emancipatory Methods, and Social Erotics." *Queer Globalizations: Citizenship and the Afterlife of Colonialism.* Ed. Arnaldo Cruz-Malavé and Martin F. Manalansan IV. New York: New York UP, 2002. 20–32. Print.

Sarria, Nidya. "Femicides of Juárez: Violence against Women in Mexico." Council on Hemispheric Affairs, 3 Aug. 2009. Web. 25 Apr. 2011.

SBI Monthly 1.1. US Customs and Border Protection, December 2006.

SBI Monthly 1.2. US Customs and Border Protection, January 2007.

SBI Monthly 2.2. US Customs and Border Protection, February 2007.

SBI Monthly 3.2. US Customs and Border Protection, March 2007.

SBI Monthly 7.2. US Customs and Border Protection, July 2007.

SBI Monthly 11.2. US Customs and Border Protection, November 2007.

SBI Monthly 12.2. US Customs and Border Protection, December 2007.

Schatan, Claudia, and Liliana Castilleja. "The Maquiladora Electronics Industry on Mexico's Northern Boundary and the Environment." *International Environmental Agreements* 7.2 (2007): 109–135. Print.

Schmidt Camacho, Alicia. *Migrant Imaginaries: Latino Cultural Politics in the US-Mexico Borderlands.* New York: New York UP, 2008. Print.

Scott, James C. *Seeing Like a State: How Certain Schemes to Improve the Human Condition Have Failed.* New Haven, CT: Yale UP, 1998. Print.

Scully, Judith A. M. "Killing the Black Community: A Commentary on the United States War on Drugs." *Policing the National Body: Race, Gender, and Criminalization.* Ed. Jael Silliman and Anannya Bhattacharjee. Boston, MA: South End P, 2002. 55–80. Print.

"Segregation Ban Decree by Federal Judge Climaxes 25-Year Fight by LULACs." *Sentinel* (Corpus Christi, TX), 18 June 1948: 1. Print.

Segrest, Mab. *Born to Belonging: Writings on Spirit and Justice.* New York: Routledge, 2002. Print.

Seper, Jerry. "Border Patrol Told to Stand Down in Arizona." *Washington Times,* 13 May 2005. Web. 20 Aug. 2010.

———. "Ex-Minuteman Members Form Group." *Washington Times,* 29 Sept. 2007: A2. Print.

———. "Gonzales Asked to Probe Prosecution of Agents; Two Were 'Doing Their Jobs' on the Border When Drug Suspect Was Shot." *Washington Times,* 27 Sept. 2006. Web. 31 Jan. 2010.

———. "Legislators Seek Review of Border Agents' Convictions." *The Washington Times,* 23 Aug. 2006. Web. 31 Jan. 2010.

———. "Minutemen Join New Organization." *Washington Times,* 21 Apr. 2005: A06. Print.

Serrano, Richard A. "US Attorney Put on Defensive; Johnny Sutton's Prosecution of Two Border Agents in Texas has Conservatives Up in Arms." *Los Angeles Times,* 18 Sept. 2007. Web. 31 Jan. 2010.

Shahani, Aarti, and Judith Greene. *Local Democracy on Ice: Why State and Local Governments Have No Business in Federal Immigration Law Enforcement.* Brooklyn, NY: Justice Strategies, February 2009. Print.

Shaw, Deborah. "'You Are Alright, But . . .': Individual and Collective Representations of Mexicans, Latinos, Anglo-Americans and Africans in Steven Soderbergh's *Traffic.*" *Quarterly Review of Film and Video* 22 (2004): 211–23. Print.

Shi, Yu. "Chinese Immigrant Women Workers: Everyday Forms of Resistance and 'Coagulate Politics.'" *Communication and Critical/Cultural Studies* 5.4 (2008): 363–82. Print.

Shome, Raka. "Outing Whiteness." *Critical Studies in Media Communication* 17 (2000): 366–71. Print.

———. "Whiteness and the Politics of Location: Postcolonial Reflections." *Whiteness: The Communication of Social Identity.* Ed. Thomas K. Nakayama and Judith N. Martin. Thousand Oaks, CA: Sage, 1999. 107–128. Print.

Silliman, Jael, and Anannya Bhattacharjee. *Policing the National Body: Race, Gender, and Criminalization.* Boston, MA: South End P, 2002. Print.

Silva, Kumarini. "Brown: From Identity to Identification." *Cultural Studies* 24.2 (2010): 167–82. Print.

Simpson, Amelia. "Warren County's Legacy for Mexico's Border Maquiladoras." *Golden Gate University Environmental Law Journal* 1 (2007): 153–74. Print.

Singer, Audrey, and Douglas S. Massey. "The Social Process of Undocumented Border Crossing among Mexican Migrants." *International Migration Review* 32.3 (1998): 561–92. Print.

The Sixth Section. Directed by Alex Rivera. American Documentary, Inc., and SubCine, 2003. DVD.

Skeggs, Beverley. *Formations of Class and Gender: Becoming Respectable.* London: Sage, 1997. Print.

Smith, Margaret W., and Linda Waugh. "Covert Racist Discourses on the WWW: Rhetorical Strategies of the Minuteman Project." *Texas Linguistic Forum* 52 (2008): 143–52. Print.

Smith, Ted. "Why We Are 'Challenging the Chip': The Challenges of Sustainability in Electronics." *International Review of Information Ethics* 11, 2009. Web. 7 Sept. 2010.

Soja, Edward. "Borders Unbound: Globalization, Regionalism, and the Post-metropolitan Transition." *B/ordering Space*. Ed. Henk van Houtum, Olivier Kramsch, and Wolfgang Zierhofer. Burlington, VT: Ashgate, 2005. 33–46. Print.

Solomon, Alisa. "Trans/Migrant: Christina Madrazo's All-American Story." *Queer Migrations: Sexuality, US Citizenship, and Border Crossings*. Ed. Eithne Luibhéid and Lionel Cantu Jr. Minneapolis: U of Minnesota P, 2005. 3–29. Print.

Sowards, Stacey. "Rhetorical Agency as *Haciendo Caras* and Differential Consciousness through Lens of Gender, Race, Ethnicity, and Class: An Examination of Dolores Huerta's Rhetoric." *Communication Theory* 20 (2010): 223–47. Print.

Spivak, Gayatri. *The Post-Colonial Critic: Interviews, Strategies, Dialogues*. New York: Routledge, 1990. Print.

Spry, Tami. "Performing Autoethnography: An Embodied Methodological Practice." *Qualitative Inquiry* 7 (2001): 706–732. Print.

Stana, Richard M. *Secure Border Initiative: Observations on the Importance of Applying Lessons Learned to Future Projects*. Washington, DC: United States Government Accountability Office, 2008. Print.

———. *Secure Border Initiative: Observations on Selected Aspects of Sbinet Program Implementation*. Washington, DC: United States Government Accountability Office, 2007. Print.

Stana, Richard M., and Evi Rezmovic. "INS' Southwest Border Strategy: Resource and Impact Issues Remain after Seven Years." United States General Accounting Office, August 2001. Print.

Stoppard, Tom. *Rosencrantz and Guildenstern Are Dead*. New York: Grove, 1967. 107. Print.

Strine, Mary S. "Articulating Performance/Performativity: Disciplinary Tasks and Contingencies of Practice." *Communication: Views from the Helm for the 21st Century*. Ed. Judith S. Trent. Boston: Allyn and Bacon, 1998. 312–17. Print.

Support Our Law Enforcement and Safe Neighborhoods Act. 49th Leg. 2nd sess. Senate Bill 1070. 23 Apr. 2010. Print.

Suro, Roberto. "The Triumph of No: How the Media Influence the Immigration Debate." Washington, DC: Brookings Institution and the Norman Lear Center at USC-Annenberg, 2008. 1–47. Web. 1 Mar. 2010.

Swift Justice: Seven Raids, Seven Hours, Illegal Immigration in America. Directed by Julie Speer and Mateos Alvarez. Little Voice Productions, 2009. DVD.

Tancredo, Thomas G. "Immigration, Citizenship, and National Security: The Silent Invasion." *Mediterranean Quarterly* 15.4 (2004): 4–15. Print.

———. "A New Strategy for the Control of Immigration." The Heritage Foundation. 26 Oct. 2006. Web. 20 Dec. 2011.

Taylor, Charles. "The Politics of Recognition." *Multiculturalism: Examining the Politics of Recognition*. Ed. Amy Gutmann. Princeton, NJ: Princeton UP, 1994. 25–73. Print.

Tenayuca, Emma. Interview with Jerry Poyo. *If the Principles are Gone*. 21 Feb. 1987. Web. 10 May 2004.

Tenayuca, Emma, and Homer Brooks. "The Mexican Question in the Southwest." *The Communist* (1939): 257–68. Print.

Ties That Bind: Stories behind the Immigration Controversy. Directed by José Roberto Gutiérrez, Elia Castillo, and Dieter Kaupp. Maryknoll World Productions, 1996. VHS.

The Time Has Come! An Immigrant Community Stands Up to the Border Patrol. Directed by Suzan Kern, James Fenian, Debbie Nathan, and René J. Cantú. El Paso Border Rights Coalition, 1996. VHS.

Ting, Jan C. "Immigration and National Security." *Orbis* (Winter 2006): 32, 48. Print.

Todorov, Tzvetan. *Facing the Extreme: Moral Life in the Concentration Camps.* New York: Henry Holt, 1996. Print.

Torres-Saillant, Silvio. "Political Roots of Chicano Discourse." *Latino Studies* 4 (2006): 452–64. Print.

Traffic. Directed by Steven Soderbergh. Performers Michael Douglas, Don Cheadle, Benicio Del Toro, Dennis Quaid, Catherine Zeta-Jones. USA Films, 2001. DVD.

Treviño, Marisa. "Immigration Enforcement Has Gone from Public Policy to Public Domain," 13 July 2010. Web. 23 Aug. 2010.

Turner, Victor. *The Ritual Process: Structure and Anti-Structure.* Hawthorne, NY: Aldine de Gruyter, 1995. Print.

The Unwanted. Directed by José Luis Ruiz; written by Frank Del Olmo. National Latino Communications Center, 1997. VHS.

Urrea, Luis Alberto. *By the Lake of Sleeping Children: The Secret Life of the Mexican Border.* New York: Anchor, 1996. Print.

US Census Bureau and the Department of Homeland Security. "NAHJ Urges News Media to Stop Using the Term 'Illegals' when Covering Immigration." *National Association of Hispanic Journalists,* 15 Sept. 2009. Web. 1 Mar. 2010.

US Customs and Border Protection. "Office of Technology Innovation and Acquisition." 2009. Web. 30 Dec. 2011.

Vachon, Michelle. "Emma Tenayuca, Community Activist." *Notable Hispanic American Women*. Ed. Diane Telgen and Jim Kamp. Detroit: Gale Research, 1993. 398–99. Print.

Vargas, Zaragosa. "'Do You See the Light?': Mexican American Workers and CIO Organizing." *Labor Rights Are Civil Rights: Mexican American Workers in Twentieth-Century America*. Princeton, NJ: Princeton University Press, 2005. 114–57. Print.

———. "Emma Tenayuca: Labor and Civil Rights Organizer of 1930s San Antonio." *The Human Tradition in America between the Wars, 1920–1945*. Ed. Donald W. Whisenhunt. Wilmington, DE: Scholarly Resources, 2002. 169–84. Print.

———. "Tejana Radical: Emma Tenayuca and the San Antonio Labor Movement during the Great Depression." *Pacific Historical Review* 66 (1997): 553–80. Print.

Vélez-Ibáñez, Carlos G. *Border Visions: Mexican Cultures of the Southwest United States*. Tucson: U of Arizona P, 1996. Print.

Vila, Pablo. *Border Identifications: Narratives of Religion, Gender, and Class on the US-Mexico Border*. Austin: U of Texas P, 2005. Print.

Viña, Stephen R. *Protecting Our Perimeter: "Border Searches" under the Fourth Amendment*. Washington, DC: Congressional Research Service, 2005. Print.

Viña, Stephen R., Blas Nuñez-Neto, and Alyssa Bartlett Weir. *Civilian Patrols against the Border: Legal and Political Issues*. Washington, DC: Congressional Research Service, 7 Apr. 2006. Print.

Wagner, Dennis. "US Cancels Plan to Build Virtual Fence along Border." *Arizona Republic,* 15 Jan. 2011. Web. 11 Apr. 2011.

Waldman, Paul, Elbert Ventura, Robert Savillo, Susan Lin, and Greg Lewis. "Fear and Loathing in Prime Time: Immigration Myths and Cable News." *Media Matters Action Network* 2008. Web. 4 Oct. 2010.

Walker, Christopher J. "Border Vigilantism and Comprehensive Immigration Reform." *Harvard Latino Law Review* 10 (2007): 135–74. Print.

Walking the Line. Directed by Jeremy Levine and Landon Van Soest. Two-Headed Productions and Filmakers Library, Inc., 2006. DVD.

The Wall. Directed by Ricardo A. Martinez. Viva Zapata Productions, 2009. DVD.

Warren, John T. "Doing Whiteness: On the Performative Dimensions of Race in the Classroom." *Communication Education* 50 (2001): 91–108. Print.

Washington, Harriet A. *Medical Apartheid: The Dark History of Medical Experimentation on Black Americans from Colonial Times to the Present*. New York: Harlem Moon, 2008. Print.

Welch, Nancy. "A Raid on a Wedding Reception." Socialistworker.org. 11 June 2010. Web. 11 June 2010.

Wessler, Seth F. "Hostile State Battles Now Define Immigration Debate." Colorlines.com, 6 Jan. 2011. Web. 14 July 2011.

———. "Welcome to the Wild, Wild South: Georgia Passes SB 1070 Copycat Bill." Colorlines.com, 15 Apr. 2011. Web. 14 July 2011.

———. "A Year after SB 1070, the Deportation Pipeline Still Begins in Washington." Colorlines.com, 25 Apr. 2011. Web. 14 July 2011.

Wetback: The Undocumented Documentary. Directed by Arturo Perez Torres. Act Now Productions and Ironweed Film Club, 2005. DVD.

"Where Is 'Away'?" *Denver Voice,* 23 Dec. 2009. Web. 7 Sept. 2010.

Which Way Home. Directed by Rebecca Cammisa. HBO Documentary Films, Good and White Buffalo Entertainment, Mr. Mudd, Documentress Films, Docurama, and New Video Group, 2009. DVD.

Wilson, Steven H. "Brown over 'Other White': Mexican Americans' Legal Argument and Litigation Strategy in School Desegregation Lawsuits." *Law and History Review* 21.1 (2003): 145–94. Print.

———. "Tracking the Shifting Racial Identity of Mexican Americans." *Law and History Review* 21.1 (2003): 211–13. Print.

Wilson, Thomas M., and Hastings Donnan. "Nation, State and Identity at International Borders." *Border Identities: Nation and State at International Frontiers.* Ed. Thomas M. Wilson and Hastings Donnan. Cambridge, UK: Cambridge UP, 1998. 1–30. Print.

Wonders, Nancy A. "Global Flows, Semi-Permeable Borders and New Channels of Inequality: Border Crossers and Border Performativity." *Borders, Mobility and Technologies of Control.* Ed. Sharon Pickering and Leanne Weber. New York: Springer, 2006. 63–86. Print.

Wood, Andrew G. "How Would You Like an El Camino? US Perceptions of Mexico in Two Recent Hollywood Films." *Journal of the Southwest* 43.4 (Winter 2001): 755–64. Print.

Wray, Matt. *Not Quite White: White Trash and the Boundaries of Whiteness.* Durham, NC: Duke UP, 2006. Print.

Yoxall, Peter. "The Minuteman Project, Gone in a Minute or Here to Stay? The Origin, History and Future of Citizen Activism on the United States-Mexican Border." *University of Miami Inter-American Law Review* 37 (2006): 517–66. Print.

Contributors

Bernadette Marie Calafell is an Associate Professor in the Department of Communication Studies at the University of Denver. She is the author of *Latina/o Communication Studies: Theorizing Performance* and co-editor (with Dr. Michelle A. Holling) of *Latina/o Discourse in Vernacular Spaces: Somos de Una Voz?* In 2009 she was awarded the Lilla A. Heston Award for Outstanding Research in Oral Interpretation and Performance.

Karma R. Chávez is an Assistant Professor of Rhetoric in the Department of Communication Arts at the University of Wisconsin, Madison. She is co-founder (with Eithne Luibhéid) of the Queer Migration Research Network (www.queermigration.com), and author of several articles on feminism, queer theory and politics, migration, and social movements. Chávez' book manuscript, *Queer/Migration Politics: Activist Rhetoric and Coalitional Possibilities,* is currently under review at a university press.

Josue David Cisneros is an Assistant Professor in the Department of Communication Studies at Northeastern University. His research and teaching explore the relationships between rhetoric, identity, and citizenship, and/in US public culture, especially with regard to race and migration. His scholarship has appeared in journals such as *Rhetoric and Public Affairs, Argumentation and Advocacy, Communication Quarterly,* and the *Quarterly Journal of Speech.*

D. Robert DeChaine is a Professor of Communication and Cultural Studies in the Departments of Communication Studies and Liberal Studies at California State University Los Angeles. He is author of *Global Humanitarianism: NGOs and the Crafting of Community* and more than a dozen scholarly articles, book chapters, and review essays. His published work has appeared in the *Journal of Communication Inquiry, Popular Music and Society,* the *Quarterly Journal of Speech, Text and Performance Quarterly,* and the *Western Journal of Communication.*

Anne Teresa Demo is an Assistant Professor in the Department of Communication and Rhetorical Studies and the School of Art and Design at

Syracuse University. Her work explores the relationship between visual rhetoric, identity, and US cultural politics. A past recipient of the National Communication Association's Golden Monograph award, her articles have appeared in the *Quarterly Journal of Speech, Critical Studies in Media Communication, Rhetoric and Public Affairs, Environmental History,* and *Women's Studies in Communication.* She is the coeditor of *Rhetoric, Remembrance, and Visual Form: Sighting Memory.*

Lisa A. Flores is an Associate Professor in the Department of Communication at the University of Colorado. Her research and teaching interests lie in rhetoric, critical race studies, and gender. She has published in *Text and Performance Quarterly, Communication and Critical/Cultural Studies,* and the *Quarterly Journal of Speech.* Her most recent work examines the rhetorical dynamics of domination, particularly as manifest in whiteness and masculinity and in historic narratives of immigrants and immigration.

Dustin Bradley Goltz is an Assistant Professor of Communication Studies at DePaul University, where he teaches undergraduate and graduate courses in performance studies, rhetoric of identity, performance of gender and sexuality, and rhetoric of popular culture. He is the author of *Queer Temporalities in Gay Male Representation: Tragedy, Normativity, and Futurity.* His research has been published in *Text and Performance Quarterly, Qualitative Inquiry,* the *Western Journal of Communication, Genders,* and *Liminalities.*

Marouf Hasian Jr. is a Professor working in the Department of Communication at the University of Utah. His areas of interest include rhetoric and law, military communication, postcolonial studies, visual communication, freedom of expression, Holocaust and genocide studies, and critical intercultural studies. He is currently working on a series of studies that investigate how members of the military rationalize the usage of key rules of engagement in Afghanistan and Pakistan.

Michelle A. Holling is an Associate Professor in the Department of Communication at California State University San Marcos. Her scholarly interests include Chican@-Latin@ vernacular discourse, rhetoric of identity, and gendered violence. She is co-editor (with Bernadette Marie Calafell) of *Latina/o Discourse in Vernacular Spaces: Somos de Una Voz?* Her scholarship appears in the *Communication Review, Communication and Critical/Cultural Studies, Text and Performance Quarterly,* and the *Western Journal of Communication.*

Julia R. Johnson is an Associate Professor of Communication, Associate Dean in the College of Liberal Studies, and Director of the School of Arts and Communication at the University of Wisconsin-La Crosse. In hir teaching and research, Julia emphasizes critical approaches to the study of communication and culture. Some of hir recent publications appear in edited volumes such as *Teaching, Learning and Intersecting Identities in Higher Education* and journals such as the *Journal of International and Intercultural Communication*.

Zach Justus is an Assistant Professor in the Department of Communication Arts and Sciences at California State University Chico. His primary research interests are rhetoric, terrorism, national security, conservative politics, and immigration. For his dissertation work Zach spent over two years as an active member of the Minuteman Civil Defense Corps, studying their strategic uses of rhetoric and qualitatively engaging their organizational practices.

Diane M. Keeling earned her PhD in Communication with certification in Women and Gender Studies at the University of Colorado Boulder. Her research interests are in rhetoric's intellectual history, posthumanist trends in rhetorical theory and criticism, and the study of rhetoric in the material world and through diverse media platforms.

John Louis Lucaites is a Professor of Rhetoric and Public Culture in the Department of Communication and Culture at Indiana University. His most recent work focuses on photojournalism as a mode of public art that serves as a key site of civic judgment in liberal-democratic public cultures. His recent publications include *No Caption Needed: Iconic Photographs, Public Culture, and Liberal Democracy*, co-authored with Robert Hariman, and *Rhetoric, Materiality, and Politics*, co-edited with Barbara A. Biesecker. He also co-hosts the blog www.nocaptionneeded.com.

George F. McHendry Jr. is a doctoral candidate in the Department of Communication at the University of Utah. He researches Critical Rhetoric and Critical/Cultural Studies, focusing on the performance of securitization of spaces and bodies in the United States of America after 9/11. This work is marked by an emphasis on resistive cultural practices. His current work focuses on using rhetorical field methods to study the rhetoric and performances of security at airport security checkpoints.

Toby Miller is the author and editor of over twenty books and hundreds of articles and chapters. His latest books are *Cultural Citizenship, Makeover Nation, The Contemporary Hollywood Reader,* and *Television Studies.* His work has been translated into Chinese, Spanish, Portuguese, Swedish, and German. You can follow his misadventures at www.tobymiller.org.

Kent A. Ono is a Professor in the Asian American Studies Program and the Media and Cinema Studies Department and affiliated faculty in the Communication Department at the University of Illinois at Urbana-Champaign. He has published several books, most recently *Critical Rhetorics of Race* co-edited with Michael Lacy. He co-edits the book series "Critical

Cultural Communication" with Sarah Banet-Weiser at New York University Press and co-edits the journal *Critical Studies in Media Communication* with Ronald Jackson.

Brian L. Ott is an Associate Professor of Media and Rhetorical Studies in the Department of Communication at the University of Colorado Denver. He is author of *The Small Screen: How Television Equips Us to Live in the Information Age* and *Critical Media Studies: An Introduction* (with Robert Mack), as well as a co-editor of *It's Not TV: Watching HBO in the Post-Television Era* and *Places of Public Memory: The Rhetoric of Museums and Memorials*.

Kimberlee Pérez is at DePaul University. Her research and teaching interests include the cultural and resistive work of performance through embodied action, narrative, queer intimacy, and collaboration. This includes interests in identity formation, particularly of queer, Latin@, and Chicana/o experience as well as transnational feminism and globalization. She has published in the *NWSA Journal, Performance Research,* and *Text and Performance Quarterly* as well as anthologies.

Mary Ann Villarreal is an Associate Dean at the University of Denver-Women's College. Her research focuses on south Texas and the formation of a Texas Mexican identity through the lens of business. She is currently working on a manuscript tentatively titled *Creating Capital: Texas Mexican Women and Family-Owned Businesses, 1930–1950*. An oral historian, Professor Villarreal has published in the *Oral History Review* and the *Journal of Women's History*.

Index